*Workers against the City*

THE WORKING CLASS IN AMERICAN HISTORY

*Editorial Advisors*
James R. Barrett, Julie Greene, William P. Jones, Alice Kessler-Harris, and Nelson Lichtenstein

*A list of books in the series appears at the end of this book.*

# Workers against the City

## The Fight for Free Speech in *Hague v. CIO*

DONALD W. ROGERS

UNIVERSITY OF ILLINOIS PRESS
Urbana, Chicago, and Springfield

Publication supported by a grant from the Howard D. and Marjorie I. Brooks Fund for Progressive Thought


1 2 3 4 5 C P 5 4 3 2 1
∞ This book is printed on acid-free paper.

Library of Congress Cataloging-in-Publication Data
Names: Rogers, Donald W., 1948– author.
Title: Workers against the city : the fight for free speech in Hague v. CIO / Donald W. Rogers.
Description: Urbana : University of Illinois Press, [2020] | Series: The working class in American history | Includes bibliographical references and index.
Identifiers: LCCN 2020023360 (print) | LCCN 2020023361 (ebook) | ISBN 9780252043468 (hardcover) | ISBN 9780252085369 (paperback) | ISBN 9780252052347 (ebook)
Subjects: LCSH: Freedom of speech—United States—History. | Assembly, Right of—United States—History. | Labor unions—Law and legislation—United States—History. | Hague, Frank, 1876–1956. | American Federation of Labor. Committee for Industrial Organization. | Mayors—New Jersey—Jersey City. | Jersey City (N.J.)—Politics and government.
Classification: LCC KF4772 .R64 2020 (print) | LCC KF4772 (ebook) | DDC 342.7308/54—dc23
LC record available at https://lccn.loc.gov/2020023360
LC ebook record available at https://lccn.loc.gov/2020023361

# Contents

# Illustrations

# Acknowledgments

Completing this book as a multicampus part-time adjunct faculty member was a challenge that I could never have met without the gracious support and encouragement from numerous individuals and institutions. (Then) Central Connecticut State University history department graduate student assistant Kira Holmes helped me to locate relevant archives, then cheered me along the whole way. Cynthia Harris and John Beekman at the New Jersey Room of the Jersey City Free Public Library guided me through that repository's Frank Hague Collection, municipal records, and newspaper collection, including what was then an unprocessed local periodical that turned out to be quite valuable. Cynthia Lutz and her colleagues in the Department of Rare Books and Special Collections at the Seeley G. Mudd Manuscript Library, Princeton University, supported my intense but happy week of research in the American Civil Liberties Union Records. The same goes for librarians Lauren Brown and Jennifer Eidson at the Special Collections and University Archives department at the University of Maryland's Hornbake Library, where I examined Congress of Industrial Organization records in the George Meany Memorial AFL-CIO Archives. Librarians at the Library of Congress assisted my look at the Harlan Fiske Stone Records and Hugo Black Papers. No less supportive were librarians at the Special Collections and Archives office and microfilm reading room at Olin Library, Wesleyan University (Middletown), Connecticut, where I examined the Arthur T. Vanderbilt Papers and the *Daily Worker*. Librarians with the Thomas Meskill Library at the University of Connecticut School of Law, Hartford, and Homer Babbidge Library at the University of Connecticut-Storrs consistently assisted when I stopped by now and again to track down various sources. Moreover, the Jewish Historical Society of New Jersey, Library of Congress, and Getty Images courteously assisted me to secure photographs. The author also heartily thanks commentators and audience members for astute comments made for papers that I presented at two meetings of the New England Historical Association, a regional gathering of the Law and Society Association in New York City, and a conference held by Connecticut State Universities history departments. Finally, the author expresses special gratitude to acquisitions editor James Engelhardt, three anonymous reviewers for the University of Illinois Press, who worked overtime to provide astute recommendations and encouragement, and copyeditor Deborah Oliver, who meticulously checked the syntax of this book. It is all the better for everyone's help, and any errors are my own doing.

*Workers against the City*

# Introduction

Early on Monday morning, November 29, 1937, dozens or perhaps hundreds of members and supporters of the Committee for Industrial Organization (CIO) converged on Jersey City in Hudson County, New Jersey, to publicize a CIO rally. Arriving from Newark, New York City, and other nearby areas, the activists headed for various plants and factories to hand out literature, most stopping off first at the headquarters of Local 73, United Shoe Workers of America, at 76 Montgomery Street to pick up handbills. Reaching their destinations was not easy. Police stopped CIO cars bearing out-of-town license plates and confiscated flyers found in those vehicles. Other officers stopped and frisked CIO sympathizers entering the Montgomery Street building. In one case, police hopped into a CIO representative's car and forced him to drive out of the city.[1]

Eventually, CIO organizers from mine, laundry, clothing, electrical, and textile worker unions arrived at the boot-and-shoemakers union office to review procedures for handing out flyers. The circulars invited Jersey City workers to attend a mass CIO meeting at People's Center on Friday, December 3, to discuss their rights under the recently enacted National Labor Relations (Wagner) Act (NLRA). "Here at last," the flyer declared, "is the great chance for every worker in Hudson County—the biggest opportunity in your lifetime—the opportunity to organize for better wages, for security of your job, and for better life under the protection of a C.I.O. contract." "Be wise—Organize! Join the C.I.O." Orchestrated by the CIO's regional director William Carney in Newark, the event was part of the CIO's initiative in 1937 to "organize the unorganized" along the East Coast.[2]

Around 6:50 a.m., a procession of male organizers left Montgomery Street and marched two by two, with leaflets in hand, several blocks to a notorious sweatshop building at Exchange Place on the harbor, followed by observers from the New Jersey Civil Liberties Union (NJCLU) and the New York City–based Workers' Defense League (WDL), a few of them women. What happened next is hotly contested. The *Jersey Observer*, friendly to the city administration, reported that police officers were waiting for marchers, having been alerted by newspaper reports that "thousands" of Carney's labor agitators threatened to "invade" Jersey City. According to the *Observer*, officers warned the marchers that they were violating a 1924 city ordinance against distributing leaflets on the streets, but marchers handed out flyers to passersby anyway, some yelling, "To hell with police," "We have a right to distribute the circulars," and "The hell with your phoney ordinance." "After repeated warnings," said the *Observer*, police picked up most marchers and either dispatched them on the Hudson River ferry to New York City or drove them to the city line. Simultaneously, police arrested organizers found distributing literature at the Westinghouse Elevator Company. In the end, police arrested thirteen marchers and quelled the event "without disorder."[3] As the *Observer* saw it, it was a routine peacekeeping operation by city authorities to enforce a lawful local ordinance against defiant lawbreakers.

Seven months later in federal court, however, marchers and observers offered a very different account: the police had wantonly assaulted them and denied their right to move peacefully about the streets and spread their message. Witnesses described how seventy-five to a hundred plainclothes and uniformed officers ruthlessly attacked them, formed a "flying wedge" to break up their lines, ripped flyers out of their hands, forced many onto the Hudson River ferry, and gave a male observer "a very sharp blow in the pit of the stomach."[4] Organizers who made it back to Montgomery Street for a fresh supply of flyers suffered as well. When they reassembled in the building, police barricaded the rear exit and compelled those leaving the front door to pass through a gauntlet of officers who frisked them, confiscated their flyers, and placed them in awaiting cars for a drive to city limits. Later, a police court judge, without allowing an official transcript, sentenced seven of the arrested marchers to five days in jail for violating the city's anti-leafletting ordinance, while he bound over six others for a grand jury indictment on the charge of illegal assembly. He concluded the proceeding by admonishing Carney—who was not present—never again to send back to Jersey City his CIO "hoodlums who are always ready to incite riots."[5]

Thus began the conflict—the Battle for Jersey City—that led to the landmark U.S. Supreme Court decision *Hague v. CIO* (1939).[6] In the months following the CIO's "invasion," Jersey City's colorful Irish Catholic, Democratic political boss, Mayor Frank Hague, virtually shut down the CIO organizing drive and suppressed subsequent efforts of CIO supporters like the American Civil Liberties Union (ACLU) to assemble and speak out in protest. Citing a 1930 ordinance, the city's public safety director denied public meeting permits to CIO organizers and their sympathizers, while police manhandled supporters who tried to assemble anyway, including Montana congressman Jerry O'Connell and the socialist Norman Thomas. The controversy became a national media sensation. Hague made headlines by excoriating the CIO and ACLU as communist fronts bent on inciting riot and disorder, but the CIO, the ACLU, and a coalition of left-leaning civil libertarians, journalists, and labor reformers seized on Hague's inadvertent comment "I am the law" to brand the mayor as an incipient dictator—the Jersey Fuehrer and Hitler on the Hudson. Hague staged an "Americanism" rally to mobilize Jersey residents against alleged CIO and ACLU communists, while opposition newspaper cartoonists lampooned Hague as a Nazi giving the "Heil Hitler" salute. The fracas culminated in federal courts, where a divided U.S. Supreme Court condemned Jersey City's actions, declared its ordinances unconstitutional, and enjoined Hague's machine from further violating out-of-doors (outdoor) expressive liberties. A constitutional milestone, the decision introduced the so-called public-forum doctrine—the fundamental right of Americans to assemble and speak in urban public places—setting a precedent for subsequent public demonstrations.[7]

Behind this battle between Boss Hague and his CIO-ACLU adversaries lay large and important questions involving assembly and speech rights that are quite familiar to us early-twenty-first-century Americans. When can people assemble on public property to express their opinions? When can labor organizers so assemble? Can they gather and speak out in any manner that they please? Can all people regardless of class, gender, ethnicity, or race have access to public space? When and how can municipal authorities regulate or even ban public demonstrations? How should authorities balance the right of ordinary people to gather and speak against cities' duty to preserve public order and safety? Like the notorious August 11–12, 2017, white nationalist rally in Charlottesville, Virginia, that turned horribly violent, or university students' raucous confrontations with radical right speakers on campus, or Black Lives Matter street meetings, or before that, antiabortion clinic protests, and even before that, anti–Vietnam War demonstrations, civil rights marches, Jehovah's Witness street appeals, mass labor rallies, woman suffrage parades, and Industrial Workers of the World (IWW) free speech fights, the November 1937 CIO event in Jersey City illustrated municipalities' long-running struggle to address these questions, with police frequently on the front line and courts standing behind them as final arbiters.[8]

While *Hague v. CIO* marked a critical development in assembly and speech rights, modern recollection of that case remains trapped in the political legend of Mayor Hague. Modern analysis of the Hague-CIO affair draws overwhelmingly on antiboss historical literature and on anti-Hague commentary generated in the late 1930s—especially the 1940 exposé *The Boss* dressed in academic style by former Democratic anti-Hague New Jersey assemblyman and (then) Dartmouth College speech professor Dayton David McKean. Evidentiary sources for the modern Hague legend are thus skewed heavily toward his opposition, and they neglect research on Jersey City's side in municipal archives, the pro-Hague press, Jersey City court filings, and the broader legal and political history in which the Hague-CIO saga unfolded. As a result, more sympathetic political studies like Richard J. Connors's *A Cycle of Power* (1971) and Leonard Vernon's *The Life & Times of Mayor Frank Hague* (2011) have been overshadowed by works that stress the Hague regime's corruption, including Steven Hart's *American Dictators* (2013), Nelson Johnson's *Battleground New Jersey* (2014), and Laura Weinrib's work on the interwar ACLU, *The Taming of Free Speech* (2016). This prevailing latter view confirms the historical consensus reported in Melvin G. Holli's *The American Mayor: The Best & Worst Big-City Leaders* (1999): that the "King of Hanky Panky" Frank Hague was the second-worst mayor in U.S. history, beaten out only by Chicago's William Hale "Big Bill" Thompson for the greatest level of mayoral infamy.

According to this prevailing school of thought, the *Hague v. CIO* decision originated in the Hague regime's arrogance, corruption and pro-business proclivities. The tall, trim, and athletic Hague—a "pushy, arrogant, and demeaning man" with a habit of punching people, says this view—ran a corrupt political machine that stayed in power through skillful use of patronage, rigged elections, and police harassment. Although he and his cronies befriended unions in the 1920s, this argument adds, Hague vowed to keep unions out of Jersey City during the 1930s Depression in order to protect sweatshop employers whose taxes were then needed to finance his bloated city payroll. Meanwhile, Hague himself received kickbacks from construction, utility, and real estate firms, enjoying a lavish lifestyle despite a modest mayoral salary. And he retained a post on the Democratic National Committee, fended off federal investigations, and received a shower of New Deal relief jobs in return for delivering New Jersey's electoral votes to Democrat Franklin Roosevelt in presidential elections. Given its corrupt collusion with employers, this literature finds, Hague's Jersey City chose to stymie CIO labor organizers when they arrived in 1937. According to the legendary view, valiant efforts by ACLU lawyers on behalf of the CIO finally challenged Hague in federal court. The ACLU's triumph in *Hague v. CIO* forced the mayor to reckon with democratic values, producing a victory for civil liberties (if not labor organizing rights) over that homegrown U.S. dictator.[9]

Our well-settled modern understanding of public assembly and speech rights today reinforces this recollection of the Jersey City controversy. Nowadays, we conceive of free assembly and speech as unchanging democratic freedoms under the First (and Fourteenth) Amendment of the U.S. Constitution. Our presumption is that Americans have long enjoyed fundamental rights to gather, speak out, and protest in public spaces, subject only to narrow content-neutral time, place, and manner restrictions, particularly restraints on "fighting words" and incitements that threaten imminent violence. In our own time, hence, we think that cities have authority only to regulate public gatherings for the purpose of facilitating traffic flow and other public conveniences, not to restrain assembly or speech ahead of time, or to discriminate against speakers on the basis of their messages. Admittedly, courts have recently excluded shopping malls and transportation hubs from assembly and speech guarantees, while social justice activists have urged that hate speech in public arenas not receive protection due to its harm to racial minorities.[10] Nonetheless, looking back with our modern legal values, we perceive that Mayor Hague's Jersey City obviously impaired the rights of workers and sympathizers to gather and speak, a violation of basic democratic principles.

This modern recollection of the Jersey City–CIO affair is compelling for its moral simplicity, but it obscures a larger story and overlooks complicating evidence. A wide range of factors all played roles in shaping the Hague-versus-CIO controversy: the roots of Mayor Hague's power in the ethnic politics of a rather typical second-generation urban machine, the broad authority that cities exercised over civil liberties under traditional municipal law, the dominance of Jersey City's Irish, Roman Catholic population in spite of demographic decline, the municipality's part in nationwide police reform, the evolution and split of the U.S. labor movement into rival American Federation of Labor (AFL) and CIO factions, the dominance of men and masculine cultures as women slowly emerged into politics, regional political competition between Hudson County Democrats and Essex County Republicans, the penetration of the nationwide interwar anticommunist movement into Jersey City politics, the rise of antifascist rhetoric among labor and reform groups associated with the Popular Front, the evolution of civil liberties from a narrow cause pursued by the ACLU to a broad popular movement, and most importantly, the massive Depression and New Deal–era restructuring of American politics and constitutional law.

To explore these larger, especially labor, dimensions of the Hague-CIO episode, this book digs deeper into Jersey City municipal records, ACLU papers, CIO archives, federal court documents, trial testimony, magazine articles, and newspaper reports. It also draws more broadly on secondary historical literature about the labor movement, urban bossism, big-city police, communism and anticommunism, antifascism, gender roles, civil liberties, and constitutional law. *Workers against the City* especially offers the first thorough review of the *Hague* case's progression through the federal judiciary from district court to the U.S. Supreme Court, illuminating the full tenor of trial proceedings and bringing out the perspective of both sides. This broader treatment shows that the grand economic, political, and legal restructuring of the 1930s was as much responsible for the CIO-Hague conflict as were the mayor's abuses and CIO-ACLU efforts to stop him. That restructuring defined modern public assembly and speech rights as much as the Hague-CIO affair itself.

Until the late-1930s, when the U.S. Supreme Court decided the *Hague* case, workers and urban residents lived in a very different constitutional world than we do today. Before the 1920s and 1930s, the U.S. Supreme Court did not apply the Bill of Rights on the state level, leaving state courts to govern speech, press, and assembly liberties. In turn, state and federal courts afforded municipalities nearly complete authority to keep order in public places, as exemplified by the U.S. Supreme Court's *Davis v. Massachusetts* (1897) decision that affirmed Boston's power to regulate or even ban speaking in city parks. State courts surely recognized speech, press, and assembly rights but construed them narrowly in conformity with broad municipal police powers, such as those exercised in Jersey City's confrontation with the CIO in 1937. If, as the *New York Herald-Tribune* said, U.S. constitutional rights were "a dead letter in Jersey City," that reflected the state of the law as much as Mayor Hague's shenanigans. Until the U.S. Supreme Court asserted federal judicial protection in the 1930s, New York City, Chicago, Jersey City, and other municipalities enjoyed virtual immunity from federal intrusion when police infringed on civil liberties.[11]

Largely free from federal judicial intervention until the 1930s, early-twentieth-century boss-led political machines like Jersey City's routinely trampled on modern notions of civil liberties, but not simply because bosses were evil. Using the moralistic language of bosses' middle- and upper-class opponents, the first generation of boss historians stereotyped city bosses like Hague that way—as corrupt, ruthless, partisan, and authoritarian enemies of democracy. Yet, as urban historian Alexander Callow wrote, city bosses were "a crazy mix," not a single type, and merely calling them "wicked fellow[s]" "does not illustrate the nature of urban politics, the way the machine developed, or the way the boss ran the machine." More recent historians, consequently, have adopted sociologist Robert Merton's "functionalist" analysis that emphasizes bosses' expediency. Although criticized for romanticizing bosses and oversimplifying urban politics, the "functionalist" approach stresses how most bosses governed cities through bottom-up, ward organizations based in immigrant, working-class neighborhoods. Bosses "functioned" in a local political culture of trust, loyalty, and ethnic camaraderie, and the constant provision of jobs, services and symbolic leadership. Parochial in outlook, they served the needs of local supporters, not the liberties of outsiders.[12]

Urban bossism has a long history in the United States, and Jersey City's Frank Hague illuminates one phase of it, the proliferation of Irish city bosses from the late 1800s to the mid-1900s. Like most Irish bosses, Hague's power lay in Irish-immigrant neighborhoods, and he maintained support there by honoring ethnic heritage, dispensing jobs, recruiting leaders, maintaining party discipline, and rigging elections, despite an Irish popular base that shrunk as Italian, Polish, Jewish, and African American newcomers moved in. Indeed, his infamous "I am the law" comment fit neighborhood politics quite well—other bosses said virtually the same thing—since it typified the boss's promise to cut through red tape and deliver the personal touch to city services. Like other Irish bosses, also, Hague exhibited masculine fighting prowess to defend his constituents. Yet, rising to power during the 1910s, he was a second-generation Irish politician who blended the rough-and-tumble style of his overwhelmingly male machine with Progressive reform, modernizing Jersey City's police and fire departments, and assimilating soon-to-be enfranchised female voters into party positions and women's auxiliaries. Like other bosses, too, Hague drew support from President Franklin Roosevelt's New Deal programs when Depression struck in the 1930s and his ethnic base declined. True, he was a corrupt boss who lived a lavish lifestyle, and he showed a special proclivity for personal violence and the muscular police tactics that were widespread at the time. Catering to his rambunctious but religiously conservative Irish Catholic clientele, Hague resembled Progressive "coercive moral reformers" who used city police to maintain order and morality. Critics might mock the diction of the sixth-grade-educated Hague when he contended that Jersey City was "the most moralist city in America," but his remark underscored how order, not civil liberties, was a central expectation of his leadership.[13]

The nationwide movement to improve police professionalism reinforced Jersey City's tendency toward coercive moral order keeping. Through the 1920s, big-city police departments around the country were riddled with incompetence, corruption, lawlessness, and violence. Jersey City officers' sometime rogue behavior and political use was commonplace. Yet, in the wake of recommendations by the National Law Enforcement (Wickersham) Commission set up by President Herbert Hoover in 1929, and in the wake of early 1930s amendments to New Jersey's 1898 Disorderly Persons Act, Jersey City's police department improved its discipline and cultivated a reputation for tough control over "racketeers" and "undesirables," then thought to be good police practice everywhere. Whatever the Jersey City constabulary's abuses, its participation in interwar police reform "functioned" to solidify Hague's hold on local constituents.[14]

Hague's controversial regime certainly created enemies, but not on the basis of civil liberties, since that issue remained marginal until the mid-1930s. The libertarian principles introduced in the U.S. Supreme Court's *Gitlow v. New York* (1925) and *Whitney v. California* (1927) cases merely offered hints for the future, while the ACLU was just emerging from World War I–era repression as an advocate of workers' right to agitate, not a defender of assembly and speech rights in court.[15] Challenges to Hague at this time thus arose as partisan causes within political institutions. After shady Hague electioneering tactics upset the reform gubernatorial candidacy of Republican Robert Carey in 1928, for instance, Republican lawmakers launched a legislative investigation of the mayor's personal finances, only to have him walk free on a legal technicality. Few civil liberties questions were raised.[16]

The CIO's November 1937 "invasion" took place in the waning days of this old legal and political environment. When CIO organizers arrived, Jersey City's parochial police supervisors assumed it as their regular order-keeping duty to stifle the potentially disruptive CIO outsiders and to enforce the city's anti-leafletting ordinance, still considered good law at the time. Under the prevailing jurisprudence of the *Davis* case, Jersey police presumed local authority to contain what they saw as CIO lawlessness. As in other municipalities, respect for nationally mandated civil liberties had not yet reached Jersey City streets. As late as March 1938, a police captain scolded two leafletters for circulating flyers at Jersey City's Journal Square, reasoning that his job was to enforce local ordinances, not the U.S. Constitution.[17]

By the late 1930s, however, the old legal world came jarringly to an end. The prosperity of the 1920s gave way to the Great Depression in the 1930s, while "new immigrants" plus African Americans increasingly outnumbered Jersey City's Irish population, causing an economic, political, and legal upheaval that reconfigured civil liberties and local police powers. Transformation of Jersey City's labor movement underlay that upheaval. During the 1920s, U.S. labor's "lean years," a small group of AFL affiliates in building and maritime trades prevailed in Jersey City and fit comfortably into Mayor Hague's local Democratic coalition. In the 1930s, however, the number of local tradesmen dwindled, while outside CIO organizers led by William Carney interjected industrial unionism into Jersey City with new labor rights protected under the 1935 NLRA. The CIO's mass organizing tactics, its class-based "culture of unity," and its spirit of "working-class Americanism," if not its traditional male-dominated gender hierarchy or minimal attention in this instance to black workers, threatened struggling AFL locals and challenged the insular Hague regime's commercial boosterism, ethnic appeals, narrow Irish Catholic base, and authoritarian style. In reaction, Hague retained AFL backing and resisted CIO unionism, apparently to defend an open-shop town.[18]

Interwar anticommunism intensified the Hague regime's reaction to the CIO incursion. Nationally, a network of anticommunist writers and agitators arose during the post–World War I years, and "little red scares" broke out repeatedly. In Jersey City, where actual communist activity was minuscule, a strong police force, robust veterans groups, old-fashioned trade unions, and pervasive Roman Catholic institutions inclined local residents to embrace this cause when striking seamen, CIO organizers, and ACLU supporters came to town.[19] Mayor Hague exploited local anticommunist sentiment for political benefit, although he did not generate it by himself. He cultivated the political language of patriotic Americanism to unite Jersey City's myriad immigrant groups behind his fight against the CIO's alleged communist menace.

Nonetheless, the slow emergence of modern civil liberties fortified the CIO's challenge to the Hague administration. Contrary to the popular impression that Hague's regime violated long-standing American liberties, the speech, press, and assembly rights involved in the CIO-Hague affair only gradually became recognized through the 1920s and 1930s. Before World War I, the judiciary was generally hostile to speech claims, and the civil liberties movement consisted of a marginal array of sex radicals, IWW agitators, and Free Speech League members who championed individual expression. After the war, in the wake of wartime suppression of dissent and the subsequent Red Scare, a new assemblage of elite law professors, dissenting jurists and rising ACLU members began to defend political speech under the national Bill of Rights, although they still operated largely outside of unsympathetic federal courts.[20] Indeed, the emerging ACLU led by founder Roger Baldwin attached itself to the cause of outdoor labor protest, due to a barrage of antilabor U.S. Supreme Court decisions, judicial labor injunctions, and local police crackdowns. Baldwin and his ACLU associates identified free speech and assembly with workers' collective actions, and they monitored an array of labor conflicts in West Virginia, California, North Carolina, Kentucky, New

York City, and New Jersey. When it got involved at this point, the ACLU typically sent representatives, including Baldwin himself, to join labor protests.[21] During Jersey City's 1934 Miller Parlor Furniture Company demonstration, for example, the ACLU dispatched New York City members to join worker picket lines.

In the mid-1930s, however, the ACLU shifted to litigation. Back in the late 1920s, the ACLU lost confidence in labor agitation and began affirming unfettered political expression as the route to progress instead, especially after court victories endorsed literary freedom and public attitudes gradually acclaimed free speech. Then in the 1930s, pathbreaking U.S. Supreme Court speech and press decisions and the passage of anti-injunction legislation and the Wagner NLRA persuaded even ACLU skeptics like Roger Baldwin that federal judges could secure civil liberties, while federal statutes could protect workers.[22] Indeed, Jersey City's conflict with the CIO in 1937–38 accelerated the ACLU's shift to judicial protection. When Jersey City blocked Baldwin from joining CIO protest rallies as he had done previously, ACLU lawyers helped CIO counsel to seek injunctive relief in federal court.

Just then, amid rising global fears of dictatorship, a popular coalition ushered civil liberties into the public mainstream. At the same time that the ACLU pursued judicial action, the NJCLU and left-labor groups like the WDL and the Socialist Party joined the civil liberties cause, bringing a few female followers with them, although few, if any African Americans. Simultaneously, the *New York Post*, the *New York Times*, *Life* magazine, and other periodicals exploded with civil liberties stories. Tightly interwoven with the Popular Front, including communists, this coalition promoted speech, press, and assembly rights under the U.S. Constitution as a public crusade. As fascist dictatorships rose in Europe, moreover, coalition members blended civil libertarianism with antifascist rhetoric in a patriotic defense of democratic institutions. Even the conservative American Bar Association (ABA) jumped on the civil liberties bandwagon in this context. Supposed dictatorships like Mayor Hague's Jersey City that adopted so-called fascist tactics became a rhetorical target for this civil libertarian alliance, although the urban machine-based Hague regime did not, as often alleged, simply serve business efforts to mobilize popular opposition against the CIO as right-wingers in other cities did.[23]

A sudden massing of state and local political opposition to Frank Hague's Hudson County political machine magnified the growing CIO and civil libertarian challenge to his leadership in 1937–38. Of course, Hague's Democratic organization had long faced political enemies, but a new surge of opponents coincided with the CIO controversy to present Mayor Hague with an exceptional political threat. Civic groups like taxpayers' associations and women's Junior Service League came out against the mayor, while regional clergymen, university professors, female activists, and labor agitators formed the NJCLU to address abuses like Jersey City's. Moreover, the CIO's political affiliate called Labor's Non-Partisan League prepared to challenge Hague Democrats' control of Hudson County, a typical CIO tactic to improve the political environment surrounding union organizing activity. In particular, outraged Essex County Republicans claimed that a fraudulent vote count from Hague's Hudson County had robbed their reform candidate of the governorship in November 1937 elections, handing that post to Hague's Democratic henchman A. Harry Moore instead. Republicans demanded an investigation of this "stolen" gubernatorial race just at the moment the CIO and ACLU arrived.[24] The dangerous political situation coupled with a shrinking Irish political base encouraged Hague's suppression of those groups.

By 1937 and 1938, hence, a political crisis loomed in Jersey City, bringing two very different political and legal worlds into collision—the insulated old ethnicity-based municipal boss system represented by Mayor Hague and the nationalized class-based new politics of labor rights and civil liberties as exemplified by the CIO and ACLU. While the struggle remained on Jersey City streets and in local courts through the fall and winter of 1937–38, the Hague administration had the upper hand. But when the conflict moved into federal court in early summer 1938, the CIO and ACLU took the advantage. Coincidentally, federal judges themselves were rethinking labor law and civil liberties.

In federal court, the CIO and ACLU attorneys sought an injunction to stop Jersey City violations of assembly and speech rights, proceedings that need to be examined more thoroughly than they have been in the past. The complete trial transcript, Jersey City's losing briefs as well as the CIO-ACLU's and the ABA's winning briefs, and the full opinion of the presiding judge all reveal an important legal battle between colliding constitutional visions, not just an exposé and rebuke of Mayor Hague's many alleged misdeeds. The testy federal district court hearing in June 1938—as fiery and dramatic as Clarence Darrow's confrontation with William Jennings Bryan in the famous 1925 Scopes trial—certainly featured witnesses who attested to Jersey City's abuses, but its real contest concerned whether the municipality had authority to do what it did, and whether federal courts had jurisdiction to protect national civil rights.[25] The *New York Times* credited Hague for doing well on the witness stand, but ultimately the judge (an Essex County, New Jersey, Republican) scoffed at Jersey City's presumptions about municipal power and issued an injunction based on CIO-ACLU lawyers' new view of civil liberties.

On appeal, the Third Circuit Court of Appeals and then the U.S. Supreme Court affirmed the trial court injunction, but in a legally murky way that revealed a constitutional transformation in progress. After almost getting derailed by one last Hague-friendly procedural maneuver in the Third Circuit, the case went on appeal to the U.S. Supreme Court under Chief Justice Charles Evans Hughes, where the high court upheld the CIO-ACLU position in a split five-to-two vote. After a long period of dormancy from the 1870s to the 1920s, when federal judges had refrained from embracing the nationalizing implications of the Reconstruction Amendments, the Hughes court adopted rising Fourteenth Amendment jurisprudence that applied federal judicial protection to assembly and speech rights on the state level, although Justice Owen Roberts's plurality decision differed significantly from Justice Harlan Fiske Stone's concurrence on the constitutional logic. Despite those differences, *Hague* arrived in the Supreme Court just at the moment when most justices were accommodating the "civil liberties revolution" that turned federal courts into guardians of insular minorities' civil rights, as celebrated in Stone's footnote 4 of *U.S. v. Carolene Products Co.* (1938). With the labor movement rising, the court also showed special sympathy for the civil liberties of workers. In *Hague*, thus, a majority of the Hughes court accepted the CIO-ACLU conception of federal jurisdiction over civil liberties and dismissed Jersey City's old-fashioned constitutionalism of municipal control, a position that only two diehard dissenting justices would have sustained.[26]

Overwhelmingly, observers today remember the *Hague v. CIO* ruling as a civil liberties victory over local tyranny, and more specifically as a CIO-ACLU victory over Mayor Hague. That impression developed largely from the public relations war that both sides waged against each other at the time, a war that workers and civil libertarians won and Hague lost. Capturing the spirit of the moment, an ACLU political cartoon depicted a humbled Frank Hague standing before federal district court judge William Clark with a pendant around his neck reading, "I was the law." "One dictator who did not get away with it," declared the caption.[27] Subsequently, CIO historians placed the Jersey City fight in that organization's successful struggle for class justice against exploitive employers and their political allies, allegedly like Frank Hague. Civil liberties historians treated the CIO-Hague controversy as a milestone in the ACLU's vaunted campaign for assembly and speech rights against domestic foes of U.S. liberties, again like Mayor Hague.

These scenarios, however, obscure as much as they reveal about the CIO-Hague controversy, and indeed obscure how American liberties evolved in the mid-twentieth century and what role workers played in that evolution. Rather than simply reflecting a final showdown with a notoriously authoritarian boss, the CIO-Hague conflict exposed the disintegration of the political and legal institutions that had sustained city bosses and their heavy-handed big city police departments during the early-1900s. Alluding to the vestiges of those old institutional arrangements, *Life* magazine got it right in 1938 when it characterized Mayor Hague as "Last of the Bosses, Not First of the Dictators."[28] Moreover, rather than just confirming traditionally hallowed U.S. civil rights, the CIO-Hague conflict marked the formulation of those rights de novo in their modern guise—the freedom to use municipal space for the exercise of assembly and speech rights under the protection of the U.S. Constitution and federal courts.

Finally, rather than overthrowing a corrupt city boss so that CIO labor organizers and ACLU speakers could exercise their constitutional privileges, the *Hague* case produced surprisingly modest political results. Because the ruling scarcely affected the basis of Hague's power in either local or national politics, the mayor easily adjusted to new outdoor speech requirements and incorporated the CIO into his governing coalition, as he often did to neutralize adversaries. Indeed, the CIO even found it expedient to endorse the mayor for reelection. Meanwhile, *Hague*'s seminal public-forum doctrine separated civil liberties from labor rights that CIO members had hoped to vindicate in 1937. The doctrine established the legal foundation for outdoor protests in the 1960s civil rights movement and beyond, but it left workers' picketing and organizing rights to develop as a separate body of law.

The *Hague* case thus illustrates the dynamic historical quality of the struggle for public assembly and speech rights in the twentieth century, and workers' place in it. In its time, *Hague* expanded national rights of workers and agitators to speak out in public places at the expense of the decaying system of municipal law and politics. Since then, however, shrinking conceptions of labor speech, narrowing judicial definitions of public places, and minority civil rights claims have pushed back against that expansion. Although cherished, assembly and speech rights have never been fixed, but have taken their meaning from the substance of law and the character of politics in changing historical circumstances. *Hague v. CIO* reflected one of those transitory moments.

# 1 The Rise of Boss Hague

## *Municipal Politics and Civil Liberties in the Old Era*

On July 16, 1919, Jersey City police inspector John J. Cody and police captain James Rooney arrested Frank A. Collins at his Brady Brass Company job during a strike. Cody and Rooney searched Collins, took him to Jersey City's second-district police station for questioning, and then released him on a $1,000 liberty bond in anticipation of his appearance before a police magistrate two days later. At the trial, the officers presented neither an arrest warrant nor charges against Collins, but simply explained that they were following orders to detain him. The magistrate found Collins guilty of disorderly conduct, suspended his sentence, and ordered him "to get out of Jersey City at once." Ultimately, however, Collins sued the policemen for false arrest and imprisonment, and won damages in a decision affirmed by the New Jersey Supreme Court. That court determined that common law restrained officers from making arrests for breaches of the peace, unless they saw defendants commit crimes or possessed judicially issued warrants. Neither was true here.[1] The case became a benchmark in criminal due process rights.

Years later, Newark labor attorney Abraham J. Isserman described the *Collins* case as an early sign of the lawless spirit that pervaded boss Frank Hague's reign as Jersey City mayor from 1917 through the tumultuous events that produced the *Hague v. CIO* ruling in 1939. Under Mayor Hague, Isserman contended, "the police, free from the normal legal restraints, stopped pedestrians on the Jersey City streets at will, searched them, sometimes ordered them out of Jersey City, or arrested them without warrant or probable cause." As such, Hague's administration typified the authoritarian and corrupt practices of late-nineteenth- and early-twentieth-century urban bosses from New York City's William Marcy Tweed to Kansas City's Thomas Pendergast.

Violation of civil liberties was part and parcel of boss rule, Isserman implied, and Hague carried bossism "to its utmost limits."[2]

Isserman's reminiscence demands respect, given his firsthand experience battling the Hague administration and his personal castigation by the mayor as the "Red counsel," but his characterization of the Hague regime obscures deeper reasons for the suppression of civil liberties in Jersey City. Isserman captured the widely accepted view that Hague was an antilabor tyrant who ran a virtual police state in Jersey City, marking him as a singular menace against American rights. Yet, a broader consideration of Hague's world shows that he was representative of his time and place, if an extreme example. The overall structure of municipal politics, U.S. law, and police culture from the early 1900s Progressive years to the early 1930s Depression period were not particularly hospitable to civil liberties. If he was an autocrat, then Hague flourished in an era that encouraged local autocracy.

* * *

During the decades preceding the *Collins* case, Jersey City emerged as a municipality that routinely trampled on civil liberties, not unlike other cities. By 1910, it had become a manufacturing center and a transportation hub in one of the most densely populated metropolitan regions of the country, no fewer than 267,779 people in a compact thirteen square miles, even more congested than New York City. Bounded on the west by streams, rivers, and bays that detached it from the mainland, and on the east by the Hudson River, which separated it from Manhattan Island, Jersey City developed as a geopolitically independent urban community that functioned as a corridor for freight traffic headed to and from the port of New York City. By the early 1900s, nine railroads crisscrossed Jersey City, claiming rights-of-way on a third of the municipality's cramped land and taking control of its harbor area, where barges ferried merchandise across the Hudson River to Manhattan docks. Simultaneously, a diverse industrial economy sprang up with foundries, meatpacking, and railroad repair, along with a smattering of lumber, electrical supply, textile, and other manufacturing firms. This dense industrial infrastructure created an austere physical environment, especially in the northeastern Horseshoe neighborhood near docks and rail yards, a "grindingly poor" area covered with shanties and tenements, permeated by saloons, drenched with effluents, plagued by disease, and tormented by roving youth gangs.[3]

This rough-and-tumble city developed a distinctive ethnic political economy that tempered civil liberties. During the nineteenth century, a haughty Republican, Protestant business elite dominated Jersey City by minimizing railroad property taxation, blatantly discriminating against new German, Irish, Russian Jewish, and Italian arrivals, and confining immigrant voting power to the oddly shaped Horseshoe district. By the early 1900s, however, Protestants moved beyond Jersey City limits, while the foreign born and their children swelled to two-thirds of the city's population. As elsewhere, Irish Roman Catholics, constituting about one-fifth of the city's immigrant-stock residents, rose to the top of the ethnic mix of Germans, Russians, Italians, and Poles, and assumed political leadership, despite a declining future proportion of city population. Their base lay in the city's tough wards of the Horseshoe, but their influence spread throughout the city as upwardly mobile Irish descendants replaced Protestants in fashionable areas. As they rose, Jersey City's Irish reshaped local political culture, overthrowing their former despised status, and proudly affirming both their Americanness and their Irish Catholic heritage.[4]

Jersey City's Irish-run political "machine" or "boss" system was a central product of these developments. As in other U.S. municipalities, machine politics arose in Jersey City during the nineteenth-century due to the inability of its weak-mayor, strong-alderman governmental structure to resolve the ethnic fragmentation or satisfy dire needs for city services. Machines addressed these problems by centralizing city politics in informal, hierarchical one-party organizations that united local grassroots ward and precinct operations under the authority of a single city boss. City machines then consolidated power by creating highly disciplined neighborhood get-out-the-vote operations that amassed electoral majorities in tenement districts in return for rewarding tenement voters with petty favors and patronage jobs, while allocating contracts to local businesses. Such interplay between bosses and local constituents was the key to machines' survival. Bosses had to pay constant attention to the needs of local voters if they were to retain their power. They never became the all-controlling tyrants that critics characterized them to be, not as biographer Alfred Steinberg said of Hague, ruling as "dictator over the lives of 300,000 subjects." According to urban historian Howard Chudacoff, the bosses' "entire system depended on neighborhood support." Machines may have thrived on manipulating the needy, he argues, but "bosses could not lead their constituents where they did not want to go." Rooted in neighborhood politics, city machines were conservative by nature and parochial in outlook, not inclined toward civil liberties.[5]

Future Jersey City mayor Frank Hague emerged out of ward-based machine politics during the late 1890s and early 1900s, an experience that shaped his attitude toward civil liberties. Initially, he advanced as a typical Irish ward politician, epitomizing the hard struggle to ascend the social ladder that his

Irish neighbors could easily appreciate. Born to Irish-immigrant parents on Tenth Street in the Second Ward of the Horseshoe in 1879, Hague was tossed out of school in the sixth grade due to unruliness and truancy, and knocked around in odd jobs before finding his home in local politics. He became a protégé of Second Ward leaders and then as an associate of Hudson County Democratic boss Robert "Little Bob" Davis, who took Hague into his organization and saved him from a double scandal involving perjury and disregard of a court summons. Ever the opportunist, Hague soon abandoned Davis to secure the lucrative city custodian's post from Democratic Jersey City mayor Otto Wittpenn, later joining Wittpenn in support of Woodrow Wilson's successful antiboss campaign in New Jersey's gubernatorial election of 1910. Although Hague's faction was soundly defeated by Davis men in the 1910 city council election, Davis's death in 1911 left his organization in disarray, allowing Hague to win election to Jersey City's Street and Water Commission that year, while Wittpenn coasted to reelection for a third term as mayor. To this point, Hague had earned a reputation as an exceptional player of factional ward politics, including the alleged Irish proclivity for him and his "boys" to use intimidation and "fighting prowess" to defeat opponents, something hardly unusual for a first-generation machine politician.[6]

The election cycle of 1910–13, however, marked a turning point in Jersey City history and Frank Hague's career. It launched what historian Steven Erie designates as a second generation of machine politics that intertwined boss leadership with Progressive reform. Hague exemplified that synthesis by blending old-fashioned roughneck tactics and neighborhood ethnic politics with new Progressive attitudes toward centralization, efficiency, and moral control. He never totally adopted the social welfare politics of urban liberalism that other urban figures like New York's Al Smith did, but he absorbed Progressive rhetoric and techniques into machine operations. Mirroring the work of urban reformers like Cleveland's Tom Johnson, Hague assumed the post of street-and-water commissioner and became Jersey City's "clean streets man," aggressively enforcing anti-littering and street-cleaning ordinances, while reorganizing his department and cutting costs. He both satisfied Horseshoe residents with sanitary improvements and job opportunities, and pleased reformers with his "efficiency."[7]

Jersey City's shift to commission government in 1913 consolidated the blend of boss and reform politics. Starting in 1901 after a hurricane exposed corruption in Galveston, Texas, commission government swept the nation as a Progressive municipal reform in midsize cities, although a few large municipalities like Jersey City adopted it as well. Strongly supported by business, commission government replaced nineteenth-century cities' inefficient maze of elected officers, councils, and boards and their corruptible ward-by-ward system of electing city aldermen with a new centralized arrangement that provided for at-large citywide elections of powerful commissions, each of whose five commissioners would administer designated city departments. With this reform, supporters hoped to remove bossism from city government, empower commissioners to run cities more effectively, and establish clearer lines of responsibility. New Jersey governor Woodrow Wilson strongly championed the reform, as did the pro-business *Jersey Journal*, but the Democratic machine (including Hague) defeated a 1911 referendum to install it in Jersey City. By 1913, however, politics changed course. Having fallen out with Wittpenn, Hague now posed as a reformer in support of commission government to counter the mayor's alleged machine. After reform passed, Hague stood for election to the new Jersey City commission, coming in fourth on a politically mixed electoral slate that included reform-minded former Republican mayor Mark Fagan, two Wittpenn men, and Wittpenn secretary A. Harry Moore. As top voter getter, Fagan was selected mayor, while Hague received the police and fire portfolio, the platform on which he began building his regime.[8]

Jersey City's commission government represented a Progressive reform that appealed especially to the local business elite. In this structural reform, centralized administration promised to respond well to commercial interests, enhance city services, and stamp out urban vice. The engraving appearing on the cover of the Jersey City commission's minutes in 1913–14 illuminated this Progressive hope. The cover pictured a gateway opening onto a bustling port with busy smoke-belching factories. A woman holding a mace labeled "commission government" had just opened the gate by using a key to unlock a padlock labeled "politics," suggesting that removal of machine politics and erection of modern city administration paved the way to commercial growth. "Jersey City: The Gateway of Municipal Opportunity" read the slogan. Commission reform and prosperity were thus tightly linked in Jersey City's political culture even before Frank Hague became the city's dominant force, and long before critics would accuse him of catering to business with his "Jersey City: Everything for Industry" slogan.[9]

Nonetheless, Jersey City was only a "weakly reformed" municipality that retained many attributes of machine politics. Like machine-run Chicago and Tammany-governed New York, but unlike Cincinnati, Dayton, and Detroit, Jersey City failed to adopt civil service reform or nonpartisan elections, leaving the bread and butter of boss politics—patronage and party discipline—thoroughly intact. Similar also to boss systems under Edward Kelly in Chicago and Thomas Pendergast in Kansas City, and even reform administrations in Hazen Pingree's Detroit and David Lawrence's Pittsburgh, Mayor Hague's Jersey City machine worked through district and ward committees to mobilize thousands of loyal city and county employees into a disciplined party operation. This included assessing 3 percent of city workers' wages (called rice pudding) for partisan purposes, much like Chicago's 1 percent levy. Similar to other Irish-run machines, too, the Hague regime reserved patronage and leadership overwhelmingly for Irish constituents, playing "recognition politics" with Jews, Italians and other new immigrants by granting only token jobs, although barely acknowledging Jersey City's growing thousands of African Americans, unlike the affinity that Republican and Democratic bosses exhibited toward black denizens in Chicago. As a result, despite the long-term demographic decline of the proportion of foreign-born and second-generation Irish-stock residents (dropping from 14 percent of the city's population of 267,779 in 1910 to 7 percent out of 301,178 in 1940, as compared to Italians' rise from 8 to 14 percent, or African Americans' growth from 2.2 to 4.6 percent), Irish Americans consistently dominated politics in Hague's Jersey City.[10]

Even so, reform was still an integral part of Jersey City's Progressive-era transformation, especially in the police department. Back in the nineteenth century, U.S. big-city police emerged gradually to keep social order in rapidly growing municipalities, but they arose largely as appendages of political machines. Numbering into hundreds or thousands of officers, police forces provided bosses with a rich source of well-paid patronage jobs to give out. In the decentralized ward system, moreover, precinct politicians controlled patrolmen more than front-office superintendents did. With little training, minimal supervision, and poor means of communication with superior officers, policemen were notorious for their brutal treatment of criminal suspects, corrupt collaboration with vice peddlers, widespread drunkenness, and neglect of duty. With all of these problems, Progressive reformers from New York City police commissioner Theodore Roosevelt to Berkeley police chief August Vollmer tried to restructure and professionalize police forces, using a military analogy to convert them into impartial agencies serving the public good. Reformers upgraded police personnel with mental and physical requirements, centralized control under tenured police chiefs, imposed military command structures, adopted new crime prevention techniques, and created special squads. Still, as late as the 1920s, city police remained captives of politics and prone to excessive force, just as happened in Frank Hague's Jersey City.[11]

When Jersey City's new commission started up in 1913, it followed familiar Progressive lines by consolidating old boards of police, fire, and other matters under a new Department of Public Safety with a single city commissioner, Frank Hague, in charge. It was a defining moment. Facing what historian Steven Hart calls a "brawling Wild West city" wherein crime flourished, Hague set about to overhaul the city's police department. In Progressive fashion, he removed incompetent patrolmen and supervisors, shifted desk officers to street duty, centralized command under the police chief and public safety director, created a special squad to monitor officers' performance, and confronted the Police Benevolent Association (PBA), a statewide policemen's mutual benefit society that stood as an obstacle to reform. When he found that the city charter limited his powers to discipline incapable officers, Hague received help from Jersey City corporation counsel John Milton to secure a clever legislative amendment that empowered the public safety director on his own to try, discipline and remove officers for violations of departmental regulations. Hague used this expanded authority to bring a "reign of terror" or great improvement to Jersey City's police department, however one looks at it.[12] He turned police reform into a crusade that fused reform, morality, and politics into a new political culture that prevailed through the 1920s and 1930s, and shaped the bounds of civil liberties in Jersey City.

Many incidents in Hague's police campaign demonstrate that fusion. On May 6, 1915, he suspended Police Chief Frank Monahan for intoxication on the job: Monahan allegedly imbibed champagne at a saloon after a political dinner in violation of Sunday closing laws, failed to arrest two saloon employees for illegally selling him the drinks, and then fell asleep drunk on the trolley car on his way home. Contradictory accounts obscure what really occurred, and politics pervaded public discussion about it. The PBA and Mayor Mark Fagan backed Monahan, while Hague advanced the case as telling evidence of the need for reform. The case boiled down to who "framed up" whom. "That there is some tall lying going on in this whole matter is evident," observed the *Jersey Journal*. In the end, the city commission exonerated the chief, forcing Hague to issue an apology, but not before he strongly defended his mandate to pursue reform. "It is my duty to see that the lives and property of the people of Jersey City are protected, and to see that every policeman in Jersey City does his duty," commissioner Hague declared. He had perhaps overreached, but still steadfastly defended police reform in high-minded terms, while benefitting politically.[13]

Other efforts to instill discipline on Jersey's police force equally showed Hague's blend of reform, politics, and moral purpose. Sternly, he put hundreds of patrolmen on trial for neglect of duty, fining many, demoting others, dismissing quite a few, and questioning their claims for special benefits. In particular, Hague demoted Lieutenant Thomas Moran to the rank of patrolman for failing promptly to dispatch a patrol car to help an ailing woman attending a Holy Name parade, although newspaper reports suggested that the unavailability of a wagon and poor communication caused this breakdown in police service. Hague's finding seemed again like overreaching, but he continued relentlessly to promote efficiency. He ended precinct captains' exemption from punching time clocks and ordered them to go out on night patrol in uniform at least once a week. He finally established the special squad called the Zeppelins, which reported directly to the public safety commissioner on internal departmental discipline. Later on, the Zeps would morph into a sinister political force, but at the time of their creation they were a common Progressive police reform designed to strengthen departments' centralized command.[14]

Hague's battle with the PBA especially blended reform, politics, and political morality. From the start, Hague described the PBA was a political rather than a benevolent organization. The association, he argued, raised huge sums of money from public charitable events on the pretext of helping widows and orphans, but actually used the funds to hire lawyers to defend delinquent officers whom Hague was bringing on trial before the city commission. The PBA countered that Hague's public safety department confiscated the cash for its own use. Yet, the dispute was less about money than about power—who controlled the police and fire departments. At a stormy city commission meeting, PBA lawyer August Ziegener accused Hague of persecuting policemen, while Hague hotly responded that the PBA should show more respect for city authority. In the end, all parties laid the matter aside, but the PBA defiantly decided at its annual meeting in West Hoboken to hold its next convention in Hague's Jersey City. "We'll show him," yelled one West Hoboken attendee, "that the PBA is still in business."[15]

The Hague-PBA conflict spilled over into the 1917 city election, wherein good government and Hague's performance as public safety director were the central issues. By this point, Hague had assembled a three-vote majority on the city commission, but incumbent commissioner Henry Byrne led a five-man slate to depose the Hague group on the grounds that it had perpetrated partisan administration, reckless public finance, and political chicanery worse than ever before. While claiming to modernize them, the Byrne slate argued, the Hague majority actually "terrorized and demoralized" the police and fire departments. It "framed up" one dedicated policeman after another, bloated the police department with an additional two hundred new officers, and turned so many patrolmen into "Hague political workers" that the number of burglaries in Jersey City spiked and gambling halls ran "full blast." The Hague slate, by contrast, portrayed the election as the "PBA vs.

the People"—that is, a choice between "shirkers" of public duty and devoted public servants. "I was elected to serve the people Jersey City and not to be controlled by the PBA," Hague declared.[16]

Some historians interpret Hague's stance as a sign of his uniquely strident antiunion views, but it was actually typical of the time. For one thing, Hague's posture mirrored Progressive reformers' resistance to a surge of police unionization that occurred during the years 1917–19, culminating with Massachusetts governor Calvin Coolidge's decree that quashed the Boston police strike. Hague's approach to running the Jersey City police department thus corresponded to growing efforts nationwide to strengthen public control over such agencies. For another thing, Hague's campaign against the PBA perpetuated the Progressive reform spirit. Already, his exploits as public safety director tracking down a murder suspect in Newark and exposing an apparent wartime German sabotage plot had established his reputation for stellar police work. His 1917 reelection campaign advertised his fight against the PBA as part of a larger plan to improve public safety: he allegedly swept aside PBA dictatorship, restored discipline to Jersey City police, and installed new communication apparatus to improve police response time. According to campaign literature, "Protection, Safety, Efficiency, Discipline" were the Hague slate's watchwords. Using the Progressive language of antibossism, "square deals," "public service" and "efficiency," and some of the substance of Progressive police reform, too, the Hague slate won the city commission election of 1917, forced the PBA completely out, selected Hague as mayor, and then handily triumphed again in another hotly contested race in 1921 on similar themes. It was "a big vote of confidence," according to the *Jersey Journal*.[17]

The Progressive character of Hague's early career has long puzzled scholars. Focusing on the Hague organization's later corruption and pursuit of power, most Hague biographers treat his early Progressive inclinations as either an anomaly, a short-lived political expediency, or a genuine pursuit that lasted only into the mid-1920s, when his politics turned reactionary. Most contend that Hague's early years were devoted not to reform but to mobilizing patronage-bound city workers into an unbeatable political organization, building the police department into a political force, and reaching out into state politics to influence gubernatorial elections and appointments. Yet, a second generation of urban historians argues that city machines like Hague's persisted despite corruption, because they remained truly "functional" in addressing their constituents' needs. This line of reasoning suggests that the Progressive aspects of Hague's police reforms were not just transitory but a foundational part of his long-term success. The reforms served his constituents while they furthered his interests as a boss.[18]

Hague's consolidation of power in 1919 and 1921 continued to mix Progressive sentiment and political self-interest. In 1919, he helped to elect Democratic banker-friend Edward Edwards as governor, leading to friendly appointments to the New Jersey Board of Taxes and Assessments and substantial property tax increases on previously protected railroad, public service, and oil companies. This achievement not only brought "justice" to city taxation but also provided an enormous new source of revenue to subsidize the city's patronage rolls and social services. In the 1921 city election, moreover, the Hague administration took credit for a modernized police department, an up-to-date fire department, a new city hospital, a new child welfare program, improved city street cleaning, and new legislation protecting rights of the city's numerous tenants. "Efficiency and Progressiveness" marked Hague's stewardship, a campaign ad said. And efficient city service remained a central claim to his political authority into the 1930s. Explaining in a 1934 speech why Jersey City residents repeatedly elected him as mayor, Hague argued that voters knew that they were getting "good government, efficient government, or whether or not the public officials are betraying them," a phrase that captures the mixture of Progressivism and bossism.[19]

Jersey City's functional combination of reform and boss politics included not only an overhaul of the police department, but also a typical Progressive police crusade against vice. According to historian Paul Boyer, Progressivism in general contained a strong moral thrust, and in cities it featured "coercive social-control crusades," wherein reformers fended off moral disasters by cracking down on saloons, prostitution, gambling, and other forms of "degeneracy." Some city bosses like Charles Murphy in New York and Edward Crump in Memphis, he added, were as straitlaced and concerned with keeping "moral order" as middle-class reformers were. Like them, Frank Hague himself became a "coercive moral reformer." Unlike dissolute boss Enoch "Nucky" Johnson in Atlantic City, Hague dressed and acted like a stern "Puritan elder." As public safety director, he set a paternalistic tone for anti-vice policing by suppressing prostitution, pornography and narcotics, banning "the back rooms of saloons where women and young girls were permitted to assemble and be served with intoxicating drinks," abolishing "cheap dance halls" in which "many young girls were ruined," and closing down burlesque theaters. A big exception was toleration of illicit horse-race betting and later bootlegging, possibly because they were controlled by Hague operatives and paid tribute.[20]

The Hague regime's cultural affinity for Jersey City's 75 percent Roman Catholic immigrant majority powerfully sustained its blend of Progressive moralism and bossism, especially due to Irish influence. According to historian James Barrett, Irish Americans "participated disproportionately in religious practice" compared to other ethnic groups (except the Poles), and their religiosity dominated urban political life, despite their shrinking portion of the city population. Jersey City consequently became, as Steven Hart puts it, a "proto-theocracy" in which lines between church and state blurred. Mayor Hague routinely named Roman Catholic clergy as city chaplains and appointed Catholics to head every major city subdivision, including the police department. In addition, his own abstemious life style modeled proper Catholic behavior. Something of a hypochondriac, Hague not only refrained from drinking, smoking and womanizing, but also staffed his administration with churchgoing family men and promoted policies that appealed to devout Irish women. After women's suffrage went through, he added ladies' auxiliaries to his organization and placed women in important party posts, most notably Mary Norton as congresswoman. Meanwhile, Hague attended mass daily, gave to local Catholic charities, marched in Holy Name parades,

Figure 1. Jersey City Mayor Frank Hague speaks at a business dinner, February 1, 1938. A Margaret Bourke-White photograph in *Life*, February 7, 1938. Image 50872167, the LIFE Picture Collection/Getty Images.

and consulted with his local pastor, Monsignor John Sheppard. In turn, ward and precinct leaders were expected to participate in the Holy Name Society or the Knights of Columbus, and attend prayer breakfasts.

Most important, the Hague administration's form of "good government" reflected the "general consensus as to a proper moral order for the community," a consensus rooted in "urban Irish Catholic morality" and Irish aspirations for respectability. Prostitution was out, but gambling within and outside of church activities was tolerable. Forceful suppression of unruly behavior was acceptable. Like other Irish Catholic residents, Hague was pessimistic about human nature and feared "the ever-present reality of sin as revealed in human conduct," according to historian James Fisher. Because of this, Hague's use of strong-arm police tactics to quell wayward activity and pacify what had once been a brawling immigrant city won him long-standing admiration. He continued to boast of this policy into the 1930s. While other cities were overrun with gangsters, racketeers and hoodlums, he claimed in his 1934 speech, Jersey City was a "moral city," the "cleanest in the country." Aggressive policing against moral disorder was thus a "functional" part of boss Hague's version of reform governance, not just political intimidation.[21]

There was, of course, a thin line between policing public order and using police to deprive political opponents of their rights to assemble, speak and picket, as Hague's regime became later known. Indeed, early on, critics complained that Hague converted police officers into political workers; over time, those criticisms grew as political challengers tried to oust his faction in city elections, outside unionists entered the city to organize maritime and factory workers, and Hague increased his use of police harassment. Yet, through the 1920s and 1930s, he appealed again and again to his widely popular mandate to preserve public order, rallying his supporters and obscuring the political dimensions of police work. Until the late 1930s, law and professional policing itself facilitated that practice.

* * *

The legal environment strongly facilitated the Hague administration's policy of aggressive policing through the 1910s and 1920s, until shifting in the 1930s—a reality overlooked by modern biographers who insist that lawlessness pervaded Hague's leadership from the start. Before 1930, U.S. law pertaining to public assemblies, street speaking, distributing handbills, and labor picketing had only begun to emerge in a modern form that would challenge municipal uses of city ordinances and police to maintain social order. First Amendment assembly and speech rights as we know them today barely existed. Federal courts would not start interpreting the First Amendment until World War I or applying it on the local level until the 1930s. State courts, meanwhile, recognized minimal common law rights to outdoor expression, but treated them as limitations on broadly construed city police powers. Moreover, free-speech debates still revolved around Sir William Blackstone's narrow old definition of speech law that prohibited prior restraint but allowed punishment for "licentious" expression that had a "bad tendency" to "disrupt peace and good order." When it came to public speech and assemblies, hence, courts acknowledged inherent rights to public expression, but still left cities with broad leeway to pass ordinances and order police suppression to restrict purportedly disruptive diatribes, assemblies, pickets, and antisocial behavior.[22]

In fact, at the start of the twentieth century, state and local law greatly narrowed the range of outdoor politics that Americans had historically practiced. In the beginning, public gatherings opposed the British Empire during the American Revolution, protested President George Washington's policies, and mobilized mass political parties in the era of President Andrew Jackson. The growth of nineteenth-century cities, however, generated a torrent of religious clashes, Civil War draft riots, labor protests and ethnic conflicts. Across the country, subsequently, political parties emerged on anti-mob and public-order planks, and municipalities responded both by enacting speaking permit ordinances and by enforcing vagrancy, loitering, and breach-of-peace laws more rigorously. Emanating from this context was New Jersey's sweeping Disorderly Persons Act of 1898, which criminalized loiterers, tramps, disturbers of the peace, and the wandering poor. "By the close of the nineteenth century," law professor Timothy Zick concludes, "a new regime of laws governing public behavior banned or severely limited assembly, expression, press and petition activities." The Salvation Army, single taxers, socialists, Industrial Workers of World (IWW) speakers, woman suffragists, and other groups might take to the streets, but they did so at governmental sufferance, not as a legal right.[23]

The U.S. Supreme Court articulated the prevailing jurisprudence that extended municipal supremacy over speech in public places in *Davis v. Massachusetts* (1897). In that case, the City of Boston arrested clergyman William F. Davis for speaking on Boston Common contrary to an ordinance requiring a permit from the mayor. Davis claimed that such an ordinance aimed at stopping breaches of peace and damage to public grounds hardly applied to his situation. He also argued that the city assumed "Princely power" to enact such a regulation, and imposed it on him in a discriminatory way in violation of the Fourteenth Amendment's equal protection clause. The U.S. Supreme Court, however, affirmed Davis's conviction on grounds laid out in the state opinion by (then) Massachusetts associate justice Oliver Wendell Holmes Jr. Without even considering Davis's constitutional claims, the U.S. Court, like Holmes, denied that citizens enjoyed any inherent right to speak on public property, "except in such mode and subject to such regulations as the legislature, in its wisdom may have deemed proper to prescribe." According to Justice Edward White, the common was the property of Boston citizens, and the Commonwealth of Massachusetts could enact legislation giving the City of Boston authority to pass ordinances managing that property, even power to exclude public speaking from the common. And if the city had authority to forbid all speaking on the common, it enjoyed the lesser power of passing an ordinance for the mayor to grant permits to allow speaking.[24] The decision left control over speech in urban public spaces fully in hands of city authorities without yet acknowledging First Amendment speech and assembly guarantees. It was a major legal pillar for the Jersey City ban on Committee for Industrial Organization (CIO) activities in the late 1930s.

As for state courts during this era, the central issue in outdoor assembly and speech cases was "the limits of municipal power," rather than constitutional rights. State judges presumed that people had common law rights to speak in streets and parks—the "poor man's printing press"—and that city governments had to treat potential street speakers equally, but state courts mainly inquired as to whether municipalities had legitimate and reasonable grounds to regulate speech-related public conduct, such as to stop littering, avoid traffic obstructions, or prevent breaches of peace. State courts assessed the extent of city powers exercised, not speech rights violated.[25]

The 1906 to 1917 socialist and IWW free-speech fights illuminated municipalities' general treatment of street speaking in this austere legal context, foreshadowing many legal issues that would arise in the CIO's battle with Mayor Hague in 1937 and 1938. The speech fights entailed efforts of socialist and IWW (Wobbly) organizers to reach working-class audiences with soapbox oratory, parades, and radical newspapers on the streets of East Coast and West Coast cities. Both groups maintained that outdoor expression was a fundamental U.S. liberty and a specific right of workers, given limited means of communication allowed them by capitalist society. Some municipal officials like New York City police commissioner Arthur Woods tolerated the socialists and Wobblies, but in most locales police officers arrested them by the hundreds on typical municipal police power grounds of obstructing sidewalks, blocking traffic, unlawful assembly, disorderly conduct, and disturbing the peace. Usually aligned with local employers, city officials convicted and imprisoned some of these agitators, released others without trial, and expelled a few by dropping them off at city limits, all tactics utilized later in Jersey

City. State appellate courts generally upheld local ordinances and agitators' convictions, but pushed back under state laws in a few cases. A Washington State court held Spokane's ordinance against street corner oratory to be unconstitutional, while the New Jersey Supreme Court vacated IWW leader William "Big Bill" Haywood's conviction for disorderly conduct in Paterson as not justified by the facts, an exemplary use of the limits-of-power doctrine.[26]

The free-speech fights inaugurated the first serious U.S. debate about the permissible legal scope of street speaking, a debate that would return in the CIO versus Hague conflict. One issue involved the nature of reasonable speech and reasonable municipal restrictions. IWW organizers claimed that they had every right to go and speak wherever they could attract people, but cities passed regulations and deployed police officers to restrict their infringement on traffic flow, private property, and public tranquility. Courts backed the cities up. In this spirit, the Jersey City commission enacted its later notorious 1924 anti-leafletting ordinance: "No person shall distribute or cause to be distributed, or strewn about any street or public place any newspaper, paper, periodical, book, magazine, circular, card or pamphlet."[27] The ordinance likely originated in the Hague administration's keep-the-streets-clean moral order campaign, but it later implicated freedom of political communication in the CIO's distribution of handbills.

The free-speech fights also provoked discussion as to whether minority speakers had to submit to majority rule. Many commentators of the time insisted that orators had to defer to restrictive laws enacted by democratic majorities that were designed for "the interest of public safety and good morals," but other observers maintained that the purpose of free-speech rights was to protect unpopular, even radical views from popular majorities.[28] This debate would resonate later in the Jersey City CIO controversy, when city officials attempted to justify their denial of speaking permits to CIO, American Civil Liberties Union (ACLU), and socialist outsiders on grounds that their radical political positions, and indeed their very presence, offended Jersey war veterans and many local residents.

The free-speech fights especially implicated the relationship between speech and disruptive or violent action. Observers roundly concurred that mere articulation of ideas was acceptable, but they disagreed as to when speech spilled over into illegal action or breaches of the public order. Some municipal authorities worried that even "peaceably" conducted rallies could stir up trouble, if speakers were known for incendiary ideas, prefiguring Jersey City's claim in 1937–38 that ACLU leader Roger Baldwin's appearance in itself would provoke a riot. Other authorities contended that Wobbly "ranters" were by their very nature "breeders of anarchy" who did not deserve free-speech rights, a rehearsal for Mayor Hague's contention in 1938 that CIO leaders were dangerous communist revolutionaries who were precluded from speech protections. Most important, many local figures despaired that the IWW's provocative words might incite a hostile reaction, again an argument that Jersey City would deploy in the late 1930s against pro-CIO speakers.[29]

The free-speech fights and subsequent worker agitation generated a series of New Jersey appellate court decisions that illustrate the limits-of-municipal-power jurisprudence that prevailed before the CIO versus Hague conflict began. Three New Jersey Supreme Court cases arose from a 1913 Wobbly-led silk workers strike in Paterson. In *State v. Scott* (1914), Justice Samuel Kalisch overturned Alexander Scott's conviction for publishing an inflammatory denunciation of Paterson police under the New Jersey Crimes Act, since Scott's intemperate remarks that city police acted like a bunch of "lawless" "drunken Cossacks" amounted only to criticism, not a plea for the forcible destruction of "any and all government." In *State v. Quinlan* (1914), however, Kalisch upheld Patrick Quinlan's conviction for advocating and encouraging workers at a public meeting to commit violent acts against silk operators, a form of direct incitement to cause injury prohibited by common law, not to mention the New Jersey Crimes Act. In *State v. Boyd* (1914), moreover, Justice Charles Parker affirmed Frederick Boyd's conviction under the crimes law for urging workers at a public meeting to sabotage or destroy silk company owners' property. The cases established a bedrock policy in New Jersey municipal law that cities could not ban public expression per se, but they could control it if it promoted disruption or crime, a policy sustained in *State v. Tachin* (1919) under New Jersey's World War I–era sedition act. In that case, the state supreme court upheld Tony Tachin's conviction for criticizing the U.S. role in World War I and declaring that Americans did not need government, but should arm themselves against it.[30]

Subsequently, the law of illegal assembly emerged as the focal point for defining the extent of New Jersey cities' authority to regulate assembly and speech. Historically, Anglo-American common law recognized citizens' right to assemble as fundamentally guaranteed, but it drew the line when three or more persons gathered to breach the peace, commit crimes by force, or behave in such a manner as to give "reasonably firm and courageous" observers fear that a riot might result. The New Jersey Court of Errors and Appeals faced this doctrine in the post–World War I Red Scare–era case of *Harwood v. Trembly* (1921), wherein socialist Fred Harwood tried to hold a street corner meeting in Rahway, New Jersey, attracting seven or eight hundred people without a permit. Fearing a riot from Harwood's anticipated remarks, Mayor David Trembley ordered the fire chief to hose Harwood off of his platform before he got a chance to speak. Ducking freedom of assembly issues, Chief Justice William Gummere used the limits-of-power analysis to rule that Trembley acted responsibly. Tracking the *Davis* ruling, he argued that "the constitutional guaranty of liberty of speech no more authorizes a citizen to appropriate to his own use the public property of a community . . . than it permits him to occupy *in invitum* the private property of a fellow citizen for the same purpose." The mayor had a civic duty to keep the streets clear, and whether or not he did so in a reasonable way was a question for a jury to decide.[31] Gummere did not confront the law of illegal assembly implicated in the case—was there really a danger of riot?—and he came down hard on the side of municipal power to restrict outdoor political gatherings. Moreover, he sanctioned prior restraint by preventing expression before it was vocalized. Harwood never got to speak.

New Jersey courts faced unlawful assembly more forthrightly in *State v. Butterworth* (1928). Here, in protest of police oppression during another Paterson silk workers strike in October 1924, labor leader John Butterworth and ACLU director Roger Baldwin led a procession down Market Street to City Hall Plaza, where they met up to two thousand followers and peacefully began to speak. Yet, police feared disorder after marchers brushed past them, gathered in a large number, and offered many "hurrahs and exclamations." Officers declared the meeting an illegal assembly, dispersed the crowd, and arrested organizers, including Butterworth and Baldwin. In a juryless trial before Passaic County's Special Sessions Court, Judge Charles Black convicted them with six other defendants under a section of the state Crimes Act codifying common law, ruling that unlawful assembly need not involve "any overt act" but could become unlawful "by such circumstances of terror as tended to endanger the public peace and excite fear." Appearing for the defendants on appeal, however, young Republican attorney (and future Hague opponent) Arthur Vanderbilt secured a reversal from Justice Samuel Kalisch and a unanimous Court of Errors and Appeals on the grounds that facts in this case did not truly evidence a disorderly meeting that threatened life or property.[32] It was an important civil liberties victory, but not a legal breakthrough. Kalisch did not affirm First Amendment rights but reevaluated facts under the old jurisprudence of unlawful assembly.

In this speech-restrictive climate, Jersey City passed two more ordinances serving to contain incendiary political expression. During the post–World War I Red Scare, a 1920 measure forbid any owner of a hall, auditorium, or other private meeting place from renting or leasing space for meetings at which speakers might talk about obstructing government or "advocating the abolition, overthrow or change" in government by unlawful means without a permit from the chief of police. Then in 1930, shortly after the *Butterworth* decision, a second measure provided that no "public parades or public assembly in or upon the public streets, highways, public parks or public buildings of Jersey City" were to take place without a permit obtained from the public safety director, who received authority "after investigation of all of the facts and circumstances" to refuse such a permit to prevent "riots, disturbances or disorderly assemblage." Tucked into city commission business with other measures that regulated parking and one-way traffic on city streets, this second ordinance seems to have originated more as a traffic than a political law.[33] Nonetheless, building on the law of illegal assembly, it gave the public safety director exceptional control over public gatherings by granting him open-ended discretion to determine when meetings threatened "riot, disturbance or disorderly assemblage." Coupled with the 1924 anti-leafletting regulation, these ordinances brought municipal power over assembly and speech to its apogee in Jersey City and set the stage for later abuses in the city's CIO confrontation.

The inclination of municipal law to favor public order over speech rights during the 1910s and 1920s extended to peaceful labor picketing. Although jurists around the country rarely denied that picketing contained speech elements, they overwhelmingly upheld laws and police actions that restrained or prohibited picketing on grounds that it was a nuisance, a threat to employers' property rights, a part of unlawful conspiracies, or a form of intimidation. Two conservative 1921 U.S. Supreme Court decisions set the tone. The first declared that the 1914 federal Clayton Act's ban on enjoining workers' peaceful persuasion during a strike did not cover nonemployee pickets or "intimidating" forms of picketing. The hotly contested 5–4 second decision struck down an Arizona antilabor-injunction law on the ground that absolute protection of peaceful picketing interfered with employers' properly rights. Such rulings encouraged strict municipal regulation of picketing. In a 1926 Passaic, New Jersey, textile workers strike, for instance, police used tear gas and clubs to enforce an anti-picketing ban. Then, in mid-1930s Jersey City, after Vice Chancellor Charles Egan condemned picketers carrying placards as intimidating, the city commission issued with an ordinance prohibiting banners or signs except for business purposes, and city police broke up picket lines not connected to recognized strikes.[34]

In many ways, then, the legal climate of the late 1910s and 1920s encouraged cities to restrain outdoor speech and assembly. While judges and municipal officials accepted speech and assembly as fundamental rights, they also held that cities carried something like ownership over public space that allowed them to curtail subversive expression, prevent gatherings seen as threatening, forestall traffic disruptions, and suspend pickets deemed too aggressive or insufficiently connected to labor disputes. In spite of lawlessness attributed to the failed Prohibition program, municipal law abetted tough policing.

The legal climate favoring municipal authority boosted Jersey City's version of "crusading government" begun by Mayor Hague in the 1910s. This crusade involved, as Steven Hart observes, "selective moralism" tailored to Hague's Irish Roman Catholic clientele. City police fought prostitution, raided bookstores for indecent literature, rooted out racketeers, and generally kept an eye out for "suspicious characters" and "undesirable persons." This resembled policing elsewhere. Even socialist Milwaukee mayor Daniel Hoan's police cultivated a tough-on-crime reputation by "picking up out-of-town suspected hoodlums on sight and either jailing them or sending them packing out of town; by cracking down hard on vice; by crushing incipient gang activity; and by harassing gamblers and brothel keepers." Yet, Jersey police simultaneously tolerated the vices of ordinary Irish Catholic residents, such as numbers running, horse race betting, illegal bootlegging, and "gaming wheels [that] ran freely at church carnivals and bingos [that] were wide open with cash prizes." Despite its selectivity, the Hague regime's moral policing sustained its "functional" agreement with voters to preserve Jersey as a "moral" town. Hague thus won reelection in 1933 on the platform of "No Vice, No Crime, No Racketeering."[35]

The legal climate also fostered Hague's well-known political uses of Jersey City police. Across the nation, Progressive reformers had hoped that professionalization would remove police from politics, but as political scientist Robert Fogelson remarks, this was impossible, because police agencies were inherently policy-making bodies that decided "which laws were enforced, whose peace was kept, and which public was served." Thus, in the permissive legal atmosphere of the time, Jersey City's modernized police department and its special Zeppelin squad became an appendage of Hague's political organization that spied on, harassed, and brutalized dissidents. Other municipalities did the same. Neighboring New York City's police force spied on political meetings, intimidated private hall owners, tapped telephones, and set up a special Industrial Squad to monitor labor radicals.[36]

Jersey City's police stood out, however, for perpetuating the nineteenth-century practice of interfering in elections. Street fighting and ballot-box stuffing had been regular features of Irish-run machines in the late 1800s, and police appointed through the Irish patronage system patrolled the polls to defend their organizations. Hague's regime kept this relic of the urban past going, as Jersey City's tumultuous election of April 1929 demonstrated. According to Republican opponent (and future city historian) J. Owen Grundy, the election followed a period when sarcastic *Jersey Journal* columnists lambasted the Hague organization and caustic anti-Hague newcomer James "Jeff" Burkitt lectured to large crowds on street corners about the Hague administration's many alleged misdeeds. A fusion ticket backed by the *Journal*, Burkitt, independent Republicans, and anti-Hague Democrats then mounted a fierce electoral effort to oust the mayor's contingent from the city commission, but police harassed Burkitt with traffic arrests and beatings, while Hague thugs roughed up other challengers and the rival *Jersey Observer* saturated downward wards with pro-Hague propaganda. As Grundy remembered it, the campaign culminated in a wild election night, when "Hague strong arm men" and "partisan police" patrolled polling places so that Hague's organization could "count itself back into office" with a dubious vote tally. Law and politics converged in the operation of Jersey City's constabulary, establishing the municipality's later reputation for "police state" and "fascist" tactics. U.S. law enforcement culture contributed to this unsavory development.[37]

* * *

Even as law and politics fostered aggressive police activity in Jersey City during the 1920s, shifting national attitudes buoyed it even more. Progressive concerns about moral disorder gave way to new worries about crime, prompting municipalities like Cleveland and Chicago to form expert crime commissions to address perceived police failures to control criminality. Cleveland's important 1922 commission report concluded that speedier processing of offenders through the criminal justice system from arrest to incarceration would deter crime, and thus it reaffirmed traditional reforms like hiring better qualified police personnel, removing obstacles to swift trial and conviction, and eliminating the corrupt influence of politics. Nonetheless, public concern about a perceived crime problem grew through the 1920s, due to gangland violence and widespread disregard of prohibition laws. In 1929, consequently, President Herbert Hoover appointed the National Commission on Law Observance and Enforcement or Wickersham Commission (after chairperson George Wickersham), which again recommended reforms, such as removing politics from policing, centralizing command, hiring better qualified officers, improving communication systems, and securing police administrators with tenure. Yet, even though the actual crime rate rose little, public hysteria about criminality festered into the 1930s in the wake of the 1932 Lindbergh baby kidnap-murder and FBI director J. Edgar Hoover's campaign against so-called public enemies.[38] Energetic crime control by big-city police departments became a central expectation of the U.S. public. Hague's 1933 slogan "No Vice, No Crime, No Racketeering" fit right in.

As city police around the country increasingly focused on crime control, most officers continued to regard the suppression of labor radicalism as part of their duties. A 1928 ACLU survey of police departments showed that the vast majority saw the control of radicals as central to maintaining public order. Most cities consequently mandated speaking permits for outdoor rallies, and some even required permission to meet on private property. The New Orleans police chief reported that he never issued permits to radicals, while Nashville (Tennessee), Pasadena (California), and Fall River (Massachusetts) did not allow street meetings at all. Across New Jersey, police in Hoboken, Elizabeth, Passaic, and other towns routinely broke up union meetings, communist rallies, and labor pickets.[39] Antiradicalism and crime control went hand in hand in police work.

City police departments ballooned everywhere in this context, not just in Jersey City. By 1930, the Jersey force had expanded to 1,398 officers and detectives, still overwhelmingly male with just five African Americans. This was a large number for a city of nearly 300,000, but quite in line with increases elsewhere in Boston (tripled), Philadelphia (tripled), Chicago (quadrupled), Denver (quadrupled), and Cleveland (quintupled). As part of large municipal bureaucracies, police forces provided hundreds of secure and well-paid positions for first- and second-generation immigrant newcomers, as well as generous pay for chiefs, lieutenants, and sergeants. Jersey City's police chief enjoyed the highest pay in the nation ($9,000 annually), but not much ahead of chiefs in Chicago ($8,575) and New York City ($8,240). The large number of officers left municipalities heavily policed, putting a cop, as Hague critic Dayton McKean said about Jersey City, seemingly on every street corner.[40]

In the midst of the national movement to strengthen law enforcement, Jersey City's police cultivated special renown for law-and-order professionalism, as illustrated by the *Police Reporter*, an in-house newsletter published in Somerville, New Jersey. Indeed, with a force so large that critics denounced it as a patronage nest bloated at taxpayer expense, Jersey City encouraged nearly a public cult of police surveillance, a refreshing contrast to early 1930s Chicago and New York, where gangsters seemingly ran amok. Consistent with Mayor Hague's policy to preserve Jersey as "the most moralist city in America," the *Reporter* praised the Jersey City police force's hard-line stance against racketeers and criminals. In a 1934 article explaining how gangsters were shifting their attention from rum running to the infiltration of legitimate businesses, (then) police chief Daniel Casey warned the "Racketeer Element" "to stay clear of Jersey City." In another 1934 essay, "The Policeman and the Citizen," police captain William V. McLaughlin maintained that the public

Figure 2. Jersey City police roll call, 1938. A Margaret Bourke-White photograph in *Life*, February 7, 1938. Image 1176830710, the LIFE Picture Collection/Getty Images.

did not fully appreciate the police officer's essential service for public order. Just as the military stood between the United States and aggressor nations, he admonished, "so too do the police departments of the nation stand between the honest citizen and the criminal element." Any letdown by police would lead to an explosion of crime, something that Jersey City's police were determined not to let happen.[41]

The Jersey City Department of Public Safety created an elaborate publicity machine to popularize this get-tough-on-crime image. In 1936, city commissioner and public safety director Thomas Wolfe set up a lecture bureau to promote public safety and publicize the police department's accomplishments. Already, the National Safety Council had awarded an honorable mention to the Jersey City police force for traffic safety work, and now the department could boast of Sergeant Malgone's success in tracking down an infamous robber in Texas. "Nothing escapes the 'Eagle Eyes' of Jersey City Police," the *Police Reporter* exclaimed. In addition, the safety department established the Jersey City Police Department Safety League, which assembled musically talented officers into a glee club and orchestra to give concerts and perform skits that educated and entertained residents (and likely sought their favor). An appreciative resident donated a "new all-white bus" for the glee club and orchestra to travel around the city.[42]

More directly connected to police work was Jersey City's Academy of Physical Training. According to academy commander Albert Thierfelder, formerly a training director at the U.S. Naval Academy, physical fitness was a vital part of a policeman's responsibilities. Jersey City consequently instituted compulsory physical training at a departmental gym both to teach men how to "take care of their bodies" and to keep them fit to do their work. As a result, Jersey City developed a masculinely muscular style of policing, as illustrated by sturdy officers who posed at the gym for photographs in the *Police Reporter*. Sergeant Henry Morse, an instructor at the Jersey City academy, stood out. Having the "grace of Apollo and the muscularity of Vulcan," according to observers, Morse was famous for using his superior strength to subdue notoriously athletic crooks like "Strangler Lewis." City authorities chose Morse as the model for a seven-foot-tall brass statue of a police officer designed by sculptor Archimedes Giacomentonio, one of whose European clients had been Benito Mussolini.[43]

Although it would be chastised later, the muscular character of Jersey City's highly visible police force during the mid-1930s was very much in keeping with Mayor Hague's long-held conception of moral policing, the masculine local culture of Irish fighting prowess, and growing national concerns about crime control. This was a tough, male-dominated, hypervigilant, law-and-order police force that strictly maintained public order and morality in Jersey City, and by physical coercion, if necessary. The police community associated this get-tough policy with Hague's leadership, as indicated by a mistaken caption in a 1936 issue of the *Police Reporter*. Under a grainy photograph of a 1916 swearing-in ceremony, the *Reporter* misidentified "Mayor Frank Hague" and "Commissioner Michael Fagan" as administering oaths to new officers.[44] Actually, gray-haired Mayor Mark Fagan was pictured (not future commissioner Michael Fagan), and Hague was still just a city commissioner, but the error exposed the widespread view of Hague as the "father" of Jersey City's modern police force and the preserver of local peace and prosperity. This blend of political lore and tough law enforcement culture prompted Jersey City's tough police reaction to striking seamen and CIO organizers in 1936–37.

And so too did a culture of police lawlessness and violence that swept the country during the 1920s and early 1930s, despite all of the reform efforts. In the course of investigating methods to improve crime control, the 1931 Wickersham Commission Report discovered rampant police brutality, violence, and abuse of criminal due process rights, especially in a practice known as the third degree. A term taken from Masonic Order initiation rites, the "third degree" referred to use of secret enhanced interrogation techniques to extract confessions from criminal suspects, such as subjecting them to bright lights, questioning them persistently for hours, flogging them with rubber hoses so as to inflict pain without leaving scars, or beating them outright with clubs, fists or kicks, all the while holding suspects incommunicado from their attorneys and the outside world without booking them, so as to avoid habeas corpus motions. Police chiefs and legal authorities denied that the practice was widespread, but the Wickersham report found evidence of it in dozens of states and cities, including San Francisco, Chicago, Detroit, Pittsburgh, New York, and Newark. The report found that police usually deployed the third degree against gangsters, poor people, and social minorities, but it also discerned that labor organizers and political radicals frequently got roughed up.[45]

Popularized by journalist Ernest Jerome Hopkins in *Our Lawless Police* (1931), the Wickersham Commission Report created a sensation and marked a watershed in public attitudes toward law enforcement. "The informed and articulate public," political scientist Samuel Walker observes, "was no longer willing to tolerate the misconduct that had been part of American policing for so long." Reformers renewed their calls to professionalize police departments, and the popular press cultivated a climate of public opinion that would oppose police brutality and misconduct through the 1960s.[46] Indeed, public outcry against Jersey officers' treatment of the CIO in 1937 and 1938 was partly a result of this emerging new outlook, one that departed from earlier concerns with social order and crime control.

Jersey City's coercion against labor organizers in the late 1930s was then as much a product of violent police culture of the time as it was the result of the Hague regime's alleged political oppression. Urban constabularies everywhere struggled with political protests and social dislocations in the emerging Depression era, frequently resorting to improper behavior to control them. Right across the Hudson River from Jersey City, for instance, the New York City Police Department (NYPD) was a showpiece for police misconduct. With a long tradition of violence again immigrants, workers, and radicals, the NYPD suppressed communist fur workers, insurgent railway laborers, and even teamsters affiliated with the American Federation of Labor (AFL) in the 1920s, and then engaged in a fierce antiradical campaign under Police Commissioner Grover Whalen in the early 1930s, highlighted by the pitched Union Square battle against communists in March 1930. Fiorella La Guardia's election as mayor in 1933 and Lewis Valentine's subsequent appointment as police commissioner abated New York police violence, but not entirely. Valentine still invited police to "muss up" crooks and gangsters. Subsequently, the ACLU took up the cause against police brutality in New York City and waged a long struggle to end police suppression there.[47]

The problem was not confined to New York. Surprise testimony before New York Republican member of Congress Hamilton Fish's committee on the communist menace in the early 1930s disclosed a "broader pattern of unprofessional [police] conduct" around the country. In their testimony, historian Alex Goodall reveals, police showed ignorance, incompetence, and prejudice, "not to mention brazen disregard for constitutional rights." Officers explained how they used petty local ordinances to arrest radicals, "knocked their heads off," and worked with conservative groups (including the Ku Klux Klan in the South) to undermine protests. The Flint, Michigan, police chief testified that he routinely arrested dissidents without charge. The Pontiac, Michigan, chief reported that his department stifled agitators by "hiding" them in the criminal justice system, "bury[ing] them within the jails so that they cannot get a writ out and get released." Meanwhile, newspapers corroborated that police often scuffled with radical outdoor speakers in the early 1930s. Police permitted many peaceful rallies to take place but acted forcefully to stop others, as when they expelled unemployment protestors from the Capitol grounds in Washington, D.C., and arrested other jobless demonstrators at a similar rally on Boston Common.[48]

The coercive inclinations of Jersey City's police flourished in this national law enforcement environment of the early 1930s on top of the infamous political machinations of the Hague regime. Growing in size, public presence, and muscular culture, the city's police department intensified its fight against local immorality and crime. The department's overwhelmingly Irish Catholic old-immigrant-stock rank and file, moreover, stood ready to clamp down on agitators of the era who espoused socialist philosophies and came from Eastern European, often Jewish immigrant backgrounds. Moreover, Jersey police officers' reliance on the Hague organization for patronage and their identification with Hague's personal leadership inclined them loyally to follow the city's get-tough law enforcement policy.

New Jersey legislation in the 1930s toughened policing even more. Following recommendations of a Washington, D.C., crime control conference, the state assembly amended the state Disorderly Persons Act to allow police powers to make arbitrary searches and arrests. Lawmakers redefined "disorderly persons" to include people "on foot or in any automobile, vehicle or public conveyance, who cannot give a good account of themselves, or who shall have no legitimate business," the last phrase revised in 1936 to read "or who is engaged in an illegal occupation" to assuage constitutional concerns. (Then) Jersey City police chief Daniel Casey praised the measure as "the most efficient deterrent to crime that has yet been devised," although he admitted that law-abiding citizens might be "inconvenienced" by getting picked up mistakenly. They "should not feel so badly about it," he remarked, since mistakes were inevitable and officers would speedily release innocent citizens "with something approaching an apology." The key thing, according to Casey, was that the law helped police to "apprehend criminals wherever they might be found." Indeed, the state Court of Errors and Appeals had already approved the routine Jersey City police practice of stopping and searching cars traveling through city streets and the Hudson River tunnels to catch criminals. In opposition, the ACLU and other civil libertarians contended that New Jersey's amended law was plainly unconstitutional, since like many vagrancy laws previously struck down, it failed to specify clear arrest standards and invited police misconduct.[49] Nonetheless, the statute remained in force through the 1930s.

An ACLU report submitted to Attorney General Homer Cummings in 1938 illuminates how the Jersey City Police Department operated in this atmosphere. Prepared on behalf of the ACLU and the New Jersey Civil Liberties Union by the Newark law firm of Isserman and Isserman, a long-time nemesis of Mayor Hague's Jersey City regime, the report aimed to enlist Cummings and the U.S. Department of Justice in the CIO's legal battle then raging with Hague. Although it was patently partisan, this advocacy brief still offers insights into the nature of Jersey City policing.

The report detailed eighty-nine instances of alleged civil liberties violations from 1930 to 1938 across Hudson County that seemingly confirmed the Hague regime's reputation for freewheeling police surveillance. Drawn from court proceedings and newspapers, the report mostly cited cases involving police interference with labor pickets, the distribution of handbills or pamphlets, and violations of New Jersey's Disorderly Persons Act, but it included a few pertaining to public meetings, the police dragnet at the skyway and Hudson River tunnels, and the suppression of radical newspapers. Overall, the cases reflect a strict police regime with a remarkably mixed agenda to sustain moral order, stop crime, restrain disfavored political groups, and use the third degree to deter antisocial behavior. In one case cited, police raided a bookstore to confiscate *The Grip of Desire*, which the Roman Catholic Church banned, along with Marxist and Leninist literature. In another, Mayor Hague told the *Hudson Dispatch* that he wanted no gangsters in Jersey City and would unleash police nightsticks to keep them away, inferring Jersey City's participation in the nationwide anticrime crackdown during the 1930s. Indeed,

Hague praised Jersey City's dragnet as a vital way to stop crime. "There are no gangs in Jersey City," he declared, "because all suspicious characters are apprehended, wherever they are seen, in automobiles, trains, or on the street." "If they have a criminal record [and] no good reason for being here and no visible means of support," he added, "we slap them in the penitentiary for 90 days. And I want to tell you[,] they stay there for 90 days. When we let 'em off the rock pile, they're not anxious to go back [to Jersey City]."[50] Hague's reference to "no good reason for being here" suggests that he was following the soon-to-be discredited phase "no legitimate business" in the 1933 Disorderly Persons Act. Although it aimed to criticize Hague's support of summary police action, the ACLU report documents his fundamental commitment to keep law and order.

Other cases cited in the ACLU report exhibit a thin line between aggressive police work and potential civil-liberties violations. For example, the report cited more than a dozen arrests for circulating leaflets and pamphlets, usually under local anti-leafletting ordinances or the state's Disorderly Persons Act. Some arrests seemed to be sensible, as in the case of a man who disrupted traffic by passing out flyers to motorists on a highway. Yet, judges dismissed others outright or found local ordinances on which they were based to be invalid. Nearly all of the leafletting arrests involved support for unpopular groups, such as strikers, bonus marchers, communists, International Longshoremen, and Jehovah's Witnesses. The report also portrayed arrests made under sections 1 and 3 of the Disorderly Persons Act as frequently questionable. Jersey City police used the statute as a catch-all to detain suspects in their Holland Tunnel dragnet, to remove traffic obstructions, and most importantly to take leafletters and picketers off of the streets in labor disputes. In one 1932 case involving the distribution of circulars, officers and magistrates obstructed attorney Sol Kapelsohn's efforts to represent his client.[51]

The ACLU report revealed police antipathy toward labor rallies and pickets. Back in the 1910s and 1920s, despite its opposition to police unions, the Hague regime had cultivated friendly relations with local AFL-affiliated labor organizations. By the early 1930s, however, police in Jersey City and other Hudson County municipalities regularly stopped gatherings of communists, unemployment protestors, antiwar marchers, the ACLU, and others, while disrupting picketers in knitting mill, restaurant, garment worker, and seamen's strikes, typically on grounds that pickets were not carried out by recognized unions, were not part of legitimate labor disputes, or were simply disorderly.[52]

Discussion in the ACLU report of so-called runaway shops especially reveals how Jersey police moved beyond keeping order to serving politics.

Marking an intrusion of regional and national labor controversies on Jersey City for the first time, the "runaways" were small struggling Depression-era, mainly footwear and textile firms that fled union contracts in Manhattan and Brooklyn by relocating across the Hudson River in New Jersey municipalities with open shop plants. The *New York Post* charged that the Hague administration made a special point to lure these companies to Jersey City with a promise of police protection from union organizers. Yet workers put up a fight. In 1934, for example, the runaway Miller Parlor Furniture Company from Brooklyn faced pickets assembled by the left-wing Furniture Workers Industrial Union in sympathy with the firm's unionized former employees. Miller secured a temporary injunction against the picketers from a local judge, but the furniture workers sought support from the ACLU, which sent Alfred Bingham and Corliss Lamont from New York City to join the prohibited pickets, resulting in those two celebrities' arrest for allegedly loitering in front of the Miller plant. Nonetheless, sensational publicity, a federal district court ruling overturning the anti-picketing injunction, local AFL unions' support of the picketers and looming November elections all caused Hague's administration to back down and permit picketing in this instance. Hague, who was conveniently out of town when acting mayor Arthur Potterton announced the concession, later denounced the furniture workers as communists and continued Jersey City's narrow policy toward labor picketing. His statement marked a turn against organized labor and one of his first uses of anticommunist rhetoric to stop it. Meanwhile, the New York–based communist newspaper the *Daily Worker* covered the story closely but evidenced no communist involvement in the Miller dispute.[53]

* * *

The Miller case signaled an important shift in Jersey City's police work that would culminate in that municipality's disruption of the 1936–37 seamen's strike and obstruction of the 1937–38 CIO organizing campaign, leading to the U.S. Supreme Court's *Hague v. CIO* decision. Nearly all observers today see these two labor controversies as shocking instances of labor suppression rooted in the authoritarianism of Frank Hague's boss regime. Yet the seamen's and CIO's conflicts were far from just the result of Mayor Hague's supposed autocratic practices or the product of police collusion with big antiunion employers as happened contemporaneously in Akron, Flint, and Chicago labor disputes. Police aggression exhibited in seamen's and CIO cases had been long in the making in Jersey City's larger political and legal culture.

For one thing, Jersey City's distinctive blend of Irish boss politics and Progressive reform concentrated municipal power in ways that made Hague's abuses in the seamen's and CIO controversies likely. Arguably, Hague stood among other powerful twentieth-century city bosses, good and bad, like New York's Charles Murphy, Chicago's Edward Kelly, Kansas City's Thomas Pendergast, and Pittsburgh's David Lawrence, who ran tight organizations, even though he stood apart for his uniquely heavy-handed style due to distinctive local conditions. Jersey City's adoption of commission government in 1913 inclined his leadership toward strict control over the city's administrative divisions, especially the Public Safety Department. Progressive-era police reform unified his command even more. Acting both as boss and as reformer, hence, Mayor Hague built his political power on Jersey City's centralized police apparatus and established the long-standing political bargain that sustained his appeal to voters. His administration would increase police and fire department payrolls to keep Jersey residents at work, while using the professionalized police force to preserve moral order and stamp out crime as Jersey City's dominant working-class, Irish Catholic denizens wanted. He did not rule just through fear, as critics charged. Indeed, public support for tough police procedures grew in the 1920s and 1930s, first to suppress gangsterism and then to contain Depression-era social unrest. This functional political arrangement perpetuated the Hague regime, even as the mayor deployed police for increasingly, and sometimes outrageously, self-serving political purposes in the late 1920s and 1930s.

Meanwhile, national legal culture symbolized by the 1897 *Davis* case sustained Jersey City's strong municipal control over assembly and speech in public places. Since the U.S. Supreme Court was only beginning to incorporate national First Amendment guarantees into the Fourteenth Amendment for application on the state level, local courts retained primary jurisdiction over outdoor assembly and speech claims, and evaluated them on the basis of the restrictive doctrines of municipal police powers and unlawful assembly. Moreover, municipal anti-leafletting laws and public meeting permit ordinances like Jersey City's proliferated everywhere, while new state laws like New Jersey's amended Disorderly Persons Act expanded city surveillance over public streets and parks. Until the mid-1930s, such a legal environment sheltered abusive municipal police departments like Jersey City's from the scrutiny of federal courts. As a result, cities exercised broad police powers over labor pickets, handbill distribution, and public rallies.

Finally, national law enforcement culture intensified tough, even violent city control over outdoor expressive activity during the 1920s and 1930s, despite decades of reform. As state crime commissions and the Wickersham report showed, Progressive police reforms had done little by the early 1930s to curtail urban police departments' routine violation of criminal due process rights and coercive treatment of "undesirables," partly because reformers and the public demanded more effective action against gangsters and crime. The modern movement against police brutality had only begun. Jersey City's oversized and muscular police department flourished in context. It was an expectation and a matter of municipal pride that Jersey police acted snappily and forcefully against unruly and criminal elements.

Up to the mid-1930s, hence, Jersey City mayor Frank Hague's administration certainly was autocratic, but it was also very much a reflection of its time. In an exaggerated way, Hague's regime embodied the peculiar mix of boss governance, premodern civil liberties jurisprudence and law enforcement culture in the interwar years that accentuated coercive municipal regulation of outdoor expressive activities like assembling, speaking, leafletting and picketing. In the late 1930s, however, all of this would change. A dramatic transformation in labor organizing, civil liberties jurisprudence, and political culture would ultimately refashion and rebrand Hague's old-fashioned disregard of civil liberties as undemocratic, unconstitutional, and even fascist.

# 2 Workers in Transition

## *Remaking Labor Unionism in a Boss-Run Town*

First there was iron worker Theodore Brandle and then there was union organizer William Carney, two formidable labor leaders who met different fates with Jersey City's strong man, Mayor Frank Hague. Brandle emerged as business agent for Ironworkers Local 45, an operative in the Hudson County Central Labor Union (HCCLU) and the New Jersey State Federation of Labor (NJSFL), and eventually a labor entrepreneur and banker. He kept up a strong partnership with Hague through the 1920s until their falling-out over unionization of the Pulaski skyway project in the 1930s. Hague pushed Brandle into bankruptcy and ruin. Carney, by contrast, arose in tough midwestern campaigns of the CIO to organize the rubber, steel, and automobile industries during the mid-1930s, and then moved east to become the CIO's regional director in Newark, New Jersey, in 1937. Cultivated in the CIO's early bravado masculine style, Carney launched an "invasion" of Hague's bailiwick in November 1937 hoping to "organize the unorganized" in spite of the mayor's opposition. Although Hague's regime temporarily stymied this effort, Carney and the CIO ultimately triumphed over the mayor when the U.S. Supreme Court ruled in *Hague v. CIO* (1939) that Jersey City had to respect worker rights to assemble and speak in public places.[1]

Brandle's and Carney's disparate experiences show how much the labor movement changed in Jersey City over the course of the 1920s and 1930s with important ramifications for Mayor Hague's treatment of worker rights and civil liberties. The long-time popular and scholarly view is that Hague's labor policy followed self-interest. While the mayor accommodated unions in the 1920s, this argument holds, he kept them out of Jersey City for fiscal reasons during the Depression-ridden 1930s—that is, he embraced a business environment favorable for luring antilabor sweatshop employers willing to pay the taxes needed to finance exorbitant city expenses. As legal historian Laura Weinrib remarks, Hague "staked the economic vitality of [Jersey City] on its employer-friendly reputation." The municipality launched its "Jersey City Has Everything for Industry" slogan at this moment.[2] Yet, political expediency alone did not produce the Hague regime's turnabout on organized labor. Equally influential were changes in the labor movement itself. The changes disrupted the city's commitment to commercial boosterism dating back to the founding of commission government in 1913. They also upset the political alliance that Hague had initially forged with labor, as Brandle's and Carney's careers showed.

Brandle illustrated the nationwide primacy of craft unions affiliated with the AFL during the 1920s, along with those unions' aversion to mass collective action and to organizing mass production workers. Locally, he demonstrated the predominance of building trades in 1920s Jersey City's diverse, small-scale economy and their inside role in helping Hague build his formidable statewide Democratic political organization, at least until the 1930s Depression decimated craft unions and pushed them into conflict with the Hague administration. As a CIO leader, by contrast, Carney marked a new generation of industrial unionists who were not natives of Jersey City but outsiders from the midwestern mining, steel, and automobile industries. His effort to bring militant industrial unionism with its masculine swagger and class-based "culture of unity" to Jersey City's low-wage factory workers conflicted with Hague's ethnicity-based ward-and-district political organization and law-and-order spirit. The shift from compatible inside craft unionism to threatening outside industrial unionism was a major reason for Hague's resistance to Carney's 1937 campaign.

The restrictive character of interwar U.S. labor law and civil liberties formed the legal context for Jersey City's reaction to organized labor's evolution, but the municipality deployed that law differently over time. Around the country through the 1920s and early 1930s, state and federal courts freely imposed labor injunctions on unions at the same time that police departments suppressed strikes, peaceful picketing, and boycotts, although court interference eased with passage of the 1932 Norris–LaGuardia Anti-Injunction Act and 1935 National Labor Relations (Wagner) Act (NLRA). In 1920s Jersey City, however, these restrictions had little impact, since Hague officials courted local craft leaders by refraining from injunctive relief and expelling outside strikebreakers that threatened local unions. In 1920s New Jersey, judges and law enforcers more readily intervened elsewhere in Paterson's and Passaic's mass textile strikes. The 1930s Depression era, however, changed Jersey City's attitude. When the severe economic downturn drove craft unions to desperate actions to survive, and then stimulated the surge of industrial unionism under the CIO, the Hague regime invoked previously neglected anti-picketing and public assembly laws to stifle the new kinds of labor unrest. This change led to Jersey City's infamous infringement on labor rights and liberties in the CIO case.

* * *

During U.S. organized labor's difficult 1920s, the convergence of local craft union needs and the rising Hague organization's political ambitions brought about a strong labor-Hague alliance in Jersey City. Craft unionism got a boost from Jersey City's post–World War I economy. Unlike postwar cities like Chicago with dominant big manufacturers, Jersey City exhibited a public sector and decentralized business sector of small and medium-size firms that employed nearly 140,000 laborers. Some Jersey City workers labored for big firms in the railroad car, meatpacking, silk goods, and electrical machinery industries averaging a hundred to five hundred employees, but most spread out among smaller foundries, machine shops, tobacco product factories, bakeries, box and paper companies, printing firms, and other establishments averaging between a dozen and five dozen laborers. Many male workers, moreover, concentrated either in skilled construction trades, or in transportation jobs such as drivers, railroad laborers, or longshoremen, while female workers congregated in tobacco products, women's clothing, telephone switchboarding, schoolteaching, and domestic service. And as of 1930, Jersey City's 4,322 male African American workers clustered in transportation or personal services, while most of the 1,993 black women laborers worked in domestic or personal service jobs. In 1930, 1,822 municipal employees—nearly all men and just five blacks—were employed as firemen, police officers, or detectives, just 1 percent of the total metropolitan workforce, a tiny number despite criticism of a bloated city payroll. Female schoolteachers easily outnumbered them.[3] Jersey City thus exhibited a diversified economy not conducive to mass unionization, but hospitable to organized local craft unions.

Conservative national attitudes toward labor relations in the 1920s also fostered cautious craft unionism. After World War I, union membership plummeted nationwide, while worker efforts to organize mass production industries collapsed. Thereafter, stagnant job growth, corporate consolidation, employers' antiunion open-shop campaigns, and an indifferent Republican administration in Washington, D.C., stifled labor activity. Most important, U.S. Supreme Court decisions under Chief Justice William Howard Taft sharply curtailed labor rights by narrowly defining legitimate strikes, rejecting "recognition" strikes, prohibiting secondary boycotts, and limiting picketing. Meanwhile, antistrike court injunctions proliferated all around the country. New Jersey reproduced these restrictions. An 1883 statute had decriminalized labor organizing, but after 1900 the state's dogmatically conservative equity judges issued sweeping injunctions that strictly limited labor activity: they defined "legal" strikes narrowly as just those involving disputes by employees of struck firms, allowed picketing only where so-called legal strikes existed, and barred pickets from obstructing streets or interfering with businesses. A 1926 New Jersey anti-injunction statute and subsequent equity decisions broadened organizing rights, but a 1937 Court of Errors and Appeals ruling restored the original restrictive view.[4]

In this context, both national and state AFL leaders refrained from engaging in aggressive collective activity. Mass job actions dropped off steeply in the 1920s, as labor leaders conserved and enlarged the gains of existing craft unions, rather than reach out to organize mass production workers. Instead, unionists in building, transportation, cleaning, food service, and other trades resorted to strategically focused strikes, boycotts, price-fixing schemes, intimidation, and even assaults against employers and nonunion workers to defend existing members' jobs and wages. Chicago employers regarded these tactics as tantamount to extortion and coined the term "racketeering" to discredit them.[5]

In New Jersey, consequently, skilled white male trade unionists dominated the state labor movement and local labor councils, including the HCCLU in Jersey City's Hudson County. Carpenter Arthur Quinn served as NJSFL president from 1913 to 1933, while iron worker Theodore Brandle ran the powerful New Jersey Building Trades Council. Simultaneously, unrest persisted among mass production silk and woolen workers in Passiac, Clifton, Garfield, and Lodi under the AFL-affiliated United Textile Workers and later the militant Amalgamated Textile Workers, but neither group succeeded in unionizing textile workers or in gaining NJSFL support. Instead, skilled workers in the booming building trades remained the backbone of New Jersey's labor movement, holding NJSFL membership steady at around 25,000 through the 1920s after a loss of six thousand constituents during the postwar recession. In Jersey City, the Building Trades Council led by Brandle remained the mainstay of the city's modest labor movement, along with teamsters who organized the city's carriers and longshoremen who unionized the waterfront.[6]

Admittedly, railroad workers, meat packers, stone cutters, and others did strike in Jersey City during the 1920s, but they still perpetuated the conservative trade union strategy of avoiding militant displays, supporting Democratic political candidates, and controlling their crafts. The NJSFL refused to endorse a socialist third-party campaign in 1920 and expelled socialists from its annual meeting. Later, the craft-union-dominated HCCLU refrained from supporting striking Passaic textile workers and declined to join protests against the Sacco and Vanzetti executions. Meanwhile, both the NJSFL and HCCLU firmly supported mainstream Democrats, held a rally for gubernatorial candidate George Silzer in 1922, and endorsed presidential candidates John Davis (rather than the AFL choice Robert La Follette) in 1924 and Alfred Smith in 1928. NJSFL and HCCLU leaders did speak out against labor injunctions and advocate the election of state judges as a way to eliminate injunction-happy jurists. Yet, Jersey trade unionists focused mostly on preserving their control over skilled labor. In 1920, for example, Brandle was indicted for disciplining workers who violated union rules by seeking nonunion-sanctioned employment. In 1926, he charged the Port Authority of New York for bidding contracts that excluded union labor. In 1927, stone cutters struck against the importation of nonunion stone for use in Jersey City public works, an action that federal courts rejected as violating antitrust laws. In 1930, Brandle and his union were investigated for an alleged conspiracy to exclude nonunion-made materials from northern New Jersey construction work.[7]

Clearly, Brandle was Jersey City's foremost labor leader in the 1920s. He demonstrated the blurred lines between trade unionism, business, and politics at the time. Starting as business agent for Ironworkers Local 45, Brandle worked his way up in local building trades councils, while assuming leadership of the HCCLU and a prominent role in the NJSFL, unsuccessfully challenging Arthur Quinn for the presidency of the latter group in 1924. He also extended his interests into business, creating the bonding company Branleygran, establishing the Labor National Bank in Jersey City, and assuming the director general's post for the Iron League of New Jersey, a trade association founded to protect structural and ornamental iron firms. He also became a "friend" and "lieutenant" of Jersey City mayor Frank Hague, who "funneled millions of dollars of city and county work to Brandle's company." Indeed, when Brandle opened his new fourteen-story Labor National Bank building in Jersey City's Journal Square in 1928, Hague was on hand to celebrate the occasion, even providing twenty police officers to guard the ceremonious transfer of $200,000 into the bank's vault. When federal prosecutors accused Hague of missing tax payments, moreover, Brandle loaned the mayor $60,000 to cover his obligation, although ironically Brandle too was charged with tax evasion in 1930.[8]

Unlike longshoremen, trade unionists like Brandle did not mesh with the ward-and-district structure of Mayor Hague's rising political machine, but that did not matter in the 1920s. Although the Jersey City Chamber of Commerce promoted the open shop among 80 percent of the city's employers, Hague cultivated ties to local trade unionists in building and transportation trades who did not interfere with local open-shop practices. On the rough-and-tumble waterfront, the local Democratic political club intertwined with longshoremen's and terminal workers' unions, while Hague allied with waterfront labor leaders to provide patronage jobs for his Democratic followers. Elsewhere in the city, he supported worker causes, despite his opposition to unionization of police and firemen. He deployed police to turn back strikebreakers arriving from New York City in a 1919 longshoremen's job action, called for judicial restraint in the use of labor injunctions, spoke at a rally of railroad strikers in 1922, and mediated local labor disputes. Most importantly, Hague sought Brandle's and NJSFL president Arthur Quinn's help to strengthen the state Democratic Party and his position in it. Both the NJSFL and HCCLU regularly supported Hague's choices for Democratic gubernatorial and presidential candidates. Both consistently supported Hague's reelection through the 1920s, including in the hotly contested 1929 race.[9]

Overall, Hague worked with labor allies through the 1920s to solidify control over city politics and bolster the Democratic Party's power in state politics, especially when a 1928–29 scandal nearly ruined his career. The mayor's state strategy was to secure the election of Democratic (or sympathetic Republican) New Jersey governors with the authority to appoint friendly judges and state commissioners wielding authority over municipal affairs. His power never extended to the state legislature, which remained solidly under Republican control. Thus, with labor help, Hague's organization elected Democratic governors Edward Edwards (term 1920–23), George Silzer (1923–26), and A. Harry Moore (1926–29). In 1928, however, this strategy failed. In the infamous gubernatorial race that year, twenty thousand Hudson County Democrats crossed over to cast ballots in the Republican primary to displace implacable Hague foe Robert Carey as the Republican nominee for the apparently weak candidacy of Morgan Larson, who was expected to lose against Hague's chosen Democratic choice, Walter Dill. Larson won the governorship anyway, and outraged Republican lawmakers led by state senator Clarence Case launched an embarrassing legislative inquiry into Hague's alleged personal and political corruption. When Hague refused to answer questions, the Case Committee called for his arrest on contempt charges, but friendly state judges exonerated Hague and ended the investigation. Perhaps in revenge, Hague's organization ran NJSFL president Arthur Quinn successfully as a Democratic state senate candidate to defeat Republican Russell Watson, the staff attorney on the Case Committee who had called for Hague's arrest.[10] Throughout all of this, Jersey trade unionists stood staunchly by Hague and the Democrats.

While Hague forged his alliance with local AFL unions, the vast majority of Jersey City's working class remained unorganized, ethnically fragmented, and largely controlled by the Hague organization. As in other urban industrial centers that historians have studied—including Chicago and Woonsocket, Rhode Island—Jersey unions represented a small sliver of skilled male Anglo and Irish workers in the 1920s, leaving the rest of the city's largely unskilled or semiskilled workers ununionized and dispersed across many trades and fragmented in social enclaves rooted in family, nationality, race and religion, especially Roman Catholicism. This included black laborers, who remained marginalized through Jersey City's whole coming struggle with the CIO. Like Chicago and Woonsocket, too, forces of modernization had started to bring Jersey City's working class out of ethnic isolation, particularly in the World War I "Americanization" campaign that generated the municipality's robust veterans' groups. Yet, unlike Chicago or Woonsocket, modernization did not incline Jersey City workers to shed ethnic allegiances and unite along class lines in the CIO during the 1930s. Instead, the powerful Hague machine perpetuated traditional identities by uniting them in an alternative culture of patriotic Americanism.

According to historian Gary Gerstle writing about Woonsocket, Americanism emerged as a political language during the interwar years that many interest groups deployed to legitimate their agendas. A vague and flexible language, Gerstle contends, Americanism connoted fealty to historic American heroes, devotion to democracy and democratic rights, faith in American progress, and paradoxically, yearning for traditional values of the past. In the 1930s, the CIO skillfully used this language to unite fragmented ethnic workers along class lines in what historian Lizabeth Cohen calls a "culture of unity" in Chicago. In 1930s Jersey City, however, the Hague regime deployed Americanism to gather the municipality's scattered ethnic groups behind a rival political culture that emboldened not class, but ethnic identification with the nation. Somewhat like conservative French Canadian leaders that Gerstle describes in Woonsocket, the Hague machine used Americanism to legitimate Irish leadership, valorize ethnic heritages, and affirm immigrant-stock Jersey residents' aspirations for assimilation and upward mobility.[11] It was with the culture of patriotic Americanism, a kind of ethnic working-class traditionalism, that Jersey City met the jarring changes in labor movement that developed in the 1930s.

* * *

The Great Depression wrecked trade unions' friendly relationship with Hague's administration. The economic collapse eliminated jobs, restructured the workforce more toward women in light industry and service work, undermined unions' ability to maintain wage levels, cut union membership, reduced income from union dues, and pushed unions into insolvency. Most labor banks created in the 1920s went bankrupt, including Brandle's Labor National Bank in Jersey City. Cutthroat competition between union and nonunion workers intensified, as trade unionists increasingly used intimidation to protect their jobs and wages. In Chicago, New York City, Detroit, Cleveland, and Jersey City, moreover, organized crime infiltrated local trade unions, both to raid union treasuries and to take over local businesses in place of bootlegging. Desperation caused lines between trade unionism and organized crime to blur.[12]

When the Depression hit, consequently, trade union and municipal priorities sharply diverged, as Hague's famous 1931 face-off with his old friend Theodore Brandle shows. Their disagreement arose over local public works projects, one of the few bright areas of employment during the Depression. The trouble started when Hague inexplicably engaged a unionized contractor who hired men not listed on Brandle's union membership rolls to construct a power station for the new Margaret Hague Maternity Hospital. To defend his members, Brandle called for protest at the power station's building site, sent members to beat up contracted men, and disrupted construction work. Hague capitulated by buying out the original contractor at great cost and then turning the work over to Brandle's men. It was a rare and humiliating defeat for Hague that provoked a fierce argument with Brandle.[13]

The falling out intensified when Hague surprisingly allowed the McClintic-Marshall Company, part of the strongly antiunion National Erectors Association, to build the Pulaski Skyway, another plum public works project in the midst of Depression. Whether an embrace of the open-shop position or just the only choice, the decision antagonized Brandle, especially after McClintic evaded his bonding company Branleygran by posting its completion bond in cash. Vowing to "unionize this job or else" and seek higher wages, Brandle resorted again to trade union coercion. His men threw up pickets and stopped work for five days in July 1931. When nonunion laborers returned to work, streets around the Pulaski site plunged into violence. A private security guard shot a Brandle man throwing rocks, and then Brandle's picketers ambushed a car carrying nonunion men, beating one of them, William T. Harris, to death. No one was convicted for the assaults. Wanting work to continue, Hague finally dispatched Jersey City police to defend McClintic-Marshall's nonunion employees. The company welcomed the officers by providing "refreshments" to keep them in "good humor." Brandle's and Hague's interests were clearly at odds.[14]

A storied three-year attack on Brandle's Ironworkers Local 45 and other local trade unions followed. Describing Brandle as "a gorilla labor leader," Hague charged with some merit that "labor racketeers" and "gangsters" had infiltrated Jersey City's union leadership and had begun using strong-arm techniques to intimidate employers and union members alike. In part, he was just acknowledging tactics that trade unionists had deployed routinely through the 1920s—tactics labeled racketeering. In part, also, his remarks recognized a new Depression-era reality—that trade unionists in construction, trucking, cleaning, dyeing, and other crafts were truly intensifying their aggressive practices, even as organized crime seeped into their operations. Perhaps out of genuine alarm about labor violence as well as for political self-interest, hence, Hague forced Brandle's Local 45 and then teamster, plumber, steamfitter, cleaner, and dyer unions into receivership. Denying that he was weeding out union men, Hague claimed that he was defending local employers and workers from outside thugs.

Some labor champions recollected later that the unions retained fat treasuries, but more likely, Depression had left those organizations insolvent and driven to desperate actions. Thus, in a local equity court, Vice Chancellor John Fallon determined that Brandle's organization had illegally engaged in collusive contract bidding, commingled its death fund with regular operating money, and unnecessarily raised costs to the public. He then ordered the union's books seized and its organization placed under new leadership. As Hague described it, these actions "disorganized" Jersey City unions, and he meant just the corrupt ones, not all of them, as the modern popular view portrays it. The nearby *Newark Evening News* praised his war against "labor czars." And in the fashionable law-and-order style of the time, Hague unleashed the city's muscular police force against alleged labor racketeers, giving it a free hand to use whatever tactics were necessary to drive them out. When it came to labor racketeers, Hague declared, "the nightstick must prevail."[15]

These events marked a watershed in Hague's labor policy, but not an abrupt turn against unions as often depicted. Overwhelmingly, conventional historical accounts treat Hague's battle with Brandle, his fight against labor racketeers, and his receivership actions all as a prelude to an all-out assault on Jersey City labor unions, an effort to turn the town into an open-shop haven. Yet, Hague's crusade actually did only target the corrupt "strong-arm crowd" among unionists, not organized labor per se. He argued that alleged labor racketeers like Brandle violated fundamental principles of collective bargaining when they adopted a bullying "do-it-or-else" posture toward local businesses and acted as though "they are law" (an ironic remark, indeed, given Hague's later reputation).[16] Otherwise, he stayed friendly with remaining local trade unions in the NJSFL and HCCLU through the 1930s, and certainly he continued to work with longshoremen's unions on the waterfront. Hague did not so much abandon his former labor allies or reject organized labor in the 1930s, as he adapted his regime's strategy to the shifting labor environment. Standing labor law provided tools for Hague's administration to do that.

* * *

After trade unionism collapsed in the early 1930s, the changing structure of labor organizing all across the nation challenged Jersey City's and other municipalities' traditional treatment of labor rights. The changes unfolded through two phases: 1929 to 1932 when a variety of local protests developed, and 1933 to 1940s when new federal laws and mildly improving economic conditions stimulated mass industrial unionism. In both phases, the changes provoked police abuses of labor rights and difficult municipal adjustments. Jersey City, while not entirely out of step with other municipalities, reacted with severity, given the Hague administration's old-fashioned machine politics, ethnic traditionalism, and tough police practices.

Around the country from 1930 to 1932, working people mobilized against the Depression locally in self-help groups, unemployment leagues, and spot strikes, while police contained these events in traditional law-and-order fashion. Unemployed men and women often led by communists in Cleveland, Chicago, Detroit, Los Angeles, New York, and other cities organized rallies and marches to city halls, where they demanded relief measures. Most of the rallies were peaceful, but some degenerated into melees as police officers used fire hoses, nightsticks, and tear gas to hold off marchers. Most notorious was the New York City Union Square rally of March 6, 1930, wherein antiradical police commissioner Grover Whalen sent a thousand nightstick-wielding officers to beat marchers back and arrest their leaders on trumped-up charges of disorderly conduct or assault. The controversy soon forced Whalen out, but the Union Square riot and similar events elsewhere exemplified how labor organizing was shifting toward mass outdoor rallies as well as strikes and pickets, thereby bringing free speech and assembly questions to the forefront. For the time being, interpretation of those civil liberties remained under state jurisdiction in the hands of city officials and judges, at least until the U.S. Supreme Court's 1931 *Stromberg* and *Near* decisions began applying First Amendment rights on the state level.[17]

In New Jersey, such developments early in the Depression evoked a tough police response. Communists rallied in Elizabeth, Newark, Trenton, and Paterson, sometimes peacefully, but they were usually busted up by police. In addition, a major silk workers strike broke out in Paterson and fomented a few pitched battles with police officers. About the same time, Jersey City police arrested workers under the broad provisions of the state Disorderly Persons Act for distributing handbills outside of a manufacturing plant, soliciting money for a miners' relief fund, and shouting an anti-AFL epithet during a strike. In each instance, city officials prosecuted workers in the manner of the third degree, finally reducing or dismissing charges. In the handbill case, the city pressured the defendant to accept representation by a Hague machine lawyer, not radical counselor Abraham Isserman suggested by communists.[18]

During the first phase of Depression-era labor protest, Jersey City's actions evinced the Hague administration's anticrime and police dragnet policies to rid the city of gangsters and racketeers, but the second phase of the national labor movement beginning in 1933 redirected Jersey City police toward containing a new kind of labor organizers. At the time, AFL trade unions shrank in force, as symbolized by the quiet transfer of NJSFL leadership from Arthur Quinn to Thomas Eames and then to Louis Marciante, and by conservative William Green's continuance in the AFL presidency. The passage of section 7a as part of the New Deal's National Industrial Recovery Act (NIRA) in 1933, however, dramatically changed the national legal landscape for labor and inspired a surge of industrial unions when it affirmed workers' right to organize and bargain collectively. With the economy slightly on the upswing and Democrat Franklin Roosevelt in the White House, labor leaders led by United Mine Workers (UMW) president John L. Lewis capitalized on section 7a by launching a long-desired drive to organize mass production workers. Even though Green declined to commit AFL resources, Lewis's UMW and several other unions quickly established a base of industrial unionism in late 1933, and then midwestern steel, automobile, rubber, and electrical workers, New York editorial writers, southern and New England cotton textile workers, Minneapolis truck drivers, and West Coast longshoremen all erupted in organizing campaigns throughout 1934.[19] Upstaging old AFL craft unionism, industrial unionism swept the nation.

The campaign for mass industrial unionization would not reach Jersey City until later, but labor agitation picked up there during 1933 and 1934, provoking city officials to clamp down. Rather than simply bust up unions threatening local firms whose tax dollars were needed to finance the large city payroll, as often charged, Jersey City officials acted more in their traditional spirit of keeping order against disruptive forces, especially from outsiders. Police arrested one worker for distributing circulars at a men's clothing store during a strike. They seized the charter of a hotel and restaurant workers union striking against the Excell Restaurant, telling its organizer to return home to Newark and never come back. Twice they arrested men who sought strikebreakers for labor disputes in New York City, and in another case they turned back out-of-town strikebreakers from intervening in a Jersey City butchers' strike. Most famously, Jersey City police disrupted picketing at so-called runaway shops, especially the Miller Parlor Furniture Company.[20]

The 1934 Miller controversy marked a turning point in Jersey City labor relations. Like other "runaways," the Miller Company had fled across the Hudson River from New York City to northern New Jersey to avoid performance of a union contract sanctioned by the NIRA's section 7a. When the firm set up shop in Jersey City and then locked its old employees out in order to hire cheaper nonunion workers, furniture union members picketed in protest. Jersey City police, however, immediately arrested fourteen of them under the state's Disorderly Persons Act and four on grounds of illegal assembly, arguing that the pickets were illegal, because the furniture workers were not in a recognized union. Meanwhile, the Miller Company secured a Chancery Court order enjoining the pickets. Critics cite the Miller Parlor event as prime evidence of Hague regime efforts to suppress unionism and attract business to depression-racked Jersey City, but the city's conservative interpretation of picketing rights and illegal assembly had long been routine.[21] Nonetheless, several aspects of the case were quite new: the entry of radical young Newark labor attorney Abraham Isserman into the case as a ubiquitous defender of Northern New Jersey labor rights; the interest that the case kindled among New York City labor activists, communists and liberals; and new federal labor regulations that the Norris–La Guardia Act and section 7a brought to union organizers. Until this time, Republicans and other local Hague opponents had complained about Jersey City police abuses in lonely isolation, but now they gained outside allies armed with new nationally protected labor rights.

Dramatizing the intervention of outside forces, the New York–based ACLU entered the Miller dispute. Still equating free-speech freedoms with class struggle and workers' rights to agitate, the ACLU national board decided to test the validity of Jersey City's ban on peaceful labor picketing and to give the Miller case national visibility. Eminent New York ACLU members joined the picket lines, risking arrest. One by one, they donned placards and picketed outside of the Miller plant. And one by one, police arrested them, including Alfred Bingham (son of former senator Hiram Bingham) and Corliss Lamont (son of J. P. Morgan and Company partner Thomas Lamont). Public safety director Thomas Wolfe dismissed them all as "publicity hunters," but the publicity achieved just what the ACLU wanted. When Lamont found no police around when he arrived in Jersey City, he drove to the Eighth Precinct police station to inform officers that he was there. His arrest soon followed. While he awaited trial, Bingham was convicted of disorderly conduct and sentenced to jail, but Isserman and Columbia University law professors had that conviction overturned on appeal. The attorneys also successfully challenged the chancery court's original injunction against furniture workers and stopped the Miller firm from getting a new one, arguing persuasively that workers enjoyed peaceful picketing rights under section 7a and the National Recovery Administration's Furniture Manufacturing Code.

Jersey City lost in court, and it lost in politics, too. A local AFL-affiliated butchers' union and the HCCLU, both ordinarily Hague supporters, came out against Jersey City's ban on peaceful picketing at the Miller plant. Meanwhile, the controversy threatened to derail Hague protégé Democratic governor A. Harry Moore in the November U.S. senatorial race. With Hague and his family on vacation in Africa, acting mayor Arthur Potterton cut Jersey City's political losses. He lifted Jersey City's ban on Miller factory picketing and declared that the city "never had nor has it now any intention of interfering with the rights of the labor." The crisis was over and Moore went on to get elected, but the Hague administration forever lost its reputation as an "erstwhile champion" of organized labor.[22] Hague's regime caught the attention of an emerging coalition of local opponents and New York liberals, radicals, and labor activists as a singular foe of labor rights.

Simultaneous with Miller Parlor events, Jersey City made political adjustments with long-term implications for labor rights and civil liberties. In 1933 city elections, the Hague administration triumphed again with its traditional "No Vice, No Crime, No Racketeering" appeal, but its long-term survival in the Depression era depended on increasing national help. Like other U.S. municipalities in the 1930s, Jersey City remained an ethnically fragmented entity sorely in need of financial assistance. Real estate taxes shrank as business contracted, and demands for unemployment relief escalated. Historians classically blame Jersey City's predicament exclusively on political corruption and a swollen city payroll, but the drastic fiscal strain that the Depression imposed on all cities was just as important. Indeed, the Depression era marked a watershed in U.S. urban history overall when city governments came increasingly to rely on federal support to sustain their operations.[23]

In the throes of the Depression, New Deal relief programs rescued many politically connected city machines, Jersey City's among them. To put masses of unemployed people to work, New Deal agencies like the Public Works Administration and Works Progress Administration dispensed patronage appointments and millions of dollars, usually distributed through state Democratic leaders and local machines. The Roosevelt administration, however, gave out the money with political benefit in mind, supporting municipal leaders like Edward Kelly in Chicago, Fiorello La Guardia in New York City, and the Democratic bosses in Pittsburgh who helped the president's fortunes, while closing out James Michael Curley in Boston and Thomas Pendergast in Kansas City, who were political liabilities. Corruption was everywhere, but the president tolerated it as politically expedient. Jersey City mayor Hague took advantage of this situation. He overcame his early estrangement from the president because of initial opposition to Roosevelt's nomination back in 1932 and became a bulwark of electoral support. Hague was a proven vote getter who consistently compiled large Democratic electoral victories in Hudson County to elect pro–New Deal U.S. senators and deliver New Jersey's electoral vote for Roosevelt in presidential elections. In return, the Roosevelt administration funneled massive amounts of relief money into Jersey City, helping Hague to put residents to work, build Roosevelt Stadium and the vaunted Medical Center, and sustain his regime's popularity.[24] Having acquired a new base of power in the national government, Hague used it both to preserve local political arrangements and to resist the new kinds of labor organizing and expressions of civil liberties that were arising.

* * *

As Jersey City and other urban governments coped with the Great Depression, labor militancy and mass industrial unionism escalated across the country. Effective July 1935, the NLRA fostered that development, partly because President Roosevelt and friendly state governors supported the law. It not only granted workers the right to self-organize and bargain collectively, and it not only restricted employers from interfering with those rights, but also it implied First Amendment speech and assembly guarantees, since the right to organize meant little if workers could not speak, circulate literature, or hold meetings. Militant labor organizers took advantage of this new legal and political situation. Maritime workers led by Harry Bridges on the West Coast and Joe Curran in the East struck for better wages and employment conditions. Moreover, textile workers set up the Textile Workers Organizing Committee (TWOC) and waged an Atlantic Coast campaign to unionize their fragmented industry and improve wage levels. Most important, the

UMW's John L. Lewis and eight other union presidents broke from the AFL in late 1935 to form the CIO, quickly establishing organizing committees and deploying hundreds of field organizers, some of them communists, all along the nation's industrial corridor from Pennsylvania to Michigan and Illinois, reaching across ethnic and even racial lines to unite ethnic and black workers in a class-conscious movement. Although collaborating with communists, CIO leaders eschewed their revolutionary ideology and took advantage of communist moderation at the time (secretly ordered by the Comintern) to get help forming collective bargaining units. Still, they followed Lewis's policy that only force would subdue fiercely antiunion big corporations. Extolling masculine strength, CIO workers staged mass confrontations with police in an Akron, Ohio, rubber workers strike, the Flint, Michigan, auto workers sit-down strike, and other events. The militancy reflected the CIO's traditional gender views that men were principal breadwinners and had a manly duty to fight for the decent family wages needed to support dependent wives and children.[25] Despite that underlying conservatism, the CIO's militant, mass unionism was still a far cry from Jersey City's staid local craft unionism.

The volatile new unionism challenged all city police departments, as the 1937 booklet, *The City's Role in Strikes* by the Chicago-based International City Managers' Association attests. Featuring essays by employers, labor leaders, city managers, and experts, the booklet demonstrated that cities were groping for new police procedures to cope with the era's vast changes in labor relations and federal labor law. A business representative argued that city police should maintain their guardianship over the rule of the law and property rights, but CIO spokesman Philip Murray contended that police now had an obligation to defend worker rights too, impartially "protect[ing] the picket line as well as . . . protect[ing] the rights of the employer." For city administrators, Donald Stone maintained that municipal police should not take sides in labor disputes, but should serve as an "impartial agency to see that . . . orderly compromises covering legal and acceptable strike methods . . . are made." In the wake of the January 1937 *DeJonge v. Oregon* U.S. Supreme Court decision upholding freedom of assembly, he added that police should respect worker speech and assembly rights to allow the venting of worker frustrations and avoid labor martyrdom. Overall, *The City's Role in Strikes* stressed that police should stay out of labor controversies and focus on keeping order to insure that disputes unfolded fairly. The booklet thus pointed away from the kind of brute force perpetrated on behalf of employers by the Chicago police in the notorious 1937 Memorial Day Massacre.[26] Quite notably, Mayor Hague's Jersey City did not embrace the booklet's enlightened new practices, but sustained old police tactics to cultivate local political support, stymie political rivals, and keep order.

A growing rift within the U.S. labor movement contributed to Hague's refusal to adjust to new labor realities. After John L. Lewis's revolt at the AFL's Atlanta convention in 1935, his CIO evolved as a bitter rival to the AFL. The CIO's formation under Lewis's guidance prompted the AFL to suspend and later expel CIO affiliates on grounds that it could not tolerate "dual unionism" or permit unions organized on an industrial basis. Nonetheless, auto, rubber, radio, steel, and other workers flocked to the CIO, causing AFL president William Green to revoke charters of CIO union locals and to order state and city labor federations to throw them out. By 1937, "peace talks" failed, and American labor split into two bitterly competing sides.[27] The Hague regime remained solidly attached to the AFL faction.

The CIO's presence as a rival to AFL unions grew slowly in New Jersey. The organization first entered the state in 1935 to help silk workers in Paterson and Passaic, and then organized RCA electrical workers in Camden. Only in 1937 did it set up a regional office in Newark, part of a CIO master plan to expand beyond its midwestern industrial base into other regions and businesses. Its aims were moderate and unrevolutionary. National CIO leaders advised regional directors and local organizers that their mission was not to challenge capitalism but to work within the system to create collective bargaining agreements under the newly created NLRA. Local organizers were to "take labor disputes off the streets and into the courtrooms and negotiating chambers," and they were to tone down their masculine fighting rhetoric and stress the formation of union contracts, not extol "picket line heroism." In spring 1937, consequently, Lewis appointed former mine worker and midwestern rubber and steel industry organizer William Carney to head the Newark office with thirty-two field representatives. Carney in turn formed the Greater Newark Industrial Union Council to spread CIO influence into Northern New Jersey and then established a field office in Jersey City led by former textile industry organizer Samuel Macri.[28]

When it arrived in 1937, the CIO held out real promise for Jersey City workers. Mostly neglected by the AFL and unorganized, many labored in medium-size industrial plants or large garment factories at low wages under austere conditions. At this juncture, the newly arrived CIO could do little more than establish its office in the city and dispatch organizers like Macri, but still it helped Jersey workers struggling to organize. Cosmetics workers at the American Home Products Company, for instance, sought CIO assistance to address "the terrible condition that existed in the plant as to low wages and abuses from the foreladies and foremen in the shop." Ninety workers employed by the Consolidated Razor Company, moreover, solicited CIO aid to inaugurate collective bargaining talks. Workers at the Standard Cap and Seal Company staged a spontaneous sit-down strike, and Macri intervened to help secure a settlement. U.S. Gypsum Company laborers gave up on their AFL union's failure to alleviate low wages, and affiliated with the CIO instead. Most impressively, Crucible Steel workers left their AFL union, aligned with the CIO, and then won a strike over contract violations. Electrical workers among the arriving CIO operatives targeted the Westinghouse Elevator Company for unionization, as they did at Westinghouse plants in other cities.[29] Despite police harassment, the CIO began making inroads.

The CIO's arrival in New Jersey instantly provoked NJSFL antagonism. In the early 1930s, the NJSFL stagnated, due both to the Depression and to the federation's dominance by Anglo and Irish building trade laborers who were neither ideologically nor strategically inclined to mobilize mass production workers, many of whom were new immigrants. When the labor movement began growing again in the mid-1930s, however, most new locals joined the CIO instead of the NJSFL. Obeying directions from AFL president William Green, the NJSFL and HCCLU reacted by disassociating CIO local unions. Organizational rivalry, not ethnicity or race, seems to have been the central issue. During December 1937, fifty local trade union leaders met in Newark to organize against the CIO challenge.[30] Although relations were fraying, the NJSFL was a natural ally for Mayor Hague against the CIO.

Anticommunism solidified that alliance and turned Jersey City's CIO controversy into one of many "little red scares" that flared up during the 1920s and 1930s, even though actual communists had only a peripheral role in that conflict. Anticommunism arose in U.S. society during the Civil War, but it did not take modern form until the 1917 Bolshevik Revolution and U.S. entry into World War I. While antilabor business barons had been the mainstay of antiradicalism before then, a broader new coalition of anticommunists emerged thereafter, including military intelligence agencies, the American Legion, the Daughters of the American Revolution, the Roman Catholic Church, patriotic groups, local police squads, conservative trade unions, and big employers, especially those involved with the antilabor open-shop movement. A large informal network including trade unions, interwar anticommunism united around an ideology that condemned communists as a fundamental threat—a Trojan horse carrying anarchy into American society as part of an international Soviet conspiracy. Anticommunists so demonized radicals as subversive that they denied them even basic civil liberties.

Integral to interwar anticommunism was the World War I–era invention of a "spider web" chart by U.S. military intelligence showing an alleged network of communist conspirators working furtively across the United States. According to historian Nick Fischer, the chart became the central way for anticommunists to spread their vision of a deadly plot by communist "spies, agents and dupes" to ruin American life. Exemplary was Illinois homemaker Elizabeth Dilling, whose widely distributed 1934 book *The Red Network* purported to show a vast Red conspiracy that included Albert Einstein, Felix Frankfurter, Eleanor Roosevelt, and especially ACLU director Roger Baldwin. Well-funded by business contributions, anticommunists were constantly ready to supply such propaganda when opportunities arose.[31] Jersey City's CIO fight would become one of them.

AFL trade unionists like those in New Jersey and Jersey City played an awkward role in interwar anticommunism. Historian Jennifer Luff contends that AFL leaders started out as "commonsense anticommunists" in the 1920s. They followed the practical policy of weeding radicals out of affiliated unions, while still defending worker civil liberties, largely in the vain hope of winning sympathy with anticommunist employers. The passage of New Deal labor laws and the rise of the CIO changed this moderate outlook. With little leverage over New Deal labor policy, the AFL objected to the administration of section 7a and the NLRA, aligning with other anticommunists who regarded the NLRA as a "Bolshevik design." Moreover, U.S. communists' decision in 1935 to work with liberal New Dealers in the antifascist Popular Front reinforced the suspicion of AFL leaders and other anticommunists that New Dealers were colluding with communists. Most importantly, the CIO's emergence with a considerable number of communist organizers, though subordinated to CIO supervision, supplied the AFL and other anticommunists with potential evidence of communists' growing labor influence. As their position in the labor movement eroded in the mid-1930s, AFL leaders embraced anticommunism as a tool to attack both New Deal labor law and their upstart competitors in the CIO. They allied with anticommunist New Deal opponents like the National Association of Manufacturers and the Liberty League, naming the CIO as a prime enemy.[32]

The intertwined evolution of the labor and anticommunist movements greatly affected Jersey City's upcoming battle with the CIO. Although increasingly reliant on federal relief money, Hague's regime was still a political machine that needed support from local constituencies that formed nearly a monolithic anticommunist front—Roman Catholic clerics and parishioners, American Legionnaires and other war veterans, tenement-district Irish voters seeking to affirm their Americanness, and AFL trade unionists. Hence, in the fall of 1937, when the Hague regime began resisting CIO organizing efforts in the language of anticommunism and patriotic Americanism, local residents including trade unionists gave the administration hearty support. Moreover, the Hague regime received outside help from anticommunists' "Red network" literature to discredit the CIO campaign. While the Hague administration had its own political reasons to oppose the CIO in Jersey City, its conflict with that group was swept up in larger fights between the AFL and CIO, and between traditional Americanism and the CIO's working-class Americanism. The politics of anticommunism infected it all.

* * *

The East Coast seamen's strike of late 1936 and early 1937 demonstrated how national labor conflicts increasingly intruded on Jersey City. In October 1936, just two years after the successful West Coast seamen's and longshoremen's strike that brought alleged communist Harry Bridges to the forefront, another West Coast maritime strike broke out and then quickly spread east. In the East, rebellious elements of the AFL-affiliated International Seamen's Union (ISU) struck against both shipowners and corrupt ISU officials. Sparked by the leadership of Joe Curran and militants including communists on the ISU rank-and-file committee, the strikers aimed to end shipowners' arbitrary employment practices, close an East Coast versus West Coast pay gap, and replace conservative and autocratic ISU president David Grange, who denounced the walkout as "communism against Americanism." The eastern strike collapsed by early February 1937, but it temporarily shut down the whole of Atlantic maritime trade, including in the ports of New York and Jersey City.[33]

In Jersey City, Mayor Hague clamped down hard on the striking seamen because they disrupted his organization's friendship with waterfront unions as well as maritime business. He issued an outright ban on seamen picketing. A large delegation of union leaders and observers then met with acting Jersey City police chief Harry Walsh to secure permission to picket, but the chief denied that a legitimate strike existed and declared that police would stop any picketing by force, if necessary. When union leaders appealed Walsh's judgment to Hague himself, the mayor insisted that no picketing would be allowed and that he would "break their heads" if they tried it. Subsequently, union leaders met with the newly created New Jersey Civil Liberties Union (NJCLU) and formed the Committee to Defend Labor Rights in Hudson County, which promptly voted to test the Jersey City ban. Defiant seamen picketed the American Export and Dollar lines in late December and early January, only to have Walsh's men—sometimes on horseback and armed with teargas—confiscate their placards, disperse them, eject them across city lines, detain a few, beat up any who remained, and temporarily shut down a shoreline tavern where union men gathered. Picketers got similar treatment northward in Hoboken and across the Hudson River in New York City. Reverend Jay T. Wright, an NJCLU observer, got a taste of Jersey City violence first hand. While he watched picketers and policemen scuffle a block away, plainclothes officers attacked him with brass knuckles. When Chief Walsh arrived moments later, Wright identified himself and complained about the assault, but Walsh grabbed him by the shoulder and pushed him down the street, telling the clergyman, "Well, for Christ's sake, get the hell out of here. Take your gospel back to church."[34]

In a formal statement a few days later, Mayor Hague defended Jersey City's ban on seamen picketing on the grounds that the agitators were communists, an exaggerated claim that avoided the real issues at stake. He admitted that all citizens, even communists, had a right to assemble peacefully, but he contended that such legal principles did not apply in this case. Communists, he said, had no intention to "meet peacefully for peaceful purposes." Their plan was "to incite disorder and encourage violence." "Revolution is their creed," he claimed. "We in Jersey City," he added, "are God-loving, law-abiding, peace-desiring Americans, and there is no place in our community for Communists or the things they stand for." First invoked in the Miller Parlor conflict, such anticommunist rhetoric was relatively new for Hague, perhaps drawn from anticommunist members of his organization like *Jersey Journal* reporter D. John Rickard, although it resembled moral rhetorical strategies used earlier to demean intruders, racketeers, and alleged perverts. His reference to "American" identity especially signaled new use of the language of patriotic Americanism to appeal to Jersey City's diverse and traditional immigrant-stock voters. Hague's contention that allegedly communist seamen were violent un-American outsiders who did not deserve free speech and assembly protections was also new, and an important legal argument that the mayor would deploy in the upcoming CIO fight. His rhetoric threw up a smokescreen that obscured civil liberties violations and effectively whipped up support, as local political opponents ruefully pointed out.

The mayor had plenty of conservative company for his views around the New York City metropolitan region. At a Catholic Holy Name Society communion breakfast in Queens, New York, for instance, borough president George Harvey portrayed communists as troublemakers who should be excluded from meeting halls and run out of town by police. At a nearby Knights of Columbus breakfast, clergymen described communists as dangerous subversives against whom Roman Catholics should stand as a "sure bulwark." At a St. Patrick's Day luncheon in Jersey City, the Right Reverend John J. Murphy told residents to be thankful that they had a mayor who told dissenters, whether "parlor pinks from Montclair, N.J. or social scum from Brooklyn, that Jersey City doesn't want them."[35]

Although Mayor Hague enjoyed regional support for his anticommunist stance against striking seamen, his actions accelerated the formation of a regional anti-Hague political coalition. Already, back in early 1936, fifteen New Jersey labor leaders from both AFL and CIO unions had petitioned U.S. senator Robert La Follette Jr.'s congressional committee on civil liberties to investigate police abuse of labor rights in Jersey City. Soon thereafter, the communist-inspired International Labor Defense (ILD) created the National Committee for the Defense of Political Prisoners, which issued a scathing report on labor violations in Hudson County. Simultaneously, the ACLU's national office in New York City recruited New Jersey lawyers to assist in its campaign for civil liberties in northern New Jersey, leading to the Newark-based NJCLU's formation around May 1936 with a board of directors comprised of clergymen, professors, attorneys, labor advocates, and two female reformers, a Mrs. Foster and soon-to-be executive secretary Nancy Cox. Meanwhile, CIO operatives led by hosiery workers union leader Carl Holderman redirected Labor's Non-Partisan League (LNPL) previously set up for President Roosevelt's reelection to challenge Hague's control of Hudson County, part of the ongoing CIO strategy to improve the political environment for labor organizing. On top of that, Jersey City resident and long-time Republican Hague opponent J. Owen Grundy quietly corresponded with ACLU director Roger Baldwin. Grundy kept Baldwin informed about Hague's political maneuvers, offered a list of witnesses to testify against police brutality, and predicted Hague's anticommunist crusade.[36] By 1937, a regional network of local opponents, labor activists, and civil libertarians had assembled against the mayor.

The ILD's and Nancy Cox's activities illustrate the role of left-leaning Newark activists in the Jersey City controversy. While the Communist Party apparently did not operate directly within Hague's municipality, its front organizations like the ILD helped to marshal anti-Hague publicity like the Committee for Political Prisoners report. Secretary of ILD's Newark branch was Robert Parker, a young communist who participated as an observer in the CIO's foiled November 29 leafletting campaign, and who befriended and soon married Nancy Cox. A direct descendant of *Mayflower* settlers, Cox was daughter of a prominent New York University (NYU) professor and ACLU board member. After attending the work-study school Antioch, she traveled to Europe in 1935 and visited the Soviet Union where she was impressed, according to historian Warren Grover, "that women had a more advanced role in society than they had in the United States." Returning to the United States, she finished her degree at NYU, joined the socialist groups League for Industrial Democracy and the New York–based Workers Defense League (WDL), and volunteered to test the constitutionality of a handbill ordinance in Edgewater, New Jersey, where she was arrested for standing on the steps of city hall handing out copies of the Bill of Rights. Due to her father's connections to ACLU director Roger Baldwin, the NJCLU then hired her at the age of twenty-three to be executive secretary, a post from which she (and Parker) observed the CIO's November 29 leafletting campaign and subsequent protest rallies. Even though she was a socialist in outlook, Grover explains, her marriage to Parker in early 1938 made her too controversial for the ACLU, causing ACLU president Harry F. Ward to arrange her departure from the NJCLU for a job with the communist-influenced American League for Peace and Democracy (ALPD). She soon led the ALPD's Newark branch and brought it to life in a fight against Nazis. Left-wing Newark agitators like Cox and Parker were drawn into the Jersey City conflict.[37]

As cooperation between Hague's northern New Jersey antagonists and the ACLU national office grew, the seamen's strike produced the ACLU's first court case against the Hague regime. The case began when Isserman, acting as the ISU's lawyer, requested ACLU assistance to secure a federal court injunction against Jersey City police interference with seamen picketing. Subsequently, ACLU general counsel Arthur Garfield Hays met in the Newark chambers of federal judge William Clark along with Isserman, acting Jersey City public safety director Daniel Casey, and police chief Walsh to discuss terms under which seamen might picket. Although an agreement seemed to have been reached, Jersey City police soon began expelling picketers again. Encouraged by Judge Clark, Hays headed down to Provost Street to investigate, along with two members of the WDL, which was testing picketing rights in Jersey City. Once there, Hays tried to join the picket line, but officers (whom Hays described as "pretty decent fellows") at first apologetically shoved him away, and then allowed him to march by himself, not with a strike placard, but just the U.S. flag. Later, Hays went to observe a simultaneous boot-and-shoemakers' picket at Exchange Place, where he found Jersey City police bodily transferring picketers to the subway entrance for a trip through the Hudson tubes to Manhattan Island.[38] Although the seamen's strike soon ended, both it and the bootmakers' strike gave the ACLU its first good opportunity to test Jersey City's ejection practices under federal law. The ACLU pursued the bootmakers' case into federal court.

The case arrived at the crucial juncture of the ACLU's ideological development, when the organization abandoned its previous attachment to radical agitation and pursued the defense of civil liberties in federal courts. Attorney

Hays was a leading exponent of the new strategy. Testifying in *ACLU v. Casey*, as the case was known, he claimed that the ACLU was not interested in labor per se but in everyone's free speech rights. In the seamen's and bootmakers' strikes, he argued, the ACLU aimed to expose the Jersey City police department's "lawless" disruption of pickets and civil liberties protected by federal law, and then to secure a court declaration affirming those freedoms. Indeed, Hays admitted that he encouraged David Clendennin of the WDL to join a bootmakers' picket line wearing a placard reading "Jersey City Police are lawless" to test police tolerance of speech rights, and agreed that the ACLU and the WDL were part of a larger campaign to challenge and change Jersey City practices. Overall, Hays asserted, the ACLU's purpose was "to persuade the courts to point out, to educate the police of Jersey City, and the Corporation Counsel's office."[39]

The ACLU also tested the legality of Jersey City's practice of ejecting or "deporting" picketers from the city rather than arresting them. On the witness stand in *ACLU v. Casey*, Jersey City assistant corporation counsel Joseph Glavin reported that the municipality found it more practical to evict than to arrest picketers, and public safety director Casey added that police had every right "to escort out of the city anyone they considered undesirable," perhaps alluding to New Jersey's Disorderly Persons Act. For the ACLU, however, Hays insisted that Jersey City's practice of eviction violated "the fundamental right to get arrested," implicating basic rights to habeas corpus proceedings, trial by jury, indeed any legal process at all. With an eye on those guarantees, even Judge William Clark was struck by the authoritarian character of ejection practices. "If you decide who is undesirable, you put yourself in the position of Hitler," he told Casey in this 1937 proceeding. In the end, Clark issued a preliminary injunction restraining Jersey City from interfering with peaceful bootmaker picketing. The city obtained a stay with its appeal to the U.S. Court of Appeals, and there a yearlong delay rendered the case moot.[40] Nonetheless, the case exposed a growing contradiction between midcentury municipal police practices and evolving federal civil liberties law, a conflict that culminated in Jersey City's clash with the CIO.

In the meantime, Judge Clark's reference to Hitler demonstrated a critical change in the political climate during the late 1930s—the rise of antifascism as a rival to anticommunism. In response to fascist regimes in Italy, Germany, and Spain after World War I, antifascism developed as a political and cultural movement in the United States, particularly during the Popular Front period from 1935 to 1939. Although fascism was European, antifascism engrossed a broad left-liberal coalition of American writers, artists, politicians, and labor leaders including communists, socialists, liberal New Dealers, CIO organizers, and ACLU activists. To them, ranting anti–New Deal figures like radio priest Father Charles Coughlin, the brutal suppression of the Southern Tenant Farmers Union, and ultimately Frank Hague's battle with the CIO all suggested ominously that fascist practices "can happen here" in the United States. In an emerging left version of Americanism, elements of the left-liberal coalition, even communists, developed antifascist political grammar that made "fascism" "a dirty word in the public imagination" and portrayed it as a danger to democratic rights and American institutions.[41]

Antifascist speech acquired special intensity among socialists in New York City, a hotbed of left-labor activity. In the city's highly contentious political environment, the New York–based Socialist Party splintered when the Old Guard wing led by clothing worker unions split away to back Franklin Roosevelt and the New Deal, while various factions of militants, communists, Trotskyists, and students jockeyed for influence in what was left of the party headed by Norman Thomas. With his party in disarray, the widely respected Thomas advanced socialism mainly as a humanitarian speaker, showing up at demonstrations, rallies, and strikes to denounce would-be fascists and defend worker causes based on socialist and U.S. democratic values. New York's *Socialist Call* echoed his sentiments. In a story by McAlister Coleman, the paper criticized New Jersey governor Harold Hoffman as the "Jersey Hitler" for belittling public relief, and condemned Queens Borough president George Harvey as "another Hitler" for telling patriotic groups that communists ought to be placed on ferryboats and sent to hell after police had worked them over with rubber hoses.[42] By 1937, antifascist and anticommunist rhetoric dominated political discourse. They framed the popular understanding of Jersey City's fight with the CIO, even today.

* * *

In 1937, pandemonium in New Jersey labor relations set Mayor Hague and the left-liberal coalition on a collision course. Early in the year, CIO organizers began making inroads among the state's oil, electrical, radio, rubber, shipyard, steel, suitcase, cigar, and clothing workers from Newark to Trenton. Sit-down strikes broke out among Newark cigar makers and Clifton clothing workers. In March, the CIO-affiliated TWOC launched its East Coast drive to organize textile workers with specific plans for New Jersey. By July, the CIO organized its regional council in Newark led by William Carney.[43]

Conflict spread throughout the state in resistance to these CIO encroachments. In February 1937, Republican Governor Harold Hoffman condemned the sit-down tactic as an un-American violation of property rights, only to earn CIO leaders' denunciation for neglecting worker rights under the NLRA.

In March, the Republican majority on the Kearny town council passed an ordinance prohibiting handbill distribution that was obviously aimed at CIO organizers, while CIO-affiliated lawyers vowed to fight it as unconstitutional. In June, Paterson postmaster Thomas Kelley refused to deliver postcards calling for a CIO-sponsored consumer boycott, but CIO leaders sent a protest letter to Postmaster General James Farley. In September, the NJSFL's annual convention rejected CIO leader William Carney's entreaties for cooperation and followed national AFL instructions to expel all member organizations with CIO connections. A deep organizational rift was developing between New Jersey's AFL and CIO unions. Not only did the CIO goal of enrolling mass production workers clash with the AFL's focus on defending skilled workers' crafts, but also more importantly, CIO organizing challenged the AFL's long-time monopoly over New Jersey's labor movement.[44]

In the middle of all this, Jersey City inducted the handily reelected Hague for a sixth term as mayor on May 18, 1937. Support was overwhelming. More than five thousand spectators thronged city council chambers and the corridor outside, while three hundred flower baskets adorned city hall. Firmly in charge, the Hague regime renewed its alliance with the local Chamber of Commerce to attract business to the financially struggling city, as advertised in the city's pamphlet *Jersey City Has Everything for Industry*. Comprised of a cross-section of the city's banking, finance, and especially small-scale manufacturing sectors, though not sweatshop clothing employers, the Chamber put out promotional literature that portrayed Jersey City as an oasis of industrial tranquility at a time of labor turmoil across the country, despite the very recent seamen's and bootmakers' strikes. The Chamber's open-shop position tolerated Jersey City's stodgy local craft unions, but it fiercely attacked the NLRA and the CIO's new kind of labor activism. Mayor Hague agreed. Together, he and the Chamber blocked an antilabor injunction measure proposed in the state legislature.[45] His administration maintained ties with the NJSFL and local AFL trade unions, and it joined business in resisting the CIO's newfangled industrial unionism then emerging.

In October 1937, the CIO and Mayor Hague directly collided. William Carney at the CIO's Newark regional office sent organizer Thomas Cometa to open a field office in Jersey City. Cometa and regional assistant director Samuel Macri then began meeting with workers at the American Home Products plant and the Standard Cap and Seal Corporation to set up local collective bargaining units. Adhering to their typically strict policy toward strangers and outside agitators, however, Jersey City police stopped Macri's car (which bore out-to-state license plates), disrupted organizing efforts at the Home Products factory, blocked attempts to rent a meeting hall, and quashed a strike at a steel flooring company. To the gruff and aggressive Carney, veteran of tough midwestern CIO organizing battles, such interference called for a militant show of labor force.[46]

Just then, the bitterly contested November 1937 New Jersey gubernatorial election complicated Mayor Hague's treatment of Carney's impending assault. The election featured a nasty contest between Republican state senator Lester Clee, a Presbyterian minister from Newark, and Democratic U.S. senator A. Harry Moore, a Hague stalwart. For his part, Clee arose from the formidable Republican organization in Essex County led by attorney Arthur Vanderbilt that was devoted to "clean government" and an end to Hague's "ruthless and corrupt" dominance of state politics. Moore, by contrast, emerged from Hague's Hudson County Democratic machine and was endorsed by the NJSFL, then battling the rise of CIO locals. From their vantage point, CIO leaders could not endorse a Republican, but they were hardly wild about the Democrat Moore. As U.S. senator, he had opposed New Deal social measures. Moreover, the NJSFL annual meeting that had endorsed him was just a "horse trading convention" that rubber-stamped Mayor Hague's choices. Still, the election held in the balance which party would control Jersey's governorship with its vast patronage powers over state prosecutors, judges and commissions.[47]

Charges of fraud ran through the whole election. In September, a local judge issued, and then mysteriously revoked, warrants for the arrest of 144 Republican and Democratic Hudson County election officials for allegedly mishandling Republican primary ballots and falsifying tallies. To prevent similar abuses in the November 2 general election, county election supervisor John Ferguson deputized 1,600 observers to monitor voting, but complaints surfaced immediately that "floaters and thugs" cast fraudulent ballots, while Hague operatives manipulated vote calculations. In the final count, Clee easily won New Jersey's downstate rural counties, as Republicans typically did, but Moore secured an astonishing 129,000 vote plurality in industrial Hudson County, giving him a narrow 45,000 vote statewide victory out of 1.4 million ballots cast. Although lack of enthusiasm for labor measures probably cost him support, Clee claimed "widespread fraud." In Jersey City alone, 145,000 ballots were cast, but Clee's advisors calculated that only around 119,000 residents could have realistically voted. Republicans later attributed thirty-two ballots to one repeat voter and numerous others cast for the dead, dying, or insane. Mayor Hague scoffed at the charges, but a big political scandal erupted. Republican assemblymen demanded a legislative investigation, while Clee submitted a petition to recount Hudson County ballots to New Jersey Chief Justice Thomas J. Brogan, a Hague minion. Brogan surprisingly agreed. Across the Hudson River, New York City newspapers marveled that Hague could pull off such a feat but supported the recount, if only to expose his regime's corruption.[48]

At this troubled juncture, Mayor Hague uttered his most infamous—and misrepresented—words, "I am the law." At a church meeting in mid-November 1937, while discussing the case of two truant lads who wanted to go to work rather than return to school, Hague described how he overrode the objections of local school officials to help the boys. When officials asserted that the boys were too young to work because it "was the law," a requirement of the New Jersey Working Papers Act, Hague exclaimed, "Listen, here is the law! I am the law! These boys go to work." Hague explained many times later that he had not meant to claim dictatorial powers. He only wanted to take responsibility for two wayward youths who might end up in a life of crime, even if that meant bending the rules, a fulfillment of a boss's pledge to do right by his constituents regardless of bureaucratic niceties. Other city bosses would have agreed. As Boston boss James Michael Curley once said, city leaders had to rule directly, "even if you have to break a few laws and tear up red tape."[49] Nonetheless, at a time when antifascist and anti-dictator rhetoric was becoming part of everyday political discourse, and at a time when Hague himself was becoming nationally controversial, his enemies seized on the quotation, and used it to caricature Hague as a tyrant. Hague's subsequent high-handed behavior in the CIO affair made the taunt stick.

In the wake of the CIO's foiled organizing efforts in Jersey City, in wake of the contested gubernatorial election, and in wake of Hague's soon-to-be infamous exclamation, the CIO's Greater Newark Industrial Council decided to take direct action, the very thing that Jersey City officials feared. Irritated by police action that shut down the steel flooring factory strike, regional director Carney planned an organizing campaign in the city. It would begin on Monday, November 29, when two thousand to three thousand CIO representatives were to enter the city and distribute leaflets announcing a mass CIO rally set for December 3 to discuss worker rights under the NLRA. Newark newspapers characterized the campaign as an "invasion," and Carney encouraged the military analogy when he depicted it as a "showdown" between the CIO and "I-Am-the-Law Hague," apparently the first use of that epithet. The planned campaign, however, precipitated a critical clash between municipal and federal law. Jersey City's ordinance of 1924 banned distribution of "any newspaper, paper, periodical, book, magazine, card or pamphlet" on "any street or public place," a common and still valid local measure, as no federal court had yet annulled it. Yet, section 7 of the NLRA protected workers' right to organize and to participate in activities aimed at organization. From the standpoint of the CIO and its supporters, the central question was whether the NLRA or local law would prevail in Jersey City. "Hague may be the law in Jersey City," Carney declared, "but he is not the law of the country."[50]

On November 29, subsequently, a small number of activists—estimates range from forty to three hundred—converged on United Shoe Workers of America headquarters at 76 Montgomery Street in Jersey City in preparation to distribute flyers. Most were out-of-town male CIO field representatives, but some were outside observers from the WDL or NJCLU, including WDL member Grace Milgram, NJCLU executive secretary Nancy Cox, and several other female activists. Based on newspaper reports, public safety director Daniel Casey expected a large crowd bent on breaking the local anti-leafletting law, so he ordered Chief Harry Walsh to detail officers to prevent commotion. As workers entered the city and approached union headquarters, hence, dozens of uniformed and plainclothes police surveilled and harassed them, picking up a few and dropping them off at city limits. Most made their way to Montgomery Street. After meeting there, workers and observers walked two by two down to Exchange Place on the harbor, where they peacefully tried to pass out their circulars announcing the December 3 rally. "TO ALL WORKERS OF HUDSON COUNTY," the flyer read. "ARE YOU satisfied with LOW WAGES, Contented with LONG HOURS, Working without PAID VACATIONS? NOW is the time Act! Be wise—organize! Join the CIO! Come to this Meeting to Find out How." The circular marked a peaceful call for a peaceable assembly. Marchers admitted later that they knew about Jersey City's anti-handbill ordinance but added that they assumed rights under the NLRA and the U.S. Constitution to circulate flyers anyway. Indeed, newspapers reported that marchers shouted, "We have the right to distribute the circulars" and "We want our rights!" According to Casey, however, police saw the action as illegal and decided to stop it to avoid "riot and bloodshed."[51] The CIO's campaign clearly ignited a clash between local law and federal law, as well as a clash of politics.

What followed, however, was no simple exercise in enforcing the law, local or federal. Under the supervision of Deputy Chief Charles Wilson, police responded to the leafletting campaign by unleashing Jersey City's characteristically muscular brand of police violence used routinely against crooks, racketeers, and intruders. As marchers entered harborside, police met them with a flying wedge and pushed them toward the ferry to send them across the river to Manhattan. Simultaneously, uniformed and plainclothes officers confiscated flyers from marchers, punching UMW representative James Sweeney in the "short ribs," and then socking Newark activist Robert Parker in the stomach as his future wife and companion Nancy Cox looked

Figure 3. Committee for Industrial Organization union organizers in Jersey City, including Samuel Macri at left under a calendar picturing CIO president John L. Lewis. A Margaret Bourke-White photograph in *Life*, February 7, 1938. Image 50872589, the LIFE Picture Collection/Getty Images.

on. Despite this treatment, most marchers returned to Montgomery Street to pick up more handbills, but as they tried to leave, police forced them through the revolving exit door one by one, searched them, and then placed them in awaiting cars to be carried out of the city. "The idea was to separate us," observed Sweeney.[52] Jersey police sabotaged the CIO leafletting operation, stifling a peaceful act of free expression.

In the melee, the police arrested thirteen would-be leafletters and then tried them in the police court of Judge Anthony Botti under irregular procedures resembling third-degree practices of the time. Cox joined Bella Kussy and Grace Milgram to check on the proceedings, positioning women as witnesses to the mostly male drama. Refusing to swear in an official stenographer—although he allowed a Mr. Winard to take notes—Botti conducted a trial distinguished by sharp exchanges between the defendants' attorney Sol Kapelson of Newark's Isserman and Isserman law firm and Jersey City assistant corporation counsel Lewis Hansen. Kapelson argued that his clients were victims of false arrest and larceny due to police confiscation of their handbills, but Hansen insisted that the city had to prosecute them to protect residents from riotous CIO behavior. In a manner that he might have applied earlier to gangsters and racketeers, Botti sided squarely with the city.

He sentenced seven of the defendants to five days in jail because they "deliberately defied the [anti-leafletting] law as proved by their own admissions." "We don't want any repetition of the violence that has taken place in Detroit, Akron and other cities," he remarked. As for the other six, he denied them a recess and then ordered them held for grand jury action at substantial bail on the charge of unlawful assembly. These defendants and their absent leader William Carney, Judge Botti said, were deliberate lawbreakers and radical disrupters of the peace. He denounced Carney and gave him his warning to keep CIO "hoodlums" out of Jersey City.[53]

Botti's comments accurately reflected the prevailing public perception of the CIO in 1937 as well as Jersey City's traditional law-and-order antipathy toward outsiders, not just a calculated effort by the Hague regime to suppress labor organizers. His reference to Detroit and Akron alluded to controversial midwestern CIO sit-down strikes and to the CIO's reputation for lawbreaking and abuse of property rights. He was surely aware of the CIO-inspired strikes and sit-downs that were occurring around New Jersey, and he probably shared Jersey City leaders' fear that such direct-action tactics could reach their city. As a result, the November 29 CIO demonstrators' defiance of Jersey City's anti-leafletting ordinance, along with CIO regional director Carney's exaggerated threat of a mass "invasion" against the city, may have persuaded Botti that the marchers were headed down the same lawless path. Like city administrators, moreover, Botti saw the marchers as outside intruders on the peace and good order that Jersey City police worked so hard to maintain. When he called Carney and his men "hoodlums," he placed them in the same category as the gangsters and racketeers whom police had run out of town a few years earlier. Others shared his view. Bayonne assistant prosecutor Jack Fineberg told a local Democratic club that Frank Hague was "the most courageous mayor in the United States." He "is not going to permit any set of men to come into Jersey City to upset our form of government and break up our industries and cause war between labor and industry here where there is peace."[54]

Yet, the violence of Jersey City's response to the CIO leafletting effort on November 29 was disproportionate to that effort's quite orderly and peaceful character. Only a few dozen leaflet distributors actually showed up, most of them hardened union men, but some were male or a few female members of the WDL or NJCLU. And while they did arguably violate the law as it then stood, the marchers walked peacefully to their destination and sought peacefully to hand out flyers with a peaceful message, only to be swarmed by police who met them with forcible crowd control measures, punches to stomachs, compulsory eviction, or unfair court arraignments. The overwrought response came from the Jersey City's long-term style of muscular policing toward outsiders and suspicious characters, its traditional limits on direct-action labor agitation, and its serious miscalculation of the actual threat that the November 29 event represented. Until the 1930s, municipal law and the national political and legal environment shielded municipalities like Jersey City from accountability for such behavior.

Changing times were about to expose and discredit Jersey City's rough-hewn tactics. In the politically liberal 1930s, mass industrial unionism rose, protective New Deal labor laws like the NLRA were enacted, a left-liberal coalition of labor supporters formed, and the modern civil liberties movement developed, thereby putting old policing practices like Jersey City's under the scrutiny of the news media, national political figures, national labor organizations, and especially the federal courts. Consequently, the old-fashioned ethnically based Hague machine confronted class-conscious outside CIO organizers and their sympathizers, not cooperative inside trade unionists; it also encountered an increasingly powerful regional coalition of political opponents, not just local Republicans and other upstarts who could be easily suppressed; and it faced federal judges, not conservative and friendly local jurists. On top of that, the scandal surrounding the November 1937 gubernatorial election weakened the Hague regime's capacity to resist the growing outside forces.

This changing political and legal landscape had enormous implications for Jersey City's and other municipalities' management of outdoor expressive activity. The legal validity of Jersey City's narrow and tough long-time treatment of public assembly, speech, and peaceful labor picketing came into question as New Deal labor laws went on the books, the CIO agitated for organizing rights, the ACLU and other groups lobbied for expressive freedoms, and the U.S. Supreme Court began applying federal civil liberties guarantees on the local level. As it unfolded, hence, Jersey City's conflict with the CIO and its supporters became part of a fundamental restructuring of municipal law and civil liberties.

# 3 Street Fight and Media Fight

## *The Battle for Jersey City*

Just a week after municipal police foiled organizers from the CIO from entering Jersey City to circulate handbills calling for a CIO rally there, the newly inaugurated newspaper the *CIO News* announced that "Dictatorship Is Proclaimed in Jersey City." The newspaper asserted that although the United States claimed to be a democracy, Mayor Frank Hague, backed by an "oligarchy of anti-union employers," had set aside constitutional guarantees with "all of the arrogance of a fascist dictator." He not only prevented peaceful picketing but also drove union organizers out of town and "denied to the working people of Jersey City the right to meet and speak their minds on union organization." A few weeks later, however, the Jersey City Chamber of Commerce passed a resolution expressing "heartfelt appreciation and gratitude" for Mayor Hague's actions. Claiming that it "never opposed collective bargaining," the Chamber explained that it supported the mayor because he had a duty to stop "disorderly elements preparing to enter the city," especially "communist radicals and outsiders bent on spreading un-American doctrines of force and violence," as they had already done in other parts of the country.[1] To outside critics of the time, hence, Hague was a European-styled fascist dictator who trampled on workers' civil liberties. To local sympathizers, he was a heroic city leader who protected his constituents from foreign radical anarchy.

These opposing viewpoints dramatized the rhetorical battle that evolved out of the CIO's fight with Jersey City, and illuminates how we remember that controversy today. At first, in the weeks and months following the CIO's unsuccessful "invasion," public attention focused on the trial of the November 29 leafletters and on Jersey City's subsequent refusal to grant the CIO permission to hold public protest rallies. Soon, the ACLU joined the CIO's fight, as did other elements of the emerging labor-left anti-Hague regional coalition centered in New York City. Jersey City denied these groups speaking permits, too. When the ACLU, labor groups, and notable orators like Norman Thomas then tried to hold a series of unauthorized rallies, Jersey City police promptly suppressed them. What began as CIO labor fight on behalf of union organizing became an ACLU-led civil-liberties campaign to secure public assembly and free speech rights for any labor-oriented group.

The conflict then spilled over into print media, radio, and public arenas where image formation became a central part of the struggle. Both sides cultivated labels and characterizations to justify their positions, castigate their opponents, rally their supporters and, most importantly, define what the lawful exercise of civil liberties really was. Ideology, not ethnicity or race, distinguished the two sides. For his part, Mayor Hague drew deeply on the rhetoric of anticommunism and patriotic Americanism to mobilize Jersey City's immigrant communities, Roman Catholics, war veterans, trade unions, and business groups, including the Chamber of Commerce.[2] He branded the CIO, the ACLU, and other accomplices as alien communists plotting social disruption, while he characterized his local constituents as true Americans needing protection. Rhetorically at least, Hague claimed that, while he did not oppose free speech as often said, outside radicals were not entitled to it. Ironically for a man of Irish immigrant stock, he expressed what law professor Stephen Feldman has described as an old-fashioned "republican" vision of civil liberties in which "free expression always remained subordinate to the overarching communal goal of the common good."[3] It was an antiquated and narrow view that critics hardly saw as libertarian.

Meanwhile, Hague's antagonists embraced the emerging rhetoric of antifascism that saw democracy at war with dictatorship. Public worries about the ability of liberal democracy to address the Depression had already raised fears of impending dictatorship; those fears intensified after 1935 when liberal New Dealers united with socialists and left-wing labor organizers in the Popular Front. In 1937, worried associates of the Popular Front began branding conservative politicians like Hague who utilized so-called fascist practices against democratic liberties as "Hitlers," "fascists," and "dictators." Thus, in the Jersey City affair, the CIO accused Hague of ignoring constitutional rights with the "arrogance of a fascist dictator," and would likely have seen the Chamber of Commerce endorsement of the mayor as evidence of how he lined up with "anti-union employers." As socialist leader Norman Thomas put it, "Hagueism Is Fascism."[4] Moreover, the fascist image of Hague served as a reference point against which socialists, the ACLU, left-leaning labor groups and the print media could articulate a working-class version of Americanism. Viewing themselves as victims of Hague's "un-American" "dictatorship," these groups used endorsements of free expression rights to claim legitimate places in the nation's democratic order. Their vision thus reflected what Feldman describes as the rising "pluralist" conception of civil liberties, wherein "democratic processes structured fair and open political battles" and "free expression became a crucial part of pluralist processes and thus developed into a constitutional 'lodestone.'"[5] Jersey Republicans joined this antifascist critique to serve their own purpose finally to bring Hague down.

Today's collective historical memory overwhelmingly embraces the critics' side of this public relations debate, recollecting Mayor Hague as an antilabor, anticommunist, and open-shop autocrat who only had contempt for civil liberties.[6] Yet, the situation was more complicated. A multitude of contemporary political struggles crisscrossed the CIO's battle with Hague's Jersey City and modulated all of the participants' attitudes toward civil liberties. For one thing, the Hague regime had to fend off nagging local political challenges, especially the Republican investigation of alleged voter fraud in the fall 1937 gubernatorial election. For another thing, labor activists still challenged Jersey City's reception of "runaway" shops that fled New York City union contracts. In addition, the Jersey City regime, like other Irish boss systems, had to contend with declining Irish political bases and the altered structure of political authority under the national New Deal state, especially under the NLRA.[7] Moreover, like other municipalities, Jersey City faced the unprecedented militancy of the emerging CIO, although it did not, as the city's Chamber of Commerce suggested, necessarily oppose collective bargaining strategies of the AFL. In turn, the CIO's so-called invasion of Jersey City provoked another conflict between the city's ethnicity-minded "insiders," particularly its Roman Catholic Irish immigrant population, and class-conscious "outsiders" associated with CIO industrial unions, socialists, and left-wing labor activists. All of these struggles blended with the rising ideological battle between anticommunism and antifascism.

Looming over these developments was the persistent old turn-of-the-century legal regime that shielded municipalities from federal judicial supervision of civil liberties. Contrary to the widespread modern perception that Jersey City's actions clearly violated assembly, speech, and picketing rights covered by federal law, the CIO's clash with Jersey City began in a legal environment that favored Mayor Hague's Jersey City. At that point, federal courts perpetuated the jurisprudence of *Davis v. Massachusetts*, elevating municipal authority over civil liberties, as courts had just barely begun to apply federal civil libertarian guarantees on the local level. The ACLU launched an initial challenge to the old jurisprudence in its suit over the bootmakers' strike in 1937, but Jersey City tied that case up in court. As late as early 1938, hence, Jersey City's actions remained technically lawful, and the assembly and speech claims asserted by the *CIO News* remained hypothetical, not yet formally affirmed by a court. Jersey City's brazen suppression of CIO expressive rights was thus still immune from federal judicial intrusion, and the struggle remained in the streets where Hague's regime had the advantage. All of this would change, however, when the U.S. Supreme Court's famed "civil liberties revolution" finally touched the Jersey City struggle with the *Lovell v. Griffin* decision in March 1938, and then ACLU and CIO lawyers finally got the CIO-Hague controversy before a federal judge in June 1938.

* * *

As Newark labor attorneys sought release of seven CIO men arrested in the November 29 "invasion," both sides began posturing for a fight. Appearing before Court of Common Pleas judge Thomas F. Meany on December 1 in an appeal of police court judge Anthony Botti's conviction of seven defendants for the violating Jersey City's 1924 anti-leafletting ordinance, the Newark lawyers and Jersey City counsel traded arguments. For the defendants, Abraham Isserman maintained that the ordinance represented an unconstitutional infringement on the men's speech and press freedoms to meet and discuss workers' rights under the Fourteenth Amendment, and that Botti presided over their trial as a politically motivated judge. For the city, by contrast, assistant corporation counsel Lewis Hansen contended that the defendants traveled to Jersey City with explicit orders from CIO regional director William Carney to disregard the so-called "'phoney' city ordinance." Having "read about the trouble that has taken place in other cities as a result of such bands of [CIO] men," Hansen said, Jersey City residents wanted Mayor Hague and police to provide protection. Hansen's assistant counsel Frank P. McCarthy added that the defendants' actions were "nothing but an out-and-out communist move and we are 100 percent against it."[8] Meany ruled in the city's favor, but rhetorical lines were drawn: speech rights against a monolithic political machine versus law-and-order rights against outside radical trouble makers.

In the month that followed, support for the mayor welled up all across the city. Pro-business motivational speaker Napoleon Hill told the Jersey City Lions Club that the country needed "more men like Mayor Hague" to confront President Roosevelt's "unholy alliance" with CIO head John L. Lewis. New Jersey Representative Mary T. Norton, a Hague associate, justified the anti-leafletting ordinance under which CIO men had been convicted as insuring citizens "peace of their homes and business relations." President of the NJSFL Louis Marciante, belying modern stereotypes of Hague as thoroughly estranged from labor, ridiculed the CIO's November 29 leafletting campaign as a "publicity stunt" and lauded Hague for supporting AFL affiliates. His remarks exposed the nationwide split within the ranks of organized labor that lurked behind Jersey City developments. Indeed, a few days later, the HCCLU commended Hague for his "fairness" toward AFL unions and denounced CIO members for acting like IWW "anarchists." For its part, the Hudson County Building and Construction Trades Council praised Hague "for his opposition to the CIO and other radical elements and for his many years supporting legitimate union interests." By December 24, other endorsements arrived from Jersey City's Real Estate Board, Lion's Club, Ladies Auxiliary of Grand Army of the Republic, Catholic War Veterans, and other groups. Historians often attribute such backing to the Hague regime's genius for coercing loyalty from city residents dependent on the municipal payroll.[9] Yet, such judgments underestimate the broad cross section of Jersey City constituents who genuinely opposed radicalism and militant unionism.

In response, the CIO mobilized its own supporters, but it lost control of its own campaign. On the day after the thwarted CIO leafletting drive, regional director Carney lashed out at Hague with typical CIO masculine bravado. "If he has chosen to throw down the gauntlet, and declare war on us," Carney proclaimed, "we want him to know right now that we have just begun to fight, too." To continue the CIO's work in Jersey City, Carney aligned with local civil libertarians, leftist labor activists in the ILD, and Newark's pro-labor law firm Isserman and Isserman to form the Hudson County Committee for Civil Rights. He then headed to Washington, D.C., to confer with CIO president John L. Lewis. Simultaneously, CIO general counsel Lee Pressman announced that the CIO's national office planned to throw its "full weight" behind the Jersey City drive, and had hired ACLU-affiliated New York attorney Morris Ernst to seek a federal court injunction against Jersey City. Previously skeptical of pro-business federal judges, CIO leaders now saw hope in seeking their support of worker rights. Once Ernst became involved, however, ACLU leaders quickly took over the Hudson County Committee and subordinated Carney to Ernst's leadership. Within days, the national ACLU office created the Committee for Civil Liberties in Jersey City, enlisting a who's who of sixty-four literary, theatrical, medical, religious, legal, journalistic, and academic figures nationwide to endorse the ACLU effort. The shift of control from the young cash-strapped CIO to the older, better organized ACLU altered the Jersey City drive's agenda. ACLU lawyers capitalized on Jersey City events to cultivate a national audience for speech and assembly rights, rather than union organizing.[10]

Rhetorical posturing accompanied organizing. As soon as Ernst and the ACLU joined the CIO struggle in early December 1937, Mayor Hague began issuing press releases alleging that ACLU "communists" stood behind the CIO campaign. Drawing extensively from New York Republican Hamilton Fish's 1931 congressional committee report and anticommunist author Elizabeth Dilling's *The Red Network* (1934), Hague tried to use guilt by association to discredit the CIO-ACLU alliance. According to Hague, ACLU founder and director Roger Baldwin, along with attorneys Arthur Garfield Hays and Morris Ernst, and the "Red counsel" Abraham Isserman, were "leading Communists in this country." They jumped into the CIO campaign, he said, to make it "a Communist fight and not a labor issue." Their assembly and speech claims were bogus, he added, because they aimed only to rationalize communists' "advocacy of force and violence to overthrow the government," not to engage in debate.[11]

Back in early 1937, Jersey City Republican J. Owen Grundy had quietly warned ACLU director Roger Baldwin that Hague might generate such a "fake red scare." How fully the mayor actually did so to protect Jersey City's "open shop" and other political interests is not clear, but his comments certainly synchronized with a growing right-wing movement. Nationwide, the informal anticommunist network begun during World War I gathered steam in the 1930s in reaction to the nationalized New Deal state, the creation of the CIO and the formation of the Popular Front. It blended with the mass "global right" that arose on both sides of the Atlantic against communism and militant unionism. Among Roman Catholics, especially, anticommunism intensified after a 1937 papal encyclical condemned communism, and the Catholic fraternal order Knights of Columbus took up the anticommunist mission. Dilling's *Red Network* captured the spirit of the movement when it warned that international communism was "a Trojan horse carrying social anarchy" and would "derange traditional American social relations and power structures." In Jersey City, patriotic old-immigrant groups like the Irish, church leaders, veterans, social clubs, women's groups, businessmen, and trade unionists heartily endorsed these views. Local clerics asserted that while labor unions were acceptable to Roman Catholics, the CIO was infested with communists and "went too far" when it "invaded" Jersey City and broke the law.[12] They agreed with Hague that CIO and ACLU radicals were beyond the pale of civil liberties protection.

The CIO countered Jersey City rhetoric first with appeals for union rights, but then with a stand against domestic dictatorship. When CIO counsel Lee

Pressman initially announced CIO plans to fight Mayor Hague's obstruction of organizers, he accused the mayor of waging a "vicious anti-union drive" to turn Jersey City into an "open-shop paradise." He then pledged that the CIO would fight back on behalf of "genuine trade unions" everywhere to establish basic union rights to hold public meetings, send organizers into communities, and peacefully set up pickets. Using antifascist Popular Front language just a week later, however, New York City CIO leader Allen Haywood denounced Hague's Jersey City as a "new Berlin" and promised that the CIO would force the "little Hitler across the river" to recognize that he was still in the United States. "We in New York," he affirmed, "are not going to accept Mussolini and Hitler right on our own doorstep." The national organization's *CIO News* concurred. By using police against union men just as fascists did in Europe, the *News* contended, the "petty dictator of Jersey City" Hague had declared war on U.S. democracy. The real question in Jersey City, hence, was whether democracy or dictatorship would prevail. CIO rhetoric thus signaled the development of a leftist working-class popular culture in the 1930s that identified the rights of workers with U.S. democracy and demonized would-be local tyrants for acting like un-American European dictators.[13]

The antifascist critique spread widely and overshadowed discourse about worker rights. Mocking Hague as "Jersey's Roi Soleil" (alluding to "sun king" Louis XIV of France), given his "I am the law" comment (similar to Louis's exclamation, "L'état, c'est moi"), the *New York Times* described the mayor as a despotic leader who did not believe in any rights. Broadcasting over New York City radio station WEVD, moreover, ACLU director Roger Baldwin denied Hague's accusations of ACLU associations with communists and then condemned the mayor for "tyranny," vowing to teach Hague himself a lesson in Americanism—that defense of civil liberties was not communistic, but a loyal affirmation of basic U.S. rights to "freedom of speech, press and assembly for all." Like the CIO, hence, the ACLU depicted the issue in Jersey City as "democracy versus dictatorship."[14] The rhetorical conflict between Mayor Hague and the CIO in Jersey City thus polarized into opposing images that dominated antagonists' reaction to the battle that followed, and the way in which we remember it today.

* * *

The media war heated up, because the legal environment in late 1937 still strongly favored Jersey City. Its meeting hall, anti-leafletting, and speech-permit ordinances, the New Jersey disorderly persons statute, and the jurisprudence established by the U.S. Supreme Court's 1897 *Davis v. Massachusetts* decision all remained good law and provided Jersey City leaders with broad legal authority to police labor protests. On December 6, city police intervened in a sit-down strike staged at the Standard Cap and Seal factory by a new CIO-affiliated union. Samuel Macri and other CIO operatives had quietly continued organizing efforts, partly due to spontaneous local job actions, even as the Jersey City–CIO conflict unfolded. Called in by plant managers, however, Police Chief Harry Walsh broke up the Cap and Seal job action, advising strikers that because they were in "Jersey City, not Moscow," they had to vacate private company property and allow only a small picket line outside without placards, the ban on placards having been affirmed by Vice Chancellor Charles M. Egan earlier that year. Walsh's order continued Jersey City's arguably still valid, if narrow policy of permitting traditional labor pickets and strike activity by existent unions, but not militant sit-down tactics or inflammatory displays. Without clear legality, moreover, the mayor's office also pressured private meeting hall owners not to rent space to CIO organizers, while police turned away others as they arrived from New York City on ferryboats and the Hudson River tunnels, a form of "eviction without arrest."[15]

In reaction, Jersey City's critics escalated negative publicity. On December 21, 1937, they held a meeting sponsored by the WDL on private property at

Figure 4. Socialist Norman Thomas addresses a packed protest meeting in Jersey City on December 21, 1937, with CIO union organizers and supporters seated on stage in front of him. Image 516524482, Bettmann/Getty Images.

St. Paul's Methodist Episcopal Church, where Hague's police could not reach them. Originally scheduled to celebrate the anniversary of New Jersey's ratification of the U.S. Constitution, the event turned into an anti-Hague rally featuring anti-Hague speakers and three hundred white, male listeners with a few women mixed in. Socialist Norman Thomas received the biggest ovation when he attacked Hague as an undemocratic autocrat who controlled New Jersey's governor, U.S. senators and state judges, and then defended CIO members' pursuit of speech rights as more patriotic than Hague's actions. If the CIO came to Jersey City, Thomas declared in a perfect expression of working-class Americanism, it "will not come here to raise the red flag. It will come here to redeem the American flag."

The critics also resorted to New York City radio stations beyond Hague's control to broadcast similar messages. In mid-December, anti-Hague activists sent a station wagon circling around city hall in Jersey City with a sign urging residents to listen to a WEVD speech by ACLU attorney Morris Ernst, brazenly parking the vehicle outside of Hague's window for twenty-five minutes. Nothing happened. In his subsequent radio address, Ernst condemned Hague as a "radical" who tore up the New Jersey and U.S. Constitutions, while his police tactics removed Jersey City from the U.S.'s democratic culture. Like Thomas, Ernst asserted that CIO speech claims showed a truer commitment to American democracy.[16]

Other political opponents on the left and right kept up attacks on the Hague regime, despite the difficult legal situation. On the left, labor activists led by state CIO leader Carl Holderman escalated the CIO's political challenge to Hague by launching a new third political party affiliated with the LNPL at a December 6 convention in Newark attended by five hundred delegates representing 150 unions from around the state. For its part, the NJSFL rejected this third-party plan in line with instructions from national AFL president William Green, but thirty-four New Jersey AFL affiliates attended the December convention anyway. The AFL-CIO split left New Jersey's labor movement politically divided over Hague's leadership in Jersey City, while political opposition to Hague in labor ranks grew.[17] On the right, Republicans continued to press the recount of November 2 Hudson County gubernatorial election returns that New Jersey Supreme Court chief justice Thomas J. Brogan had allowed to commence. While it was doubtful that Brogan as a Hague ally would permit the recount to proceed far enough actually to jeopardize Democrat A. Harry Moore's victory, the situation still threatened the Hague regime's statewide dominance just at the moment that it faced the CIO challenge.[18]

A war of words between ACLU attorney Morris Ernst and Mayor Hague added vitriol to the conflict. Appealing for National Lawyers Guild's support in Washington, D.C., on December 17, Ernst denounced Hague's administration as "a symbol of real dictatorship." "So far there has been no evidence of machine guns," he reportedly stated, "and I hope there will be none, because I know we would be playing into the hands of Mayor Hague." If Hague were allowed to tear up the Constitution and the Bill of Rights, then any other mayor could do the same thing against the CIO, the AFL, or anyone else. Hague responded in kind. In spite of "red ranters" like Ernst, he observed, "no machine guns will be used by Communist invaders in Jersey City," because it was an American town of law and order, "never an adjunct of Russia." And if Ernst ever wanted to bring "his gang" with machine guns into Jersey City and repeat his speech there, Hague warned, "I guarantee . . . that his friends will not see him for a long time."[19] The bitter give and take reinforced the clash between competing visions of the controversy—American democracy against dictatorship versus American law and order against foreign radicalism.

In this polarized atmosphere, the CIO and its allies loosely associated with the Hudson County Committee for Civil Rights began seeking various kinds of relief within the limited channels available to them at the time. Isserman and Isserman lawyers filed briefs before the New Jersey Supreme Court to reverse convictions of seven November 29 CIO leafletters. Newark Law School dean and municipal law expert Spaulding Frazer joined the legal team with promises to file an application for a CIO speaking permit with Jersey City public safety director Daniel Casey. CIO organizers prepared to meet workers in front of their plants and to distribute flyers in Jersey City. And activists began gathering information for a report to be submitted to the U.S. senator Robert La Follette Jr.'s Committee on Civil Liberties. With attorneys in the lead, the CIO coalition began turning the Jersey City struggle into a legal campaign for free speech and assembly rights.[20]

Reading about these plans in the newspapers, especially CIO regional director Carney's alleged statements that CIO members would gather in Jersey City regardless of municipal consent, the city's corporation counsel James Hamill fired off a letter to advise Carney about municipal regulations. In careful detail, he reminded Carney first about Jersey City's January 22, 1924, ordinance that prohibited any person from "distribut[ing] or caus[ing] to be distributed any newspapers, papers, . . . circulars, cards or pamphlets" in any public place or on any street. He then asked Carney to recall the April 15, 1930, ordinance that forbade "public parades or assemblies" in public places "until a permit shall be obtained from the Director of Public Safety," a permit that director could refuse, if he determined after investigation that there was need to prevent "riots, disturbances or disorderly assemblage." Hamill added that New Jersey statutes also banned unlawful assemblies based on the common-law prohibition of gatherings that endangered "tranquility and peace" or had "a natural tendency" to strike fear in "rational, firm, and courageous persons." In a spirit of "fair warning," he treated CIO organizers as outsiders who needed a lesson in local law and a stern reminder that Jersey City would enforce it.[21]

After talking with Carney about Hamill's letter, Spaulding Frazer issued a reply suggesting a more open view of CIO speech rights in the city. Observing that Hamill's letter seemed to be swayed by "the hysterical outbursts of your Mayor," Frazer contended that the CIO men arrested on November 29 had every right to circulate handbills under the Wagner Act, and that if littering were really a problem, then the CIO could assign people to pick up any flyers dropped. In any case, Frazer said, the real issue was not CIO lawbreaking but politics. CIO organizers had no intentions of violating the law, but only wanted to assemble peacefully and discuss an end to arbitrary police arrests and a repeal of the anti-leafletting ordinance. On the very day that he wrote, Frazer noted, he was submitting the CIO request for a public meeting permit from public safety director Casey, something that CIO members had a lawful right to get. As Frazer had it, Jersey City needed the civics lesson. Yet, Hamill answered back on December 27 that Jersey City intended to apply its ordinances equally to all, including the CIO.[22] The Frazer-Hamill exchange illuminated the fundamental CIO–Jersey City legal dispute that pitted assembly-and-speech rights against municipal police authority.

Still, city officials gave both CIO and ACLU representatives the runaround. On December 17, Isserman and Isserman attorney Samuel Rothbard made an application to safety commissioner Casey for the ACLU to hold a rally on the steps of the courthouse, but then got bogged down in an exchange of letters over Casey's request for a list of speakers. Simultaneously, Frazer filed his own request for a CIO meeting permit, stating that the CIO proposed to lobby the Jersey City Board of Commissioners for a modification of the city's leaflet ordinance and for an end to police harassment. He listed Montana Representative Jerry O'Connell, Roger Baldwin, William Carney, and others as likely speakers. Casey promptly responded that he was investigating Frazer's request, but then he strangely delayed any further answer either to Rothbard's original ACLU inquiry or to Frazer's CIO filing.[23]

Casey's delay signaled the city machine's typical manipulation of municipal police powers but still raised a significant issue in law. In this instance, Casey had to decide how to apply Jersey City's 1930 public meeting permit ordinance stipulating that he could refuse a permit, if he determined that a proposed public rally threatened "riots, disturbances or disorderly assemblage." That provision drew on English common law rules predating the U.S. Bill of Rights that were still in effect in December 1937, although the U.S. Supreme Court's *DeJonge v. Oregon* (1937) ruling had just begun applying the First and Fourteenth Amendments to local assembly cases. *DeJonge* held that people had a fundamental right to assemble peacefully and assert grievances without specifically applying that right yet to public streets or parks. The common-law tradition, however, still drew the line at "unlawful assemblies" wherein groups of three or more persons gathered so as to disturb the peace or provoke others to do so, a principle affirmed in New Jersey's 1928 *State v. Butterworth* decision.[24] Jersey City's 1930 ordinance carried that concept of illegal assembly forward with the proviso that speaking permits could be denied when the safety director found a threat of "riots, disturbances or disorderly assemblage." Casey exploited the "riot" provision of the 1930 ordinance to justify suppression of the ACLU and CIO rallies.

Casey's and Jersey City's proof of threatened violence was an alleged outcry from the city's veterans. On December 27, the Committee of Veterans of Jersey City sent Casey a letter expressing strong opposition to any speaking permit allowing a rally that included the ACLU's notorious "slacker," "draft-dodging," and "un-American" leader Roger Baldwin. At the 113th Regiment Armory on the following evening, three thousand veterans from the American Legion, Veterans of Foreign Wars, Jewish War Veterans, Catholic War Veterans, Italian-American War Veterans, Polish Legion, and other groups endorsed resolutions making the same point. The gathering reflected how wartime Americanization had bonded Jersey City's many ethnic groups along patriotic lines, not the class-conscious lines that marked the CIO. Articulating themes of the interwar anticommunist movement, the vets favored "decent" treatment of working people but asserted "utter opposition" to the "Communist CIO with its record of armed mobs, [mass] intimidation . . . seizure of property, defiance of the courts, bloodshed and death to those who oppose its doctrines." They consequently condemned "any elements coming to Jersey City preaching the gospel of Communism." No surprise then that veterans supported Mayor Hague's policy of excluding Baldwin and CIO agitators from the city.[25]

Critics complained with good reason that Hague's regime orchestrated the veterans' outburst, but there was more to it. The mayor's office issued an "Important Notice" on December 28, 1937, urging that "All Veterans Report at Armory Tonight," many veterans being city employees dependent on the Hague organization for their jobs. Yet, the veterans' expressions were not simply the product of city hall machinations. Veteran Clarence Squires wrote to the *Jersey Observer* to insist that he went on "my own free will" along with "hundreds of [other] veterans who were not on the city payroll," because he did not want Roger Baldwin or the CIO to get a foothold in the city. Thus, contrary to the stereotype of Hague as the masterful dictator who controlled everything in his city, the veterans' rally showed how his administration vented larger social forces. For one thing, the veterans' meeting revealed Jersey City as a hotbed of anticommunist sentiment. While closely allied to the Hague machine, the city's fragmented ethnic minorities, conservative Irish Catholic leadership, local AFL-affiliated trade unions, and post–World War I patriotic groups were all constituencies that robustly opposed communism and CIO activities. For another thing, Jersey City leadership intertwined with the fiercely anticommunist American Legion and Veterans of Foreign Wars, as signified by architect and World War I infantry officer Hugh Kelly's multiple roles as rally chairman, local American Legion commander, and assistant to Hague follower, Governor Harry Moore. Moreover, Mayor Hague's long anticommunist newspaper exposés against ACLU and CIO activists were hardly written by the sixth-grade-educated mayor himself, but drew directly from national anticommunist literature. And Jersey veterans' endorsement of a national American Legion resolution evidenced their deference to the organization's nationwide anticommunist campaign.[26] The Jersey City veterans' anti-CIO meeting was thus not just a politically manufactured affair but a reflection of deep-seated local political culture.

Two days after the veterans' rally, Casey finally sent Frazer a letter refusing the CIO meeting request on the grounds that it threatened "riots, disturbances or disorderly assemblage" as prohibited by city ordinance. He cited the veteran's committee letter, the large tumultuous veterans rally, incendiary rally speeches, and stern objections by both the city's Chamber of Commerce and its Central Labor Union all as evidence of impending disorder. Assuming that violence threatened by potential listeners could justify prior restraints on public speakers, Casey claimed that he was only doing his duty to keep city peace. An exasperated Frazer replied on January 3, 1938, that Casey's three-day wait before responding looked suspiciously like a delaying tactic to allow veterans to mobilize. He added that Casey had bowed "to the mercies of a riotous mob" rather than enforce the constitutional rights of Baldwin, the CIO, and others who planned only to petition the city commission peacefully. In reality, Frazer said, Jersey City was fomenting mob action to deny free speech. Indeed, a CIO organizer who managed to attend the veterans' rally (before being spotted and arrested) later testified that anti-CIO and anti-Baldwin resolutions were passed at the meeting "under pressure" from rally leaders. "Is it," Frazer asked Casey, "that you tolerate mobs instructed to do your bidding and heroically suppress and oppress by public and private force all individuals who disagree with or oppose you?"[27]

Casey's and Frazer's verbal duel exposed prevailing ambiguities in the law of assembly. Their give and take evoked the same question that arose earlier in *State v. Butterworth*—how to balance citizens' common-law right to speak and assemble against local government's inherent power to prevent disruptive gatherings—but the issue remained fluid at the moment. The U.S. Supreme Court's *Gitlow*, *Whitney*, *Stromberg*, and *Near* rulings had all established threshold principles for extending First and Fourteenth Amendment protections to the state and local level, but the court had only just begun its long string of modern assembly-and-speech cases. In its January 1937 *DeJonge* decision, the court first applied federal protections to local peaceful assemblies, and in its April 1937 *Senn v. Tile Layers Protective Union* case, it addressed peaceful picketing. Numerous questions remained. How much authority did municipalities have to control speech in public spaces (would *Davis*, 1897, stand)? When could local ordinances allow public officials to require permits to exercise outdoor expression (*Cantwell*, 1940)? When might courts hold those assembling and speaking guilty of provoking disorder with "fighting words" (*Chaplinsky*, 1942), incitement (*Feiner*, 1951), or provocative speech (*Terminiello*, 1949)? In what public places must public authorities allow people to assemble and speak (*Edwards*, 1963)? In what public places might officials exclude speakers (*Adderly*, 1966)? And in what circumstances might courts find that public officials used claims of peacekeeping just as a pretext to suppress unpopular views (*Hague* itself, 1939, and then *Edwards*, 1963)? In December 1937, CIO and ACLU attorneys advanced a new libertarian argument to answer these questions based on the Bill of Rights and the NLRA, but in formal law the questions remained unsettled in court.[28]

The absence of clear federal law regarding public assembly and speech issues left the CIO's struggle with Jersey City in the turbulent realm of politics where challenges to Hague's organization were mounting. For years, Hague had kept local opponents like James Burkitt and local civic groups like the New Jersey Taxpayers' Association and women's Junior Service League at bay.[29] Yet, by the winter of 1937–38, not only were CIO organizers trying to enter the city, not only were militants affiliated with the CIO trying to form a rival New Jersey labor party, and not only were Republicans contesting ballot fraud in the fall 1937 gubernatorial election, but also unrest was growing among ethnic outsiders in Jersey City's Jewish and Italian communities, and among a few Roman Catholic clerics, if apparently not African American residents, even as Mayor Hague's Irish political base contracted. Jersey City's squabble with the CIO thus blended with a larger political crisis. The Hague regime met that crisis by consolidating its local political support in an infamous Americanism rally on January 6, 1938.

The rally emanated from the Jersey City Chamber of Commerce. On the morning after the veterans' meeting, the Chamber set up a committee of local bankers and businessmen headed by Commercial Trust Company vice president Robert Carmichael to assemble local civic groups for the occasion. The Chamber proposed to bring the whole Jersey City community together "to back up Mayor Hague in his fight against the threatened invasion of the CIO and Communistic elements into the city." Notably, the HCCLU sent a large delegation to the Chamber parley, having passed a resolution the night before that refrained from endorsing the Chamber's policies, but vowed to "drive out a radical outfit that seeks to destroy the legitimate unions in Jersey City." Representatives from the Holy Name Society, American Women against Communism, and other groups also supported the Chamber's plans, and even staunch Hague opponents like Republican former judge Robert Carey joined the Chamber's cause. Meanwhile, letters endorsing Hague's anti-CIO stand rolled into city hall from ethnic, business, and veterans groups. The pro-Hague *Jersey Observer* heartily supported the mayor as well. "The CIO is anathema to Jersey City," an *Observer* editorial read, and consequently Mayor Hague was "fully justified" in meeting the CIO threat "with forthright action." Indeed, Hague himself published an "Appeal to the People" exhorting city residents that it was their patriotic duty "to lay aside all other business in order that you may be present to testify your loyalty to the City . . . and to the principles of Americanism."[30]

Jersey City's Americanism rally did not just represent the "marriage of high capital and popular mobilization" attributable to other right-wing or "fascist" efforts to suppress industrial unionism at the time. Elsewhere, in Gastonia (N.C.), Flint (Mich.), and the Mohawk Valley (N.Y.), big corporations worked with local law enforcers and communities to stop CIO organizing, but in Jersey City, Chamber members were weaker than businesses elsewhere, and the Hague organization loomed as the predominant institution. Jersey City's Americanism rally was centrally about Hague's political power. Moreover, while Hague worked closely with the Chamber to stage the rally, the scope and depth of anti-CIO sentiment suggests that the event was more than just a politically orchestrated "fake red scare" foisted on the people by the Chamber or Hague. The AFL-affiliated HCCLU joined the rally against the CIO as a result of the AFL-versus-CIO split, while the city's veterans, Roman Catholics, and immigrant communities participated to defend local traditions against alleged CIO radicalism. Most important, the

Hague regime had a strong interest in encouraging traditional community values to maintain his power. Hague used the language of Americanism, family, God, and country to unite Jersey City's diverse local groups behind his leadership, and to resist the class-conscious Americanism and culture of working-class unity promoted by the CIO.[31]

As the Chamber readied its rally, Jersey City delivered the emerging anti-Hague coalition a major public-relations setback. After Hague's opponents united in the Hudson County Committee for Civil Rights in late December, ACLU director Roger Baldwin mapped out a detailed battle plan to fight Jersey City violations in a "Dear Friends" letter. The message contemplated pursuit of a federal court decree, a congressional investigation, attempts to secure rally permits, plans to set up pickets and distribute flyers, and efforts to organize disaffected Jersey City residents. At a January 3 conference, moreover, Baldwin and Ernst plotted an all-out assault on the Hague administration that included a lawsuit before federal district court judge William Clark in Newark, test cases on the right to picket, an invitation to Representative O'Connell to speak in Jersey City, the formation of local and national protest committees, and an appeal to the Democratic National Committee to remove Hague from his post as vice chairman. On the very next day, however, the mayor's office stunned the ACLU-led coalition by releasing a photostatic copy of Baldwin's "Dear Friends" letter to local newspapers. Hague claimed that the letter provided proof "beyond question" of "a definite tie-up between the CIO and the Communist Party." Baldwin and the ACLU were mere fronts for the party, the mayor maintained, and Baldwin's letter revealed that he was "directing the whole CIO program" "from behind the scenes." Hague's characterization of the letter added force to the local anti-CIO furor and drowned out well-placed ACLU charges of mail tampering. The ACLU filed complaints with the U.S. Justice Department and Postmaster James Farley, who was reportedly advised by President Roosevelt just to tell Hague to "knock it off." The incident illuminated how FDR's expediency protected Jersey City from federal intervention, although Hague eventually had to answer to a federal grand jury.[32]

With support from city police and municipal officials, subsequently, Jersey City's Chamber of Commerce brought a massive crowd of a hundred thousand residents together at the armory on January 6 to oppose the CIO and communism in the name of Americanism. Someone arranged buses to bring residents from four locations to the armory and set up amplifiers to broadcast proceedings onto streets after first-come, first-served attendees filled the auditorium's twenty thousand seats. Dozens of the city's business associations, labor unions, civic leagues, Holy Name societies, ethnic clubs, veterans groups, and women's organizations were represented. Officers of teamsters' unions, railroad trainmen, laundry worker groups, the NJSFL, and the HCCLU turned out en masse. An American Legion band entertained the crowd, while organizers prepared to broadcast speeches nationally from Mutual Broadcasting System's Newark radio station WOR. Most remarkably, a bipartisan array of dignities sat on the stage to make introductions and give speeches, including Chamber vice president Carmichael, governor-elect Harry Moore, Representative Edward Hart, Republican ex-judge Robert Carey, and of course Mayor Hague, all men. Newspapers marveled that arch enemies Carey and Hague cordially shook hands and then sat next to each other as they waited to speak, an action for which fellow Republicans later criticized Carey.

Organizers framed the gathering as an affirmation of true Americanism against alien communism as represented by the CIO. Banners strung up around the auditorium read "Jersey City—One Hundred Percent American," "Time to Strike Against the Red Invasion," and "Mayor Hague Appeals to You to Remain. Don't Leave. Your Presence Registers Your Americanism." Republican speaker Carey epitomized the rally's bipartisan tone when he observed that while he had many political differences with Hague, he stood together with the mayor when it came to opposing communism's foreign threat to the city. "This is an American night in Jersey City," he declared, capturing the *Jersey Observer*'s contention that "politics went out the window." Speaker after speaker contended, moreover, that Jersey City's Americanism did not oppose "lawful" labor organizing, such as that practiced by AFL-affiliated unions, but the "lawless" disruption promoted by "Reds" in the CIO. According to governor-elect Moore, "These radicals have no right to come into our city to browbeat our people," and "we have a right to protect the people from such outrages." Indeed, a banner hanging in the armory urged Jersey residents to "Drive Communism Out of Labor," while Representative Hart's statement that "this meeting is not one against organized labor" evoked loud applause. The real fight was against the "Red Menace," as Mayor Hague explained in a "fiery" address. Claiming that he had a long history of supporting "adequate wages" and "fair conditions" for workers, a long friendship with the AFL, and a long record of promoting labor peace, Hague asserted that Jersey City's battle did not involve rank-and-file CIO members but was instead against the "communistic elements" that had seized control of that group. "As long as I am Mayor of Jersey City," Hague proclaimed, "I will . . . oppose their invasion of the city. They shall never come into our city and destroy industry." Reacting to all of this from New York City, real communists at the *Daily Worker* castigated the mayor's speech as a bunch of "wild lies" that fomented a "vigilante spirit" of "physical violence" against upstanding unionists.[33]

Figure 5. Jersey City Americanism rally held at the armory by Mayor Frank Hague and the Chamber of Commerce on January 6, 1938. A Margaret Bourke-White photograph in *Life*, February 7, 1938. Image 1176831282, the LIFE Picture Collection/Getty Images.

In years that followed, critics denounced Jersey City's Americanism rally as "a macabre image of total, arrogant political control" by the Hague regime, but a closer look shows that the event exhibited broadly conservative anti-CIO sentiment across Jersey City businesses and working people. For instance, with a board of directors laden with banking, financial, and utility companies, as well as small manufacturers and professionals, though no sweatshop garment firms, the Chamber of Commerce had for years been cultivating Jersey City's reputation as "an ideal industrial center" largely due to its labor peace, something disrupted by the CIO's entry into the city with support from the "viciously one-sided" Wagner NLRA. For their own reasons, AFL Jersey trade unionists agreed. When CIO organizers moved into Jersey City and other East Coast territories previously dominated by the AFL and tried to secure recognition under the newly created NLRA, NJSFL president Marciante—like national AFL president William Green—fought off CIO encroachment. Trying to explain away the CIO's allure to some laborers, Marciante condemned that group as a communist-infested force that undemocratically coerced workers into membership and interfered with orderly trade union practices. No mere puppets of Hague's regime, the Chamber and local AFL leadership shared an aversion to CIO activities at the January 6 rally.[34]

For cultural reasons, local veterans, Roman Catholics, and Irish also held that aversion. From the post–World War I Red Scare onward, the American Legion and Veterans of Foreign Wars stood nationwide as bastions of the interwar anticommunist movement, and Jersey City veterans sustained this sentiment against the CIO. According to a resolution passed by a Hudson County committee of the American Legion, legionnaires did not regard the CIO as a true representative of legitimate trade unionism but saw it as a group of "anti-American agitators" who were trying to "conceal their subversive designs" by masquerading as labor organizers. Like Mayor Hague, consequently, the Hudson County Legion called on public officials to refuse such agitators any privileges of citizenship "which may be distorted to an improper purpose." Moreover, Jersey City's Roman Catholic clergy and parishioners also rejected the CIO as a radical force—almost unanimously. Robert Lynch, the Irish Catholic president of Jersey City's Central Labor Union, denounced the CIO as a "Red army." Catholic War Veterans mobilized as a vigilante force against the CIO. Jersey City's Irish especially resisted the CIO. Like Irish elsewhere, they were "steeped in the parochial culture of their parishes and voluntary associations," and were tightly interwoven in churches, craft unions, veterans groups, city government, and police. They saw the CIO as a threat to their whole way of life.[35] Together with the Chamber of Commerce, Jersey City's veterans, Catholics, AFL members and Irish formed nearly a united front against CIO organizers even without the Hague administration's centralized direction.

The close "fit" of the Hague political machine with Jersey City society, according to political scientist Richard Connors, largely explained the mayor's political staying power. The character of the community that he bossed was just as important as Hague's bossism in sustaining his long ascendancy and ability to stifle civil liberties. Disgruntled Republican and city historian J. Owen Grundy found Hague's rapport with local industrial and banking interests to be "nearly perfect."[36] The mayor's rhetoric of Americanism appealed widely to Jersey City veterans, Catholic organizations, trade unionists, and ethnic communities, especially the Irish. The united outburst against the CIO at the armory reflected Jersey City's thoroughgoing commercial and social conservatism as much as it exhibited the Hague regime's ability to command support. The CIO and its partners were thus fighting not only Hague, but a whole community.

* * *

In the weeks following the armory rally, local political support for Mayor Hague's fight against the CIO and its ACLU allies continued to run wide and deep. Endorsements of his "courageous" and "heroic" stand emanated from local newspapers, Knights of Columbus, Holy Name societies, veterans groups, Jersey City democratic political clubs, the dean of Jersey City's John Marshall Law School, the New Jersey Association of Professional Engineers, and speakers at the Essex County Jefferson-Jackson Day dinner in Newark, though no black groups for or against. Across the board, these groups maintained that communism, not legitimate labor organizing was at issue, and that Hague was only doing his duty to preserve law and order. Speeches by New York Republican Representative Hamilton Fish and Mayor Hague himself amplified this position at a packed Jersey City Chamber of Commerce dinner attended by six hundred adoring Rotary, Lions, and Kiwanis Club members on January 12, 1938. Fish warmly endorsed Hague's policy, warning that communists had infiltrated CIO leadership, disturbed CIO unity talks with the AFL, and threatened to derail the U.S. labor movement. In tones prefiguring the coming McCarthy era, the mayor added that Americans "had better wake up" to the way that communists were infiltrating basic American institutions. According to Hague, Jersey City was a "moral," "clean," and "peaceful" industrial center that did not hamper legitimate labor activity, even when carried out by the CIO. Indeed, he had nothing against rank-and-file CIO members, the mayor insisted. The real danger, he affirmed, came from communist agitators like maritime labor leader Harry Bridges, CIO officials William Carney and John Brophy, and ACLU activists Roger Baldwin, Morris Ernst, and Arthur Garfield Hays. Hague avowed that these men would assert "constitution rights, free speech and the free press" to obscure their subversive purposes. "Every time I hear these words, I say to myself 'that man is a Red, that man is a Communist,'" Hague asserted. "Drunk with power," such figures would claim constitutional rights as a pretext to launch mass picketing, upset labor relations, and destroy property, as they already had done in San Francisco and Detroit. This rhetoric by Hague did not, as pervasively misquoted later, reject all free speech, just its abuse by subversives. Yet, by condemning CIO and ACLU opponents as disruptive subversives in such sweeping terms, he effectively stifled their discourse in the rather authoritarian tones for which he was known.[37]

The nearly monolithic local front that Jersey City put up against the alleged invasion by supposed CIO and ACLU communists helped Hague to repel local political threats. On the very pages that featured outpourings of local political support, newspapers reported on Republicans' ongoing challenge to the 1937 gubernatorial election. With defeated Republican candidate Lester Clee's ultimately unsuccessful recount under way, Republican state lawmakers formed an investigative committee and began subpoenaing Hudson County poll books, but Hague's police stymied the inquiry by impounding election records. On top of that, a political flap erupted when newly elected governor Harry Moore named Hague's legal advisor John Milton to fill Moore's vacated U.S. Senate post. Milton was deeply implicated in many Hague scandals, including alleged payoffs, the denial of civil liberties to labor organizers, and the tainted 1937 election. The New Jersey CIO's political wing, the LNPL, lobbied hard to secure a Senate investigation before Milton was seated, contending that corruption negated his fitness to hold office. Yet, the U.S. Senate's Democratic leadership declined to pass judgment on Milton and allowed him to take his seat. Bolstered by the immense local backing generated by the anti-CIO campaign, Hague quashed Republicans' bid to upset the 1937 gubernatorial election and dissuaded congressional leaders from questioning his organization's choice for senator.[38]

Nonetheless, agitation against Hague's anti-CIO stand festered all around in local, regional and national politics. Dissident northern Jersey Protestant and Roman Catholic churchmen spoke out against suppression of CIO speech rights, including local Democratic critic and Italian Holy Name Society leader John Longo, whose appearance indicated the rise of ethnic outsiders as challengers to Hague. Meanwhile, the national Jesuit weekly *America* along with Monsignor John Ryan dismissed the fuss over communism in Jersey City as a "red herring" that obscured the real struggle over civil liberties. In addition, New York–based socialists, the *Catholic Worker*, the Association of Catholic Trade Unionists, the WDL, and the ILD increasingly treated the Jersey City fight as a proving ground for labor rights nationwide. The WDL, in particular, teamed up with the NJCLU and its executive secretary Nancy Cox to test the constitutionality of local anti-handbill ordinances. Moreover, the CIO continued political efforts to displace Hague as mayor, submitted a bill of complaints about Jersey City's labor law violations to Congress, and staged rallies in Newark and other nearby communities to mobilize public opinion and raise money. Finally, in press releases, radio addresses, public speeches, and pamphlets, the ACLU's Hays, Ernst, and Baldwin all denounced Hague's civil liberties violations, even though some CIO officials criticized Ernst's attacks as "undignified" and neglectful of worker rights.[39]

While united in their opposition to the Hague administration and its tactics, however, CIO and ACLU leaders differed markedly over what was at stake in Jersey City. To CIO officials, the fracas was all about their organization's right to unionize a population of exploited workers under the recently enacted and upheld NLRA, despite the opposition of a corrupt mayor doing the bidding of local businesses. Without reaching out to particular ethnic groups or blacks, the CIO described Jersey City as an "open-shop heaven" dominated by sweatshop employers who sought refuge from modern labor laws so that they could pay Jersey City's suffering (largely female) workers sometimes as little as $3 to $5 a week and leave them to live and work in substandard "fire traps." The communist *Daily Worker* corroborated these claims, although few communists were parties to the CIO–Jersey City struggle. In interviews with Jersey sweatshop workers (who frequently requested, "don't use my name"), *Daily Worker* reporter Art Shields exposed cramped workspaces, long hours, abusive shop foremen, and pay insufficient for food and rent, particularly among female and African American laborers. His attention to blacks showed communists' exceptional concern for African American workers but no evidence that communists were organizing them in Jersey City. Overall, according to the CIO, Jersey workers were "prisoners of despair" who desperately wanted to be unionized, as evidenced by the quick formation of local unions shortly after CIO organizers moved in. With ties to big corporations, textile factories, garment firms, and chemical companies, the mayor tried to stop them with police spies and other forms of coercion. Yet, a *CIO News* editorial cartoon captioned "Trying to Stop the Flood!" predicted that Hague would fail. It showed him with his finger in a Jersey City dike futilely trying to hold off an unstoppable CIO flood, while shielding himself with an umbrella labeled "police coercion," as a fat man labeled "sweatshop employers" looks on in alarm, money bag in his hand. The CIO thus saw Mayor Hague's "ballyhoo campaign against radicalism and communism" as "nothing more than a subterfuge to protect Jersey City employers." The AFL aggravated the problem, CIO writers added, by siding with Hague and serving as tools in the anti-CIO campaign.[40]

ACLU spokesmen, by contrast, brushed off charges of communism and emphasized respect for civil liberties as the issue at stake. Hays, Ernst, and Baldwin all disavowed any personal affiliations with communists and condemned Hague as a petty local dictator who used the "bogey of communism" to divert attention from his civil-liberties violations. They described the January 6 anticommunist armory rally as an event orchestrated by Hague himself, not a genuine reflection of public concern, and they perpetuated the mischaracterization of his "I am the law" statement by declaring that he was "not the law" but subject to the U.S. Constitution. Importantly, ACLU leaders signaled their shift in philosophy away from previous commitments to labor agitation and toward neutral civil liberties. They explained their entry into the Jersey City as purely a fight to uphold the law and enforce rights guaranteed to all citizens, not to serve the CIO or other labor groups. They aimed to secure free speech, press, and assembly for all.[41]

To this point, the Jersey City controversy remained a political power struggle in which Hague and his associates easily sabotaged opponents. Meeting hall owners still denied rental space to CIO operatives, and city police still disrupted efforts to pass out circulars. Meanwhile, the Hague organization demoted two of Chief Justice Brogan's relatives on the city payroll, when the jurist issued an adverse ruling in the gubernatorial election recount case. Then, when Bayonne public safety director Horace Roberson, the only Republican on that city's commission, spoke out against Hague's abuse of CIO speech and assembly rights, and even permitted a Bayonne rally at which Roger Baldwin spoke, Hague-allied Democrats on the Bayonne commission promptly had Roberson removed, along with nine policemen and firemen he had hired. And, of course, Jersey City public safety director Daniel Casey continued to deny CIO and ACLU orators speech and assembly permits.

Hague opponents thus struggled against a seemingly impregnable wall of pro-Hague support. On the municipal level, overlapping constituencies of Roman Catholics, Irish residents, veterans, AFL union members, city employees, Democratic party workers, local newspapers, and local businessmen remained thoroughly within the Hague camp, allowing city administrators (with much police help) to conduct a "reign of terror" that subdued the Jersey City taxpayers association, Republicans, and non-Irish insurgents like John Longo and James Burkitt, not to mention CIO organizers and ACLU speakers.[42] On the state level, the stalled recount process seated Democratic Hague ally Harry Moore securely in the governor's chair. On the national level, Congress refused to intervene in Hague minion John Milton's U.S. Senate appointment, while President Roosevelt remained silent. Long stymied by these political arrangements, Hague opponents by the late 1930s turned to national institutions that would ultimately prove capable of penetrating the Hague regime's local bastion of power—the federal courts and the press.

In what would turn out be a pivotal event, Spaulding Frazer filed a complaint for the CIO and its ACLU supporters in federal district court against Hague, Daniel Casey, and other Jersey City officials on January 7, 1938. Dismissing any power that those officials might claim to regulate CIO and ACLU activities under municipal law, the complaint boldly staked out a new legal scheme to defend liberties. It contended that Jersey City violated civil rights under a panoply of federal laws, and requested that the district court enjoin the municipality from interfering with CIO and ACLU members' access to city streets, ability to hold public meetings, attempts to distribute literature, and efforts to rent meeting halls.[43]

The lawsuit opened a new battle front in the larger war between the CIO and Jersey City. For their part, CIO attorneys described the suit as "the spearhead of a legal attack on Hague," while CIO regional director William Carney characterized it as a way to advance national CIO organizing efforts. Alluding to the mayor's anticommunist harangues, the city's anti-CIO rallies, and the veterans' central role in them, he claimed that "no rabble-rousing appeal to passion, no organization of vigilantes will stop the forward march of the CIO from Atlantic to Hudson County." After the suit was filed, consequently, CIO leaders convened a meeting of CIO president Lewis, CIO legal counsel Pressman, United Auto Workers head Homer Martin, electrical workers leader James Carey, Jersey regional director Carney, and Newark attorney Samuel Rothbard in Washington, D.C., to confer about legal strategy. For his part, Mayor Hague dismissed the suit as a change of tactics for people who were still insurrectionaries. Observing that the CIO entered "every other city" with violence and riots, the mayor found the CIO's sudden embrace of "peaceful methods" to be deceptive. "Now they come with a lily in one hand," he remarked, "and a bomb in their other concealed behind their back." He was not fooled. Even though the CIO was "adopting peaceful methods for a change," Hague said, he was "ready to fight them on this court issue." He saw the suit as a new political trick, not appreciating how the shift of venue into federal court would disarm him and give critics new legal weapons under national judicial authority.[44]

Simultaneously, the print media emerged as another national challenge to the Hague regime. By the mid-1930s, Hague had coopted his city's major dailies, the *Jersey Journal* and *Jersey Observer*, although nearby newspapers in Newark and New York City more freely criticized his administration. Jersey City's suppression of the CIO's "invasion" on November 29, however, ignited what *Life* magazine called a "battle of the headlines" that stimulated regular press coverage all over the country. The "battle of Jersey City" became a national story, and a series of muckraker-style exposés on the Hague regime flowed forth from the *New York Post*, *New York Times*, the *Daily Worker*, *Literary Digest*, *New Yorker*, *Time*, *Newsweek*, *New Republic*, *Nation*, *Forum and Century*, *Life*, *Christian Century*, *Readers' Digest*, and *Saturday Evening Post* from December 1937 through 1940, when the penultimate Hague exposé, Dayton David McKean's book *The Boss* appeared.

Journalistic coverage in these years solidified the contemporary perception of the Jersey City-versus-CIO struggle that still prevails today. Written very much in the antifascist idiom of the time, that coverage exuded both fascination and dread that an authoritarian figure like Hague could emerge in U.S. democracy, a big concern in 1938, given public uncertainty as to whether democracy or dictatorship would triumph during depression. Newspaper and magazine accounts typically described Hague's rise from humble beginnings to political power, his strong-armed and corrupt political methods, his extravagant and apparently ill-gotten lifestyle, his genuine contributions to the city's well-being like the medical center and elimination of vice (except horse race betting), the high tax rate and squalid living conditions that most city residents endured, his reputation for maintaining an open-shop town, and, most importantly, his authoritarian leadership style associated with the "I am the law" claim. More nuanced articles like *Life*'s questioned whether Hague really was a dictator or just "the last of the bosses," but the majority of journalists equated Hague with Hitler and other fascists across the Atlantic. A letter to the editor of *Life* included a photograph of Hague with a Hitler mustache penciled in. Overall, the national press depicted the CIO fight as the product of Hague's arrogant reaction to a group that dared to challenge him. In a city where Hague declared "I am the law," Sutherland Denlinger explained in *Forum and Century*, the law caused the arrest of men who attempted to distribute anti-Hague literature and the law suppressed CIO and ACLU public meetings—"the law" in this case being Mayor Hague.[45]

Journalistic reaction to the Hague-versus-CIO controversy played a huge role in shaping popular understanding of civil liberties, a form of "popular constitutionalism" that sent public opinion racing ahead of contemporary courts of law in determining the meaning of constitutional rights. When assaying the Jersey City affair, writers placed the Bill of Rights with its guarantees for free speech and assembly at the center of American democracy and its constitutional scheme. Could democracy be upheld, asked Russell Porter of the *New York Times*, by "withholding civil liberties under the Bill of Rights from any minority no matter how unpopular with the people of [Jersey] city?" There is "no democracy without civil liberty," a Norman Thomas magazine article declared. Hague's alleged danger, hence, was that he defied the rule of law and muzzled the kind of free expression that made American democracy vibrant. As journalists saw it, Hague was un-American and Jersey City was not truly part of the United States. Hague "is a weed in our somewhat trampled democratic garden," *Forum and Century*'s Denlinger wrote, "and should be torn up by the roots, paternalistic virtues along with the rest of the plant."[46]

The journalistic narrative, however, did not match legal realities in early 1938. As outrageous as Jersey City's actions toward the CIO and ACLU seemed to critics then, and to us today, the city was not entirely out of step with municipal law, labor law, or civil-liberties law as courts construed them at that moment. Public outcry certainly protested Jersey City's abuse of CIO speech and assembly rights, while the CIO bill of complaint alleged specific violations of the rights to picket, rent meeting halls, distribute circulars, hold outdoor rallies, and conduct labor organizing activities. Yet, in a practical legal sense, these charges remained just accusations in January 1938. No state or federal court had yet ruled that Jersey City lacked the authority to enact its meeting hall, anti-leafletting, and meeting permit ordinances, or that any of those measures were invalid. Nor had any courts yet decided that public safety director Casey lacked discretion under those ordinances to deny meeting permits, or that police officers lacked power to remove "undesirable" people from city limits or shut down allegedly illicit labor pickets, or as a matter of fact, that Jersey City officials abused any of these powers. *State v. Butterworth*, *Davis v. Massachusetts*, and the legal infrastructure supporting municipalities' autonomous power to police public order remained intact. The Hague regime's actions toward the CIO, ACLU, and other political opponents were thus still "lawful" in the sense that they conformed to contemporaneous jurisprudence and did not defy any court orders. Legal conservatism shielded Hague's abuses for the time being.

In the absence of judicial intervention up through the winter of 1938, Hague opponents focused on molding public opinion. At the same time that the CIO's organizing campaign expanded around the country, regional director William Carney linked his own local drive against the Hague regime to national CIO efforts in a fund-raiser, "CIO Theater Night: Bring Democracy to Jersey City," held in Newark on February 20, 1938. Carney could not get CIO head John L. Lewis to attend, but he did persuade CIO union affiliates of automakers, miners, furriers, dyers, printers, textile workers, and other groups to insert greetings and buy advertisements in the "Theater Night" program. He also secured the sponsorship of forty-six notable liberals from around the country, including Roger Baldwin, Malcolm Cowley, Dorothy Kenyan, Corliss Lamont, Oswald Villard, and Orson Wells. Squarely part of the CIO's "cultural front" that deployed literature, theater, and music to advance industrial unionism, Carney's "Theater Night" aimed to rally CIO unionists and liberals behind the CIO campaign against Hague. The program included orchestral music, negro spirituals and work songs, dancing, and tunes from labor's popular musical reviews *Pins and Needles* and *The Cradle Will Rock*. The core, however, rested in speeches by Montana's Democratic Representative Jerry O'Connell and Carney on the union struggle. As Carney explained, the CIO was fighting an "American Hitler" in Jersey City who was denying residents basic speech and assembly rights to discuss their problems, especially horribly low wages. The CIO was trying to organize these workers to secure better treatment, he said, but "I Am the Law" Hague deployed city police to disrupt union activity. If Hague's tough antiunion activities were not stopped, Carney warned, his tactics would spread elsewhere. The Jersey City fight implicated the CIO cause nationwide.[47]

On the following Saturday, civil libertarians under the auspices of the Hudson County Committee somehow managed to rent space for their own protest meeting at Jersey City's Fairmount Hotel, a private establishment out of bounds for Jersey police. Characterized by an ACLU press release as an "invasion" into Hague territory, the meeting brought more Hague opponents together, including Representatives O'Connell and John Bernard (Minn.), Reverend William Kiernan of Bayonne, and Rabbi Benjamin Plotkin, James "Jeff" Burkitt, and John Longo of Jersey City, although no CIO representatives, and no female or black speakers. O'Connell opened with a withering attack on Hague's "Charlie McCarthy governor" A. Harry Moore, whom he argued had never been elected but took office in a vote stolen by the Hague organization. Then, mixing local politics with global affairs, he denounced Hague as a corruptionist and fascist who suppressed worker civil liberties in the manner of Hitler and Mussolini. He concluded that Jersey City's struggle marked the "greatest crisis" in U.S. history, determining whether fascism or democracy would prevail in the nation. Viewing the Jersey City situation mainly as a trade union fight, Representative Bernard added that Hague's actions toward the CIO marked a nationwide drive to crush unionism. He urged Jersey workers to take up the fight just as black and white sharecroppers were doing in the South, and steel and auto workers had done in Detroit, Flint, Akron, and Toledo. The meeting showed how the Jersey City affair united an array of critics around civil liberties and labor concerns.[48]

Then, momentously, the legal tide began to turn. On March 28, 1938, the U.S. Supreme Court handed down its pathbreaking *Lovell v. City of Griffin* decision that nullified a City of Griffin, Georgia, ordinance requiring that persons distributing circulars, handbooks, advertising, and other literature within municipal limits first to get written permission from the city manager. The ruling obviously implicated Jersey City's 1924 anti-leafletting ordinance, as well as similar measures throughout New Jersey and around the country. Nonetheless, when WDL activists Grace and Morris Milgram attempted to pass out circulars advertising a socialist meeting at Journal Square the next day, Jersey City police confiscated the flyers and told the Milgrams that regardless of the *Lovell* decision, "we are enforcing the Jersey City ordinance, not the [U.S.] Constitution," a reflection of the old legal view that municipalities were not affected by the federal Bill of Rights. A few days later, however, Jersey City corporation counsel James Hamill offered second thoughts in an advisory opinion. Although *Lovell* did not rule directly on Jersey City's 1924 ordinance, he conceded that the measure did fall under the scope of the high-court decision. Consequently, he advised public safety director Daniel Casey to start allowing the distribution of literature on Jersey streets, but he listed tight restrictions that kept the CIO's November 29 action illegal. "Under no circumstances shall mass demonstrations such as were attempted by the CIO and other groups several months ago be tolerated," Hamill wrote. Still, the ruling marked a turning point in the CIO's Jersey City struggle, as it began to break down the edifice of conservative municipal law that had long sheltered city police practices. At last, journalist McAlister Coleman rejoiced, "Jersey Joins the Union." Seizing on the opening, the NJCLU issued instructions to leafletters on how to behave on the streets and how to deal with police officers who challenged their newly established right.[49]

The federal courts now protected literature distribution on city streets, but local governments still controlled speeches and rallies. Princeton students and a New York City speakers' association found this out when Jersey City refused them assembly permits. So did Hague critic James Burkitt when he stood atop an automobile in Journal Square on April 16 to deliver an oration on behalf of Democratic activist John Longo, who was awaiting trial on trumped-up election fraud charges. Having been denied a permit under the 1930 city ordinance, Burkitt attempted to speak anyway. Fifty police officers showed up and pulled Burkitt off his car as he began to talk before a jeering crowd of perhaps a thousand people who shouted, "Let him speak" and "Let's hear what he has to say." Before Burkitt could utter more than a few words, officers grabbed him, dumped him into a police car, and drove away.[50]

Socialist Norman Thomas also learned that speaking and meeting still lacked federal protection. His effort to address an anti-Hague rally at Journal Square on Saturday, April 30, triggered a wild five-week street struggle in the absence of federal oversight. Having been denied a speaking permit after veterans submitted a 158-page petition against it, Thomas traveled over to Jersey City after May Day celebrations in New York to give a speech about civil liberties nonetheless. As the crowd awaited his arrival, *Catholic Worker* editor William Callahan and WDL representative Morris Milgram tried to distribute handbills, but police confiscated those flyers in defiance of the recent *Lovell* ruling. When Thomas arrived at 8:00 p.m., Milgram tried to clear the way for his car, but officer 191 (otherwise unidentified) socked Milgram in the eye and knocked him to the ground, while other policemen whisked Thomas into a nearby sedan that took him to the Hudson River ferry. Lawyers Guild member Ashley Carrick witnessed all of this from the nearby crowd, and when he resisted police efforts to push the crowd back, he too got punched and taken to the ferry for transportation across the river to New York City. The incident sparked wide criticism. Former Republican presidential candidate

Alf Landon denounced it as a violation of sacred American speech rights. The *New York Times* said that Hague's administration was acting like Adolf Hitler's regime and that it was time for some outside agency to determine whether Jersey City maintained a "republican form of government" as required under article 4, section 4, of the U.S. Constitution. This observation astutely signaled the rising view that the old state-federal constitutional structure had to be revised to protect civil liberties. If local freedom was to be cherished, the *Times* asserted, "local tyranny is something in which the whole country has an interest."[51]

The Thomas "deportation" stirred up a political firestorm in which statements from both sides "flew thick and fast." While an uncharacteristically shaken Hague testified before a grand jury down the hall on mail-tampering charges, Thomas and his attorney Arthur Vanderbilt appeared in Newark's federal court house to file kidnapping charges and seek damages from Jersey City, a complaint that the FBI was also pursuing. In Jersey City, meantime, corporation counsel Hamill countered by asserting that Thomas had gotten what he legally deserved. The city's public safety director had acted fully within his discretion to deny Thomas's speaking request, Hamill contended, and if Thomas wanted to contest that decision, he should have filed a test case in court, not defy it with an unauthorized street meeting. Since Jersey City mayor Hague had given instructions to protect citizens from "Red agitators," he concluded, Jersey police "had a legal right, and in fact a duty, to prevent the violation of the city ordinance."[52]

More skirmishing over the right to assemble, speak, and pass out leaflets in Jersey City followed. Representative Bernard announced plans to speak at an ILD event at Journal Square on Saturday, May 7. A new group called the Hudson County Committee for Labor Defense and Civil Rights (HCCLDCR) had requested an assembly permit on the ILD's behalf, but public safety director Casey refused it. Nonetheless, two thousand veterans led by Hugh Kelly—with Casey's acquiescence—staged a "patriotic" rally of their own to denounce the "radicals." Speakers at the veterans gathering argued that "the time has come to stop talking and do something," and Kelly himself urged veterans to "spare no efforts" "to keep this Red group from appearing on our public streets." In this tense situation, the ILD tried to hold its event anyway, but a scuffle broke out when policemen and crowd members stopped three *Catholic Worker* representatives from distributing flyers. ILD leader Vito Marcantonio then hastily called the meeting off for fear of "another Memorial Day Massacre." Meanwhile, non-Irish Hague opponents suffered in torment: Longo was convicted and awaited sentencing; Burkitt languished in jail on a hunger strike; and Rabbi Plotkin's congregation was threatened with eviction from the Jewish Community Center. And Thomas continued his challenges to Jersey City actions. He formally sued the city in federal court for his April 30 "deportation," then applied for another speaking permit. Predictably, safety director Casey denied it on grounds that he had received "thousands" of protest letters against it and had seen a newspaper picture of (the decidedly anti-Soviet) Thomas raising a clenched-fist "Red Russia" salute at the New York May Day rally. Casey claimed that serious disturbances would inevitably result from a Thomas appearance.[53]

Despite all of this, the HCCLDCR tried again. The committee asked safety director Casey for a permit to allow Representatives O'Connell and Bernard to appear at Pershing Field on May 27, but Casey once more turned it down. If the two representatives took up the Hudson committee's defense of "reds, radicals and communists who violate the criminal laws of our country," he admonished, Jersey City residents would rise up in "disorder and riot." The committee prepared to assemble anyway, while Hugh Kelly called out veterans yet again for a counterdemonstration, advising them that "don't let us start anything, but we'll finish it if they start anything." When the rally finally took place, reportedly five hundred police officers under Casey's command patrolled the field, harassing and punching anti-Hague protestors, including ILD leader Robert Parker and CIO organizer Samuel Macri, the latter of whom was knocked out cold and sent to the hospital. Like Thomas before him, O'Connell was rushed by police into an awaiting car and "deported" to New York City, all for his own safety, city officials said.[54]

Thomas then shifted his rally to Military Park in nearby Newark on June 4, but even that did not work. Newark granted Thomas a permit, but when his day came to speak, crowd members identified as veterans pelted him with eggs, while an American Legion band stood in front of the rostrum blaring out patriotic music to drown out his address. Mayor Hague had arranged with an associate from rum-running days, Newark gangster Abner "Longie" Zwillman, to call out enforcers to sabotage the event. City officials were embarrassed. Thomas complained that Newark police mishandled the situation, prompting Newark's safety director to launch an investigation. The NJCLU and Newark's ministerial association warned that the June 4 "riot" showed that "Hagueism" had spread to their city. Newark issued Thomas a new permit to speak at Washington Park on June 25.[55]

Despite these relentless challenges, Jersey City residents turned out in a massive display of support for the Hague administration in an "American Rally" on June 6 that would, according *New York Times* reporter Foster Haley, have credited "P. T. Barnum, Tex Rickard, Mussolini, Hitler or Stalin." The previous Friday, Hague had issued a press release vowing that he would "fight to a finish" his struggle against communists and the CIO, including those who "hid behind the false cloak of free speech." The June 6 event endorsed this policy. As many as a hundred thousand cheering onlookers lined Harrison and Bergen Avenues where Hague led a parade of sixteen thousand veterans and other marchers, American flag in one hand, fedora hat in the other, smiling, bowing, stopping to kiss a little girl. "Attaboy, Frank!," yelled crowd members. Perhaps, as skeptics charged, the swollen ranks of municipal employees protecting their jobs inflated the crowd. Yet, as the *Times*'s Haley observed, the huge turnout revealed a deep reservoir of local patriotism beyond anything that Hague's machine could manufacture. Haley noted the festive Fourth of July spirit of the rally, even in a city where a fifth of its residents were foreign born. Americanism united Jersey City residents across ethnic lines and gave them a sense of community consciousness as opposed to class consciousness. By joining the rally, they simultaneously affirmed American principles and celebrated their own ethnic, often Irish identity, reacting enthusiastically when bands struck up "The Wearin' o' the Green." As Haley observed, the main attacks on Hague and demands for free speech came from outside of the city. A tense atmosphere developed against outsiders, as police routinely jostled New York City news reporters and crowds greeted pro-CIO speaker Jerry O'Connell with cries of "Kill the bum!" and "Run him back to Russia!" Outsiders also sensed antisemitism, although Police Chief Harry Walsh denied it. The June 6 rally showed again that the battle for Jersey City was not just a struggle between an authoritarian mayor and labor-oriented free-speech advocates, but also a cultural fight between insulated Jersey residents espousing patriotic Americanism and an array of modern, libertarian outsiders avowing a left-leaning working-class version of Americanism.[56]

Undaunted, the news media and political adversaries continued their antifascist attacks on the Hague administration. Opposition cartoonists presented Hague as an un-American dictator—signing a "Rome-Berlin-Jersey City" treaty; throwing a man labeled "free speech" off a Jersey City pier into the Hudson River, as an appalled Statue of Liberty looks on; rejecting a scroll containing the First Amendment as "more radical stuff." The *New York Times* cartoon "Der Big Boss Fuehrer" portrays Hague in a Nazi jacket with fascist salute (although also dressing him in golfing pants, as a taxpayer caddy looked on, to mock his corruptly financed Florida vacations). In an accompanying article, the *Times* argued that dictatorial disregard of civil liberties had been an integral part of the mayor's leadership from 1918 onward, as he persistently denied civil rights and subjected opponents to deportations and other forms of suppression. Labor activists also equated Hague with fascist leadership. According to Norman Thomas, Jersey City government was "pint pot Hitlerism." Just like Hitler, he said, Hague popularized himself in a battle against communism, organized a mob to bully political dissenters, staged "bread and circuses" to distract citizens from real issues, aligned middle and upper classes against labor organizers, and appealed to patriotism to create a mass movement under his control—all to sustain a corrupt regime in which sweatshops prospered, taxes were high, and Hague lived a life of luxury. A WDL pamphlet *Hagueism: What Is It?*, agreed. When "Fuehrer Hague" was caught in election fraud, it said, he proclaimed that "the Reds are coming!" to ensure that voters forgot that outrage. "Out came the bands, the faithful Legion, the flags. Out go civil liberties." In an editorial titled "Heil Hague," the *CIO News* made the same point. Just like German and Italian fascists, Hague created a "mythical 'Red Scare'" and used "unscrupulous lies" to discredit defenders of democracy as communists, while staging a "big show" to give the appearance of democracy, when he was actually running a dictatorship.[57]

This antifascist rhetoric illuminated political agendas within the labor-left coalition, although racial justice was not among them. For the CIO and the WDL, the Jersey City battle was part of a bigger program to secure worker rights to protest, picket, and organize into industrial unions. For the ACLU and other liberals, the fight against Hague advanced a broader crusade for free-speech rights. For Norman Thomas, the Jersey City battle figured into a greater campaign to advance socialism at a time when the Socialist Party was declining. By standing up to the Hague administration, Thomas elevated socialists as moral leaders who countered the scourge of autocracy that afflicted not only Jersey City, but also Tampa, Kansas City, New Orleans, and other municipalities. Opposition to Hague's alleged fascism thus allowed the CIO and its labor-left allies to legitimate their own programs and claim a rightful spot in the American political nation, a political posture that resonated mightily in the late New Deal years when the Roosevelt administration and Congress both drew on working-class support, spewed antibusiness rhetoric, and produced a stream of pro-labor statutes.[58]

By framing their battle against Hague in fascist terms, the CIO, ACLU, Thomas, and other elements of the labor left projected the lasting image of what the Jersey City struggle involved. The antifascist image identified the lawless strongman as the central threat to democratic processes and labor rights. When Thomas remarked that "there is no democracy without civil liberty," he meant that democracy could not exist where authoritarian regimes suppressed rights essential to popular government, such as freedom to speak, freedom of the press, freedom from false arrest, and freedom to circulate pamphlets and assemble on public streets. This powerful left version of Americanism built on earlier antiboss stereotypes, indelibly coloring popular views of the Jersey City–CIO affair down to today.

Yet, behind the popular images, mundane political and legal realities were more decisive. More than "fascism," the battle of Jersey City revolved around questions of local municipal authority, the appeal of boss politics, and the jurisdiction of federal courts to impose national civil liberties at the local level. As late as the mid-1930s, municipalities retained enormous power within the national political system, as exhibited by the central role that local organizations like Hague's in Jersey City and Edward Kelly's in Chicago played in FDR's and the Democratic Party's national governing coalition. Those organizations provided vital electoral support and congressional Democratic majorities for New Deal programs.[59] Hague's seat on the Democratic National Committee and congressional Democrats' acquiescence to Hague protégé John Milton as U.S. senator acknowledged that reality. So too did FDR's toleration of Hague's shenanigans and decision to stay publicly out of the Jersey City fracas (until midsummer 1938). In their fight for civil liberties, hence, the CIO, ACLU, and their allies were up against not only the Hague regime and Jersey City but also municipalities' entrenched role in national politics.

The CIO and its partners also ran up against the continued functionality of boss politics in Jersey City. Like middle- and upper-class reformers who opposed urban machines in the late nineteenth and early twentieth centuries, Hague's critics then and now emphasize the corruption, voter fraud, and suppression of opponents that typified his organization, while ignoring the actual roots of Hague's power in ward politics. Critics may be correct that the Hague administration bullied citizens and masterminded political events, but they overlook the Hague regime's strong continuing appeal based on traditional urban-machine practices. Hague continued to garner support with lavish patronage and a heavy police presence against racketeers, gangsters, and other "troublemakers" who threatened the local moral order. Just as in New York, Chicago, or Pittsburgh organizations during the Depression years, moreover, his regime made classic use of patronage to put residents to work in New Deal projects, fulfilling the boss's promise to provide employment. And finally, in the usual boss way, the Hague organization formed ethno-cultural ties with city residents, especially with struggling Irish residents who aspired to upward mobility and respect as U.S. citizens.[60] Like other city machines, Hague's administration excelled at local politics, creating a bulwark of local support that opponents inside and out found hard to surmount.

The CIO and allies especially faced traditional legal edifices that protected city regimes like Jersey City's, although those edifices were about to crumble.

As late as the spring of 1938, the 1897 *Davis v. Massachusetts* decision recognizing municipalities' nearly absolute control over streets and parks remained good law, while "limits of municipal power" analysis and common-law unlawful-assembly doctrines restrained local courts' intervention into cities' regulation of public gatherings. In that legal environment, Jersey City police officers still freely used their discretion to regulate street behavior, powers enlarged by the municipality's still valid 1930 speaking permit ordinance and New Jersey's Disorderly Persons Act. Whether arrests of CIO pamphleteers or deportation of opposition speakers constituted an abuse of those laws, or whether those laws themselves were defective, were important questions of fact and law yet to be decided in court. Until federal courts addressed these matters in the summer of 1938, Jersey City and its antagonists fought it out in the press and on the streets.

Still, the Jersey City struggle encouraged the development of a new popular conception of civil liberties, just at the moment when the CIO suit for injunctive relief finally went to trial in June 1938. Hague's opponents prepared public opinion to view that trial before Judge William Clark as a hearing to affirm civil liberties against a would-be local tyrant. With the danger of fascism made vivid by caricatures of Hague as a dictator, ACLU activists, CIO labor organizers, socialist speakers, and the press all conveyed the theory that outdoor street speaking, public rallies, and circulation of leaflets were fundamental elements of American democracy threatened by Hague. In their language of working-class Americanism, CIO activists specifically attached that threat to the rights of workers. However, the rising new popular civil libertarianism advanced the novel constitutional view that federal courts were empowered to enforce those rights on state and local levels, sweeping away old post-Reconstruction conceptions of federalism that had insulated municipalities from federal intrusion. How fully Judge Clark would accept these propositions remained in doubt. Civil liberties law was in flux during the summer of 1938.[61] *CIO v. Hague* would be an exercise in making civil liberties law, rather than just applying it to Jersey City.

# 4 Into Federal District Court

## *Municipal Power and Civil Liberties in a New Forum*

As most people remember it today, the June 1938 injunction proceeding against Jersey City and Mayor Frank Hague in U.S. district court in Newark—then known as *CIO v. Hague*—was a final reckoning. After brazenly denying fundamental civil rights and liberties to CIO activists and their supporters, this story goes, Hague and his regime finally found themselves in a legal forum that they could not control: a federal court. Subsequently, according to this account, that tribunal vividly exposed Jersey City's blatant civil-liberties violations and predictably gave the municipality a stern rebuke. Hague's outspoken five-day testimony on the witness stand did as much as anything to convict his administration for its brashly unconstitutional misdeeds.[1]

Yet, this view of *CIO v. Hague* lacks historical insight. It takes modern conceptions of civil liberties developed largely by the winners in the wake of the trial and reads them back into the story of the trial itself, neglecting the losers' legal perspective as well as the unsettled character of law at the time. Actually, the full trial record shows that the Jersey City losers gave as good as they got. They offered significant legal defenses for their actions in opposition to CIO and ACLU claims. Meanwhile, federal courts had yet to rule definitively on the speech and assembly rights implicated in the case, much less decide what that meant for traditional municipal powers. The hearing consequently did not just hold Mayor Hague and his administration culpable under existing law, but more importantly it determined what the law really was. It adjudged the clash between Jersey City's old-fashioned municipal law and the CIO-ACLU team's modern civil libertarianism.[2]

Beyond that, the proceeding brought two very different worlds into conflict. On one side, the plaintiffs included an array of industrial unionists—the

CIO; steel, rubber, and electrical worker unions; CIO regional director William Carney; and many field representatives—along with the ACLU. They represented the rising industrial union movement protected by new federal laws such as the Wagner Act (NLRA) and the growing civil-liberties crusade rooted in federal civil-rights laws, the Fourteenth Amendment and the Bill of Rights. Also, they displayed a culture of working-class unity and manly breadwinner prerogatives, as well as a commitment to civil liberties. On the other side, the defendants were municipal officers of Jersey City—Mayor Frank Hague, public safety director Daniel Casey, and Police Chief Harry Walsh, plus the city's board of commissioners collectively. They reflected old-fashioned city machine governance and traditional police practices that had been historically shielded from federal judicial oversight, and they sustained a localistic culture steeped in traditional ethnic, religious, and family allegiances.[3] The collision of these worlds at trial was a fiery affair, indeed. CIO-ACLU cocounsel Spaulding Frazer and Morris Ernst sparred fiercely with defendant lawyers James Hamill and John Matthews. Frazer's and Matthews's courtroom references to each other as "Spauld" and "Sir John" were not terms of endearment but signs of grim familiarity between rival lawyers. Verbal sparks flew freely, especially when Ernst interrogated Mayor Hague on the witness stand, showing deep personal dislikes and mutual disrespect for the separate moral and legal universes that each represented.

This shift into court marked a critical change in the CIO–Jersey City struggle. The CIO-ACLU plaintiffs adopted the ACLU's emerging legal tactics, rather than rely on the muscle of outdoor direct action, the bread and butter of CIO industrial unionism up to this point. The change came about, largely because the battle of the CIO and its allies on Jersey City streets stalled, and because ACLU efforts to secure the intervention of Attorney General Homer Cummings and U.S. Senator Robert La Follette Jr.'s civil liberties committee failed, not to mention the ACLU's own transition from agitation to litigation. By embracing the legal strategy, the CIO and ACLU moved their fight off of the streets, where municipal authorities and police had the upper hand, and into federal courts, where judicial procedures and federal law gave trade unionists and civil libertarians the advantage. That Republican judge William Clark from Essex County, a rival to Hague's Democratic Hudson County, presided over the trial tilted proceedings in favor of the CIO and ACLU even more.

Yet, a CIO-ACLU legal victory was not a sure thing. The ACLU had already tried judicial action to defend worker freedoms in *ACLU v. Casey*, but that 1937 bootmakers' case was delayed on appeal and would become moot in the end. In addition, federal law was only beginning to show promise for worker rights and civil liberties, leaving worker rights unclear, especially in the municipal context. The labor law revolution and civil liberties revolution as we know them today were just beginning, and how they would unfold could hardly have been certain for participants in the *CIO v. Hague* case during the summer of 1938. True, the 1935 NLRA had created new rights for workers, and the U.S. Supreme Court had not only upheld that statute in April 1937 but also decided in *DeJonge v. Oregon* (January 1937) and *Herndon v. Lowry* (June 1937) that working-class agitators enjoyed protection from state encroachment on free-assembly and speech rights under the Fourteenth Amendment. Nonetheless, previous Supreme Court decisions in *U.S. v. Cruikshank* (1876) and *Davis v. Massachusetts* (1897) that respectively restricted federal speech and assembly protections on the state level and upheld municipal authority over those rights in city parks still remained intact. Even as the civil liberties revolution was starting, remnants of the long federal judicial tradition of staying out of civil-liberties questions on state and municipal levels lingered on.[4]

At trial, consequently, Jersey City attorneys and witnesses defended the municipality against CIO-ACLU charges as if the old laws were still in place. Yet, their legal position crumbled as the hearing unfolded, leading to some desperate courtroom ploys. At first, when CIO-ACLU attorneys called witnesses to substantiate Jersey City's harsh treatment of CIO organizers and their supporters, Jersey lawyers offered the traditional defense that the city was merely carrying out its municipal function to stop law violations, particularly CIO disregard of the anti-leafletting ordinance. But then, when Judge Clark ruled that the ordinance did not apply to the CIO's passing of political handbills, Jersey lawyers fell back on the argument that CIO operatives and supporters were subversive communists whose speaking requests the city had to deny to preserve peace and order. CIO-ACLU plaintiff attorneys certainly assailed this defense on behalf of CIO assembly and speech rights, especially when they interrogated public safety director Daniel Casey. Even so, when Hague took the witness stand, the mayor forcefully expanded on that defense, drawing on the literature from interwar anticommunism to warn against an ACLU-led communist conspiracy, something that Jersey City attorneys tried to support with an astounding subpoena for CIO and ACLU records. Ultimately, Judge Clark summarily rejected Jersey City's contentions and, very importantly, the law they were based on. Embracing the CIO-ACLU legal position almost completely, he not only granted the CIO-ACLU injunction, but also began reconfiguring municipal law and civil liberties in a modern way.

* * *

In a January 15, 1938, press release, the ACLU characterized the joint CIO-ACLU complaint against Jersey City as an "omnibus injunction suit," and "omnibus" it surely was. Submitted by Spaulding Frazer in U.S. district court on January 7, 1938, the complaint maintained that Jersey City flagrantly violated CIO and ACLU members' speech, assembly and organizing rights in many ways. According to the complaint, Jersey officials intimidated private hall owners from renting to CIO members under a 1920 city ordinance that was unconstitutional; it refused to allow pickets on the capricious ground that they were not part of legitimate labor disputes; it obstructed peaceful CIO distribution of flyers based on the city's 1924 anti-leafletting ordinance that was itself unconstitutional; it illegally expelled many CIO organizers on the New York City ferry; it encircled CIO headquarters on November 29 with police who subjected members entering or leaving to unlawful searches and seizures; it assigned police officers to intimidate and harass workers who expressed sympathy for the CIO; and it arbitrarily denied CIO as well as ACLU requests for public meeting permits under New Jersey's unlawful assembly statutes and the city's 1930 public meeting ordinance, the latter of which was also constitutionally suspect. All in all, the complaint charged, Jersey City's actions constituted an "unlawful conspiracy" to deny CIO and ACLU plaintiffs their rights to meet and discuss the work of the CIO and the rights of workers under the newly enacted NLRA. Concluding that the plaintiffs all suffered a loss of federally protected rights and privileges, and financial harm above the statutory requisite of $3,000 needed to justify federal jurisdiction, the complaint asked that the court enjoin the Jersey City defendants from interfering with the plaintiffs' access to streets and highways, their efforts to hold meetings in private or public spaces, and their attempts to distribute leaflets and other printed matter. The complaint also requested that the court enjoin the city from enforcing its three ordinances in any ways that interfered with the rights that the proposed injunction aimed to protect.[5]

Central to the CIO complaint was its argument that the injunction suit lay under federal law and the jurisdiction of federal courts. For its part, the ACLU had long argued that federal judges could apply the Bill of Rights on state and municipal levels. The federal courts, however, had just begun to adopt this view during the 1930s. Just before the Jersey City case, the U.S. Supreme Court's *Palko v. Connecticut* (December 1937) decision and its famous footnote 4 in *U.S. v. Carolene Products* (April 1938) introduced the ideas that the U.S. constitutional scheme created a hierarchy of fundamental rights, and that the Fourteenth Amendment's due process clause drew on some of the guarantees listed in the Bill of Rights for protection against state encroachment. Speech and press rights were at the top of the hierarchy.[6] The Jersey City case thus tested whether federal courts would assert jurisdiction over these new liberties at the municipal level.

In his complaint for the CIO against Jersey City, attorney Frazer put forward four reasons to justify a federal claim and the federal district court's authority in the case. The complaint asserted that the plaintiffs were protected: by article 4, section 2.1, of the U.S. Constitution entitling citizens to the privileges and immunities of the several states; by section 1 of the Fourteenth Amendment guaranteeing due process and equal protection as they pertained to speech, press, and assembly rights; by the NLRA provision that promised workers "full freedom of association [and] self-organization . . . for the purpose of negotiating the terms and conditions of employment"; and by Reconstruction-era civil-rights laws (Ku Klux Klan Acts) that criminalized conspiracies to injure persons exercising their civil rights.[7] The complaint registered an innovatively nationalistic view of civil liberties protection.

In their answer on February 19, 1938, however, the Jersey City defendants not only disputed factual allegations of civil liberties violations against CIO members and supporters, but also presented a more traditional view of the constitutional scheme that denied federal jurisdiction. The defendants denied any knowledge of abuses charged—in essence, asserting that they had not happened—and argued instead that the CIO plaintiffs themselves had conducted an unlawful invasion that violated Jersey City's anti-leafletting ordinance with the unlawful purpose to create "disorder, confusion and riot." The plaintiffs' contention that Jersey City ordinances were unconstitutional, the answer continued, were "mere conclusions of law" and "improperly pleaded." According to the answer, moreover, Jersey City officials themselves acted in a "perfectly lawful" way under local ordinances to have police maintain order and later deny speaking permits to plaintiffs who seemed determined to cause disorder. The only real question in the case, the answer concluded, was the constitutionality of Jersey City's several ordinances, but that was not for the U.S. district court meeting in equity to decide. The defendants denied the district court's jurisdiction in the matter, since the plaintiffs had not met the statutory minimum of $3,000 in damages and no "real or substantial Federal question" was involved.[8]

Whatever the merits of this controversy, hence, the CIO-ACLU injunction suit legally entailed far more than just calling the Hague administration to account under accepted civil-liberties law, as the media portrayed it. Instead, as a judicial proposition, the suit invoked a contest over a basic question of fact: whether the CIO fracas involved ruthless city suppression of workers and allies who were innocently trying to exercise speech, press, and assembly rights, or did it entail a lawful attempt by city authorities to keep order against invading radical law violators? Beyond that, the case raised two important legal questions. One was whether Jersey City's meeting-hall, anti-leafletting, and speaking-permit ordinances unconstitutionally infringed on civil liberties, and in any case, whether city officials abused their authority under them. The other was whether federal courts enjoyed oversight over these questions. In historical hindsight, after the "civil-liberties revolution," answers to these questions seem like foregone conclusions. But in the fluid moment of June 1938, they were all up for grabs.

* * *

On March 28, 1938, as both sides prepared for the injunction hearing, the U.S. Supreme Court dropped its *Lovell v. City of Griffin* bombshell. One of several Jehovah's Witnesses cases, *Lovell* unanimously struck down a Georgia municipality's ordinance requiring distributors of circulars, magazines, or pamphlets first to secure the city manager's permission before giving out their material. For the Court, Chief Justice Charles Evans Hughes determined that Griffin's ordinance amounted to licensing and prior restraint in violation of the First Amendment freedom of the press guarantee as incorporated into the Fourteenth Amendment's due process clause. The ruling had big implications for the pending CIO–Jersey City case. It certainly called Jersey City's anti-leafletting law into question along with similar measures in other New Jersey communities, as evidenced by reaction to the suppression of Grace and Morris Milgram's efforts to circulate flyers on Journal Square on March 29, 1938. When the ACLU's Roger Baldwin and the CIO's William Carney informed the city that it could no longer ban such activities under *Lovell*, corporation counsel James Hamill responded with his advisory opinion that admitted to *Lovell*'s relevance, but still warned against leafletting as a pretext for mass demonstrations and other disorder. The street battle over leafletting continued. More important was Hughes's legal reasoning. Building on the string of U.S. Supreme Court cases extending from *Gitlow v. New York* (1925) through *Stromberg v. California* (1931) and *DeJonge* (1937), Hughes's incorporation of First Amendment rights into the Fourteenth Amendment set the precedent for federal courts to apply those guarantees locally.[9]

Meanwhile, an atmosphere of "terror" filled Jersey City streets. On April 14, Rabbi Benjamin Plotkin told the NJCLU that "the people in Jersey are so terrified by what happened in [Jersey City] and the ever-present threat of what is to come, that they have lost all their spirit, and make no attempt to fight for what they know to be their rights." The April 30 rally from which

Norman Thomas was "deported" likely intensified those feelings. So too did the May meeting proposed by the ILD at which U.S. Representatives Jerry O'Connell and John T. Bernard were to speak, only to have it broken up by war veterans who vowed to stop "red groups on the street."[10]

As tensions festered on May 26, lawyers for Jersey City and the CIO-ACLU team appeared in the U.S. district courtroom of Judge William Clark in Newark to argue the CIO-ACLU injunction application. Appointed to the federal bench by President Calvin Coolidge in 1925, the Newark-born Clark was a well-connected Republican typical of the Protestant Yankee elite in New Jersey's Essex County that included figures like Hague foes Lester Clee and Arthur Vanderbilt. Known for independent thinking and a proclivity for controversies, he likely had little sympathy for CIO direct-action strategies, but neither an affinity for Democratic Irish Catholic boss leadership in Hudson County.[11] He had already shown sympathy for the ACLU and skepticism toward Jersey City in the earlier *ACLU v. Casey* case.

While three hundred observers packed the courtroom and two hundred others waited outside, Jersey City's James Hamill stood before Clark and stunningly opened the trial by offering a settlement. Running down the list of complaints, Hamill denied most of the CIO's and ACLU's allegations, contended that the leafletting issue was no longer relevant due to the *Lovell* decision, and stated that the only real dispute concerned Jersey City's refusal of CIO and ACLU speaking permits—an issue that he proposed to lay over for further argument. Otherwise, he said, Jersey City was ready to agree on an injunction restraining the city from interfering with street access, leaflet distribution, and meetings in private halls, assuming that the city admitted no wrongdoing. Appearing for the plaintiffs, Spaulding Frazer initially objected on the grounds that Jersey City was trying to wiggle out of a confrontation with CIO charges and to avoid an embarrassing hearing that would expose all of the city's brazen civil-liberties violations. Nonetheless, he retreated with Hamill to hammer out a consent injunction. For a day, it seemed that Jersey City and the CIO-ACLU had achieved a "truce."[12] There, the whole spectacle could have ended in compromise. Jersey City would have to allow CIO street activities, leafletting, and private gatherings, but *Lovell* already required much of that. Both the CIO and ACLU would have to forego publicizing Jersey City abuses and an immediate ruling on speaking permits, but the CIO would gain access to organize.

However, Mayor Hague balked. "I will not under any circumstances enter into any compromise with these red groups," he declared.[13] His legal team had given him an escape hatch, but he inexplicably refused to climb through it. Why would the city's corporation counsel pursue a consent injunction if the mayor were going to reject it? Seemingly, with local anticommunist sentiment roiling, Hague chose to stand on, or perhaps decided that he could not back down on, his reputation for defending the city from outside radical agitators. He would fight in court to exclude the "Reds" altogether. Missing signs like *Lovell* that the legal tide was flowing against him, he made a serious political miscalculation.

* * *

The injunction proceeding commenced in U.S. district court on June 1, 1938. Hague arrived in a "smartly tailored dark suit," having been subpoenaed by plaintiffs to testify, but Judge Clark released him until a later day. Hamill then started with a typical motion to dismiss the case. He said that it did not belong in a federal equity proceeding, that plaintiffs had not met the $3,000 threshold of damages, and that *Lovell* rendered moot the circular distribution issue. This signaled Jersey City's basic argument that federal courts lacked jurisdiction, but Clark denied it and invited Frazer to call the plaintiffs' first witness.[14]

Frazer opened by summoning a parade of witnesses who attested to police officers' repeated disruption of CIO efforts to meet, circulate literature, and speak on Jersey City streets from the CIO's initial organizing activities in the fall of 1937 through the ILD rally in early May 1938. His interrogation strategy aimed to evince a pattern of police abuses that demonstrated an ongoing Jersey City policy to suppress the speech, press, and assembly rights of the plaintiffs, a problem needing judicial restraint. He started with witnesses who related the familiar story of police interference with the November 29 leafletting operation. CIO organizer Dan Foley, for instance, described police encirclement of the Montgomery Street union headquarters, police confiscation of circulars at Harborside, the officers' dispatch of marchers on the New York City ferry and in automobile rides to city limits, and the trial of leafletters in Judge Anthony Botti's court, where the judge denounced William Carney and CIO members as "hoodlums" from the bench. In his cross-examination, Hamill countered by trying to elicit Foley's admission to a radical background and malevolent intentions, particularly that he attended a meeting in Newark that planned to violate Jersey City's anti-leafletting ordinance intentionally. Hamill tried to establish deliberate violation of Jersey City ordinances as a CIO motive.[15]

Before Foley left the stand, Judge Clark and the attorneys sought to clarify just what the Jersey ordinance required as compared to the City of Griffin ordinance struck down in the *Lovell* case. Clark determined that Jersey City's regulation, unlike Griffin's ordinance, did not require a permit, but banned all literature distribution outright. Jersey's was an anti-littering law, Clark concluded, not one that covered the conveyance of circulars hand to hand, as Foley was trying to do. Such an interpretation undermined Jersey City's contention that the CIO leafletting campaign violated local law. Hamill fiercely objected. The Jersey ordinance flatly banned all "distribution and litter," he argued, rendering CIO actions lawless.[16] Ruling against that view, Clark gutted a central legal premise of Jersey City's case.

And so it went with other plaintiff witnesses. They all testified in devastating detail about police disruption of leafletting efforts and disregard of basic criminal due process procedures: police stops and searches of cars without warrants, police confiscation of circulars, officers' use of a flying wedge to bust up the Harborside leafletting operation, and police herding of leafleters onto the New York City ferry. WDL observer David Clendennin indicated that police stopped him and searched his suitcase when he arrived at the Montgomery Street union office, and just laughed when he complained that the process violated constitutional search-and-seizure rights. UMW representative James Sweeney said that police struck him in the stomach, and NJCLU executive secretary Nancy Cox reported that she saw the same thing happen to Robert Parker. And witnesses who made it to the police court arraignment of thirteen leaflet distributors related aberrations there, especially Judge Botti's refusal to swear in an official stenographer, although he did allow a Mr. Winard to take notes. Even Judge Clark found Botti's action extraordinary. "Surely no court in the world is entitled to refuse a stenographic record." Frazer asked Clark to admit Winard's transcript into the record, and over Hamill's objections, the judge allowed it.[17]

As he had with Dan Foley, Jersey City counselor James Hamill and his colleague Joseph Glavin tried to discredit these witnesses by extracting testimony that exposed unlawful motives. They asked observers from the WDL about the origins and purposes of their organization, probing for evidence that they operated illegally in Jersey City. Across the board, these witnesses disavowed any communist connections, expressed concern for workers subjected to "mistreatment, terrorism and other forms of official brutality," and stated they traveled to Jersey City on November 29 only to observe and take notes. Unitarian minister Aaron Gilmartin did admit that he decided to participate in the literature distribution himself to raise a legal test, even asking one officer to arrest him. Under close questioning by Glavin, however, he denied having gone purposefully to Jersey City just to violate the law.[18]

Compared to testimony evoked by the plaintiffs' attorney Spaulding Frazer that documented massive police suppression of the CIO distribution effort, the defense cross-examinations of early witnesses hardly revealed a broad

CIO campaign to break the law, just a small, peaceful leafletting activity that technically violated a minor local ordinance whose scope and constitutionality were questionable. The CIO-ACLU case was prevailing at this point, and Jersey counselors began grasping for straws—in this case, the straw of anticommunism. When Judge Clark began asking each witness about his or her religious and political beliefs, Hamill objected that the judge was allowing plaintiff witnesses to throw up a smokescreen to obscure their radical affiliations. If the judge permitted plaintiffs to affirm belief in some party or philosophy, Hamill argued, "then every Red in the country, by this simple trick . . . could divest himself of any culpability for belonging to the Communist Party." Hamill and Clark reached an agreement that Hamill himself would ask witnesses about their backgrounds. The exchange illuminated what was rising as Jersey City's central defense in the case, now that its original charge of violating the anti-leafletting ordinance had lost force—that CIO organizers and their supporters were unruly communists.[19]

From peripheral positions, several women testified for the plaintiffs, but evidently no African Americans did so. NJCLU executive secretary Nancy Cox attested to seeing instances of police violence, while she and her assistant Frances McKee reported difficulties in renting meeting halls and securing assembly permits. Moreover, Grace Milgram from the WDL described police disruption of leafletting efforts, and her WDL colleague Bella Kussy recounted her detention and expulsion by police on the Hudson River ferry. Their testimony showed opportunities again for activist women to rise up as supporters in left-wing groups, but not directly in the CIO, which generally excluded women from leadership posts and treated them as subjects to be helped in the CIO's larger unionization campaign. CIO counselor Frazer called no female CIO organizers to testify, hence, but only four young Italian female slipper and garment sweatshop workers. They all reported paltry pay averaging eight dollars a week for forty to fifty hours of labor until they were hired at unionized plants, which lifted their wages to twelve or fourteen dollars. Seemingly, Frazer sought testimony to show need in Jersey City for the CIO to unionize female new immigrant workers, a group neglected by the city's Irish machine. Meantime, Frazer neglected to call African Americans to the witness stand. Although several thousand black laborers resided in the city's working-class wards, they were a marginalized group that the CIO lawyers ignored in this controversy.[20]

Frazer then turned to the April 30 Thomas rally and the May 7 O'Connell and Barnard rally. Again, witnesses painted an ugly picture. They described going to the Thomas meeting, being punched and struck by police billy clubs as officers whisked Thomas away, and then being harassed for handing

Figure 6. Nancy Cox of Newark, New Jersey, executive secretary of the New Jersey Civil Liberties Union, 1937. Warren Grover Collection, courtesy of the Jewish Historical Society of New Jersey.

out flyers before being expelled on the New York City ferry. In his cross-examinations, Hamill probed witnesses for illegal reasons for attending the Thomas rally, but he only got them to say that they went to hear Thomas's view of the Jersey situation. As for the O'Connell and Barnard assembly, the NJCLU's Cox reported that she saw hundreds of police officers swarming there under the direction of public safety director Daniel Casey, and that one of them came over and socked her husband Robert Parker between the eyes. The three *Catholic Worker* representatives then attested that police officers confiscated their circulars "in no mild manner," despite the *Lovell* ruling, and took two of the men away without arrest. The remaining man tried to pass out literature later, but when policemen came up to remove his leaflets and crowd members apparently from the Jersey City veterans' committee approached, he decided to leave. Hamill's cross-examination insinuated communist connections to the *Catholic Worker*, but not convincingly.[21]

Plaintiffs' attorney Frazer finally called CIO field organizer Samuel Macri to the witness stand, summing up the CIO's whole ordeal in Jersey City. A textile worker and organizer by background, Macri testified that CIO leaders in Washington, D.C., had sent him to assist William Carney in "organizing the unorganized" throughout New Jersey. In Jersey City, he indicated, he and other CIO operatives diligently tried to bring workers into unions, but police thwarted them. Police detectives interfered with his efforts to organize cosmetics and metal fabrication plants, and arrested him during the November 29 CIO leafletting drive. Although he consistently tried to steer workers toward the formation of stable unions and collective bargaining relationships rather than spontaneous strikes (the official CIO policy), he added, city police stymied his efforts. On one occasion, Macri tried to persuade a police captain that city interference violated workers' "constitutional rights" "to peaceful assembly, free speech and freedom of the press" but was told by the officer that he did not follow the Constitution, but a local court ruling holding that organizers could not talk to workers without a bona fide strike, a sign of Jersey City's behind-the-times legalism. To the end, Macri avowed, Jersey police obstructed his work. They upset his efforts to organize laborers at a gypsum plant in March 1938. It was likely they who slugged him from behind at the May 27, 1938, Pershing Field rally, which put him in the hospital.[22]

At this point in the trial, tough-talking Essex County Democrat John Matthews joined defense counsel to bring out the plaintiffs' alleged radical ties in pointed cross-examinations. He questioned Macri closely about his checkered early career, probed for communist connections, and then interrogated Macri about his involvement in several Jersey City strikes. When Macri balked, with Judge Clark's agreement, at naming employees he met at the unsuccessful American Home Products strike, Matthews objected that Macri was trying to obscure the fact that he and his colleagues were radical rabble rousers, not true trade unionists. And Matthews insisted, "no Communistic group is going to persecute labor while I have a tongue in my head." Echoing Mayor Hague, he warned the judge not to be fooled by communist trouble makers who hid behind claims to labor rights and civil liberties. "Why is it, your Honor, today, that in this case the CIO people, who sat down all over the country and destroyed the working man in the eyes of the public, are now glorified under the false issue of free speech?" He was laying out Jersey City's main line of defense—that CIO organizers were communist insurgents who used civil liberties as a smoke screen to obscure violent intentions. Yet, in witness Samuel Macri's case, he was unable to obtain corroborating testimony. When Matthews tried to get Macri to admit that he fomented a sit-down strike at the Standard Cap and Seal Company, for instance, Marci explained that the sit-down started spontaneously, that police intervention worsened it, and that Macri helped to resolve it.[23] The hearing was turning into a rout for the CIO-ACLU plaintiffs.

* * *

Things worsened for Jersey City when the plaintiffs called Director of Public Safety Daniel Casey to testify, in effect, putting the Jersey City police department's whole policy toward civil liberties on trial. With their own sharp-tongued lawyer Morris Ernst now doing the questioning, the plaintiffs asked Casey about an array of Jersey City police policies, hoping to evoke testimony that exposed a pattern of Jersey City police abuses that would justify a court injunction. On picketing, for instance, Ernst got Casey to articulate Jersey City's traditional narrow view. "If there is a strike they [workers] got a perfect right to picket," Casey asserted, but "If there is no strike, I figure that there is no need of pickets." He stated emphatically that he would not allow pickets to persuade people to unionize a plant, showing complete unawareness of the new Wagner NLRA's effect on picketing in "recognition" strikes. Indeed, Casey admitted under Ernst's interrogation that he was not familiar with that law, but he added (correctly) that a new city ordinance banned "carrying placards on peaceful picket lines."[24] On picketing, Casey's testimony exhibited a parochial persistence of old-fashioned police policy, not a petulant resistance to labor organizing. Jersey City had not kept up with new labor legislation. Casey's outdated views coincided with those of officers who told the Milgrams and Macri that Jersey City police were obligated to enforce municipal law, not federal constitutional law.

Casey's testimony on the controversial Jersey City police practice of "deporting" suspects beyond city limits also evidenced an old-fashioned, parochial outlook. Perhaps thinking of New Jersey's Disorderly Persons Act, he described Jersey City's practice of identifying and removing "suspicious characters" and "undesirables" from the municipality in order to prevent crime, disorder, and violence. Casey explained that Jersey City posted four police squad cars in specific spots to identify "suspicious" vehicles and persons, and gave officers full discretion to stop and search such vehicles and people at will. He added that patrolmen had standing orders to warn, arrest, or "shove around" people when they caused disturbances, including "escort[ing] anyone from the seat of danger" for his own good. Casey insisted that removing "undesirable" persons protected the city. "If we decide we can get along better with [the undesirable person] out of the community and he is going to cause trouble for us[,] we keep him out, if he don't belong there."[25] This explanation emphasized the Jersey City police force's long-standing law-and-order policy of excluding troublesome crooks and racketeers, but it obscured police policy toward labor organizers. When was an "undesirable" person a CIO man or an ACLU member whom police decided Jersey City could "get along better without," because he "did not belong there"? Casey evaded the politics of deportation in the CIO case.

He also evaded politics when he discussed police treatment of the November 29 CIO circular distributors. Under questioning by Ernst, Casey maintained that the November event marked a classic example of peacekeeping. When he saw newspaper reports about an impending "invasion" by "two thousand strong" CIO organizers, Casey explained, he told Police Chief Harry Walsh that he did not want any disturbances and directed him to detail policemen to deal with the situation. It was a matter of law and order. "I guess two or three hundred strong marched down Montgomery Street; it was illegal," Casey testified. "Before there was a riot these people were taken to a certain part of the city and released. It was [for] their protection, to stop riot and bloodshed."[26] Of course, earlier testimony that workers marched peacefully and police started the trouble flatly contradicted Casey's description. With the case finally in federal court, rather than in the muddier court of local politics, he could no longer hide such ugly facts.

The gap between ugly facts and Jersey City rhetoric grew wider when Ernst grilled Casey about his refusal to grant permits to CIO and ACLU speakers and supporters. The question implicated Jersey City's April 1930 ordinance requiring permits from the public safety director, and Ernst questioned Casey as to how he administered this law. First, he wanted to know how frequently public safety directors had denied such requests before 1937. Once produced, public safety department documents showed that Jersey City had rarely turned down speaking permits before then, marking Casey's decisions against the CIO, ACLU, and their supporters thereafter as an abrupt change in policy. How did Casey go about determining that he should refuse a permit due to the laws' disavowal of riots and disturbances, Ernst further inquired. The safety director explained that he investigated each group that filed an application, considered who was listed as speakers without reviewing speeches, and assessed the likely community impact by reading local newspapers. His main concern was "the good of the city" and the protection of life and property.

Then, in a heated exchange, Ernst turned to how Casey applied this procedure to the specific permits that he had refused from December 1937 through May 1938. In regard to the ACLU rally permit requested by attorney Samuel Rothbard on December 17, Ernst questioned Casey's return request for information about the purpose of the meeting. The ACLU attorney saw this as tantamount to asking an applicant in advance, "what are you going to say?," so that Jersey leaders could deny a request if they disagreed with the speaker's message. "If that isn't pre-censorship of free speech," Ernst exclaimed, "what is?" To do his duty, Casey replied, he had to know something about the purposes of the proposed ACLU rally, since he had received citizen complaints about outsiders coming into the city to utter undesired rhetoric. He worried about a violent reaction. When Ernst then asked Casey whether it was right for a hostile mob to stop a speech, Casey responded, "well, when [a speech] will draw a crowd that is hostile—mob psychology is a terrible thing, . . . it would take a regiment of soldiers to stop them from committing riot and violence and this is what we are trying to stop." In this case and others involving speakers like O'Connell and Thomas, hence, Casey insisted that danger of violence, not the content of speech, was his main concern. "It wasn't what they would preach," Casey asserted, "but how the mob that went there would take it." And when Ernst asked him why Jersey City's notoriously large police force could not control crowd reaction to public oratory, Casey responded that he still had to deny the permit requests because he feared that angry crowds might swell beyond police management.[27]

The examination of Casey turned nastiest when Ernst inquired about the Hague administration's possible role in stirring up the veterans' protest against public meeting permits requested by the ACLU and the CIO in mid-December 1937. Ernst wanted to scrutinize the origins of the veterans' protest and their rally on December 28, but Casey obstructed that inquiry. To test his theory that Jersey City manufactured the protest, Ernst showed Casey the public notice from the mayor's office calling on all veterans to meet at the armory on the evening of December 28 and postcards from local Democratic clubs urging veteran attendance as well. Casey denied having anything to do with these items, or having even seen them ahead of time. Then questioning revealed that Jersey City had not fully complied with a subpoena duces tecum to produce records shedding light on the extent of grassroots veterans' protest. With Ernst's motion to hold him in contempt hanging over his head, Casey made a quick telephone call to his office during a recess and had the rest of the needed material delivered. And it was damning. The material included only three protest letters from December 1937, just a single one from a veterans group, hardly a sign of a mass veteran outrage. Evidence that the Hague administration instigated the veterans' rally was powerful.[28] It undermined Casey's danger-of-mob-reaction justification for denying meeting permits and showed that the danger of CIO-induced violence was exaggerated or even fabricated. Jersey City's defense continued to crumble.

* * *

As the hearing moved toward its culminating event—Mayor Frank Hague's appearance on the witness stand—skirmishing between the two sides continued outside and inside of the courtroom. On the streets, Jersey City police continued to disrupt efforts of CIO organizers to hand out pamphlets and to hold meetings, prompting Frazer to file an amended complaint on June 10 to reinforce the CIO-ACLU's original injunction request, an amendment that Judge Clark accepted over Matthews's objections. Inside the courtroom, the plaintiffs called witnesses who attested to telephone calls and a secret meeting at a Newark city commissioner's office evincing a conspiracy between Jersey City officials and Newark authorities to disrupt Norman Thomas's rally at Military Park in Newark on June 4, 1938, at the same time as the trial. Lucky for Jersey City, Judge Clark disallowed the testimony, but it exposed Jersey City's unseemly and even desperate campaign to stop the CIO and supporters.[29]

Then, in a stunning courtroom maneuver, Jersey City's defense team served an omnibus subpoena duces tecum on CIO regional director William Carney, ACLU leader Roger Baldwin, ACLU attorneys Morris Ernst and Arthur Garfield Hays, and ACLU president Dr. Harry F. Ward. The subpoena requested that the named parties produce a sweeping array of documents, including all of the "files, records, membership lists and the like" that the CIO and subordinate unions had accumulated after their arrival in New Jersey, plus all records that implicated left-wing ACLU associations, such as those with the Garland Fund, the ILD, the IWW, the magazine *New Masses*, the communist newspaper *Daily Worker*, and the ACLU itself. Seemingly based on connections outlined in Elizabeth Dilling's *The Red Network*, the subpoena aimed to build an evidentiary record showing that the plaintiffs were not really parts of the labor movement but elements of a communist conspiracy. Proof of a conspiracy, Jersey City lawyers argued, would undermine the plaintiffs' eligibility for constitutional protection and equitable relief on grounds that they violated New Jersey's 1902 criminal anarchy law. It would also show that there were good public safety reasons to suppress the plaintiffs.

Taken aback, plaintiff attorneys moved to quash the action. Frazer remarked that he had never seen such an "impertinent" subpoena. It required that the CIO bring practically its whole office over to the courthouse, something that was inconvenient to the court, not to mention unfair to the plaintiffs. Ernst objected that the documents requested were "fabulous in size" and an inherent violation of civil liberties. Moreover, he rejected a central theory underlying the defense subpoena—that local listeners' potentially violent reaction to outside radical speakers should guide the treatment of civil liberties. Such a theory, he complained, would give any city official an arbitrary right "to clamp down on free speech and the bill of rights" at any time. As Judge Clark saw it, subsequently, the subpoena raised an important issue of law. He speculated as to whether, under the law, "authorities need not permit [speakers'] views to be expressed on the public streets or public parks," "if the persons who live in the city object to the views." The U.S. Supreme Court would not address this "hostile audience" problem until the *Hague* case itself and post–World War II rulings, especially in the civil rights era.

The defense subpoena foundered on a practical matter, however. Was the subpoena directed to the right persons, and could those persons actually produce the documents requested? Sorting through the subpoena's various requests one by one, Judge Clark found mostly not. In an effort to paint Ernst as a communist mastermind, for instance, the subpoena treated that ACLU lawyer as a conduit between the ACLU and communist or radical groups. Clark determined, however, that he had no access to most of the papers requested. Ernst had once been an IWW member, but that group was defunct. He also had no links to the *Daily Worker*, which, if anything, was persistently "riding" Ernst for his *anti*communist stance. In the end, Clark disapproved most of the defense subpoena. He decided that the request to Roger Baldwin to produce Communist Party records should be tossed out, and that subpoenas for the ILD, *Daily Worker*, CIO affiliates, and other groups should all be addressed to other parties. He exposed the defense subpoena as a fishing expedition, and plaintiff attorneys surely agreed. Seeking all records requested, Ernst remarked, would be like subpoenaing all of Mayor Hague's correspondence, including that with the "bookies." This last quip brought a chorus of objections from the defense table.[30]

* * *

On Thursday, June 9, 1938, the trial reached its culmination when the plaintiffs called Mayor Hague to the witness stand. As he entered the court, Hague tried to lower expectations by telling news reporters to forget the story—"put away the pencils, boys," he told them—but plaintiffs saw his appearance as an opportunity to let Hague convict himself on his own arrogance and bombast. Indeed, historians recollect that Hague did just that. As they see it, he pontificated at length, often against the advice of his lawyers, offering one embarrassing admission after another. In fact, plaintiff counsel relentlessly badgered him. In a legal fishing expedition of their own that resembled Clarence Darrow's interrogation of William Jennings Bryan in the 1925 Scopes trial, plaintiff attorneys Spaulding Frazer and Morris Ernst grilled the mayor about questions far beyond the grievances listed in the CIO bill of complaint. Seemingly, they aimed as much to put Hague on trial for his reputation as the "Jersey dictator" as to document civil liberties violations. Their strategy caused a tumult, provoked a torrent of objections from defense counsel and drew sharp and often effective ripostes from Hague himself. "Go the limit," he told Ernst at one point. "Don't spare me, . . . because I am not going to spare you. . . . Take off the gloves."[31]

Frazer set the tone for the plaintiffs' examination of Hague when he asked the mayor to define communism, or more specifically "Hague communism." The insinuation that Hague had an eccentric view of the matter, however, brought a mixture of applause and hisses from the courtroom crowd and objections from defense attorney John Matthews. He accused Frazer of the "ungentlemanly act" of casting aspersions on the mayor. "There is no such thing as Hague Communism," Matthews observed. "There is Hague decency and Hague order." On the witness stand, the mayor then responded by defining a "communist" as "a man who is subject to Russia, a radical who is opposed to American principles and American institutions, whose sole purpose is to overthrow our government." Many of the CIO's leaders and supporters fell into this category, he added, including "Mr. Ernest" sitting at the plaintiffs' table. In subsequent testimony he explained that the Jersey City had a quarrel not with the CIO per se, nor with its rank-and-file members, nor even with leaders like John L. Lewis, but with "Reds" who had captured control of the CIO's Jersey City labor campaign. "Now the CIO has apparently disappeared," he argued, "but this whole affair is continuing and has continued for the last three or four months, under the leadership of the counselor sitting at the table there, your associate counsel [Morris Ernst]."[32]

Of course, Hague was correct that Ernst and the ACLU had taken over the court case for the CIO, but his charges of communist influence were fantastic, drawn more from the script of interwar anticommunism than from the facts at hand. There is virtually no evidence of communist influence in the Jersey City–CIO affair. Under Matthews's cross-examination, however, the mayor claimed that he had discovered a Red network imperiling Jersey City. His regime's concern about communism began in early 1937, he asserted, when Jersey officials learned from West Coast authorities that alleged communist longshoreman Harry Bridges was behind an ongoing East Coast maritime strike. From that point on, Hague testified, Jersey City gathered information on the communist menace and then prepared for any disorder that might develop from it. According to Hague, the 1931 Fish Committee Report prepared by right-wing New York Republican Representative Hamilton Fish (a favorite text among interwar anticommunists) tipped Jersey City off regarding the Garland Fund created by wealthy left-wing Bostonian Charles Garland. It was a central sponsor of communism, said Hague, especially through the ACLU. Plaintiff attorneys questioned this testimony's relevance, but Matthews defended it as demonstrating what information shaped Mayor Hague's state of mind. A key point, Matthews stressed, was the Garland Fund's role as a communist bulwark. It financed many left-wing publications and causes, including communist "boring in" organizations like the ACLU. Indeed, ACLU counselor Morris Ernst was the Garland Fund treasurer. When he resumed his testimony, hence, Hague stated that all of this information helped him "to form the opinion" that Ernst and the ACLU were communist in affiliation, that the CIO "invasion" was a communist event, and that Ernst was an "undesirable" speaker.[33]

To the critics, Hague's characterization of CIO leaders and ACLU supporters as communistic was calculated bombast, a cynical pretext to cover up his actual motives to crush the CIO on behalf of local business and political interests. Yet, from the standpoint of Jersey City's insular political culture based on its combination of local commercial interests, AFL trade unions, ethnic Catholic social life, and Hague administration strict policing policies, the mayor's portrait of an orderly city embattled by subversive outside forces made sense. Law and order had long been part of Jersey City's governing practices, as had the expulsion of suspicious outsiders (and political opponents). Economic and political self-interest figured into Hague's testimony, but so too did his defense of local unions, churches, and ethnic culture. Whether a federal court would accept this defense was questionable.

Protection of Jersey City against disruption by outside communist intruders framed just about every response Hague gave to questions about police actions. When Frazer asked him why he had called the November 29 circular distribution campaign an "invasion," Hague replied that he was referring to CIO regional director William Carney's threat to send in "3,000 [men] strong" to disrupt the city regardless of the law. For many years, Hague asserted, Jersey City had enjoyed friendly relations with AFL local unions—"never had any disputes"—and indeed (overlooking testimony of Samuel Macri and others), the CIO itself was initially welcome in the city as a law-abiding group, maintaining three headquarters there. Because of CIO sit-down strikes in Detroit and other Midwestern cities, however, Hague decided that the CIO had become dangerous, and "that for them to invade a city meant serious trouble." The intervention of "Mr. Ernest" into the CIO controversy aggravated the situation. As he saw it, leftist leaders had turned the CIO into a disruptive labor group and Jersey City had to protect residents from the chaos that it would bring.[34]

When Frazer pressed Hague on the details of how Jersey City police had treated the leafletters on November 29, the mayor maintained that the officers had acted appropriately. Admitting that only two hundred CIO representatives showed up to distribute circulars, Hague argued that the police still had to act forcefully in light of Carney's earlier threat of a large invasion "for the purpose of defying law and order." Even so, Jersey police showed restraint, the mayor asserted. They did not want to arrest anyone for violating a small ordinance like the anti-leafletting measure, so they deported offenders as a "neighborly" way to keep public order. Police would "mildly enlighten" leafletters of local law by pushing them out of the city for their infractions, and detain just the "ringleaders" for prosecution. When asked about police violence on November 29, however, Hague implausibly claimed, "I never heard of it."[35]

Throughout his testimony, Hague insisted that CIO unions were "welcome in Jersey City as long as they are law abiding," and offered an example suggesting more truth to this contention than historians nowadays allow. Not totally excluded, the CIO managed some organizing activities throughout the city, despite its squabble with Hague. Hague thus described how a CIO-sponsored strike at Jersey City's Crucible Steel plant in January 1938 was settled in an orderly way. According to Hague, eight hundred "high-class, hard-working men" went on strike and threw up mass pickets, although the city adjusted the number of marchers with the men's agreement. Soon thereafter, the strike was settled to the benefit of the strikers, much as an earlier strike had been resolved back in 1932 when the firm had an AFL union. The *CIO News* celebrated this successful job action as a CIO victory right in the middle of Hague territory, but to Hague, the quick resolution demonstrated Jersey City's facility at labor relations, even with CIO unions. Indeed, a local union officer publicly complimented the city's handling of the strike until CIO leaders "went after" him and forced a retraction.[36] With its own propaganda machine, the CIO tried to obscure anything positive in Jersey City's labor record and cultivate a thoroughly antilabor image of the town.

This CIO rhetorical strategy underlay Frazer's ongoing examination of Hague. Reviewing labor controversies in Jersey City over the previous ten years, Frazer tried to build a record showing that the Hague regime consistently denied labor rights. On the 1936–37 seamen's strike, Frazer tried to get the mayor to admit that he falsely used the specter of communism as an excuse to intervene in that affair, but Hague insisted that alleged radical Harry Bridges caused the trouble. On the 1934 Miller Parlor Furniture Company strike, Frazer tried to get the mayor to agree that he had interfered with civil liberties to defend a runaway shop, but Hague described it as a matter of policing the annoyance of outside New York City labor agitators (furniture makers union) and "publicity seekers" (ACLU members), not admitting that the city backed down under negative publicity. Hague then agreed that he broke up a truck drivers' strike in 1932 and a teamsters and chauffeurs strike in 1934, but he contended he did so because "gangsters" were running the unions. On the 1931 McClintic-Marshall strike that had culminated in the ouster of labor leader Theodore Brandle, Hague described Jersey City's intervention not as instance of union busting but as a matter of restoring law and order where there had been mayhem and murder.[37]

Regarding the widely asserted charge that Hague systematically lured "runaway shops" to Jersey City with the promise of suppressing labor problems, the mayor concurred that his administration did invite businesses to Jersey City on grounds that there would be labor tranquility, but he added that his regime advised firms not to bring labor troubles with them. When Frazer pointedly reminded him that notorious runaway firms exploiting low-wage labor like the Uneeda Slipper Company did indeed move to Jersey City, Hague contended that was not what his administration wanted. Uneeda, Hague said, "has given us a lot of trouble." "We try to discourage all those sweatshops, we don't allow it." He agreed with Frazer that labor organizing was one possible way to address the sweatshop issue but argued that organizing should not be done by outsiders. "Why," he protested, "don't they do it with local groups, why do they come from Brooklyn and New York, and why don't they let the American Federation of Labor and Jersey City do it?"[38] Hague stated that it was not labor organizing per se that bothered Jersey City leaders—he accepted local AFL unions—but organizing by disruptive outsiders like the CIO.

Overall, Hague's testimony blunted Frazer's effort to show that Jersey City's history of labor affairs was just one long string of abuses, thereby challenging Hague's image even today as monolithically antilabor. Hague argued persuasively in some cases that his administration treated labor issues with sympathy, made reasonable efforts to work with local, especially AFL unions, and tried to root criminal elements out of local labor leadership. Characteristically, he drew the line at labor outsiders like the CIO that brought in direct action strategies. He was quite unpersuasive, however, in explaining away November 29 police abuses or in justifying anti-CIO actions in the hysterical terms of warding off subversive communist influence. These failures doomed Jersey City's defense case.

Spaulding Frazer's and his colleague Morris Ernst's subsequent interrogation of Hague on the suppression of speech and assembly rights during months from December 1937 right up to the trial in June 1938 proved to be especially devastating. Frazer began by asking the mayor about his apparent complicity in the veterans' rally of December 28, 1937, which safety director Casey had used to justify denial of CIO and ACLU speaking permits. The mayor denied collusion. According to Hague, alert newspapermen informed veterans about the CIO and ACLU applications, and the former servicemen then spontaneously turned out in protest. In a long exploration of how

Jersey City's political machine operated, however, Frazer drew testimony from Hague showing how his administration's patronage system and close association with local Democratic ward clubs, veterans organizations, and business groups gave it tremendous leverage over public sentiment, even without giving direct orders. In a famous example, Frazer got Hague to admit that neither his administration nor the police department had to order meeting hall owners to deny the CIO rental space, because hall owners already knew what kind of "distasteful" groups that Hague wanted excluded. And when the plaintiffs' attorney queried the mayor about the postcard urging veterans' attendance at the December 28 anti-CIO-ACLU rally, he denied that it emanated from his office.[39] According to Hague, veterans' hostility toward the CIO and ACLU festered naturally. True enough. Still, other testimony had shown that his regime mobilized that sentiment into action.

In further questioning, Frazer asked Mayor Hague to discuss why Jersey City so repeatedly denied speech rights to the CIO and its supporters after November 29, evoking some of his most inflammatory statements. The mayor denied that Jersey City stood against free speech or public meetings per se, and he patiently explained once again that he had not aspired to dictatorship when he exclaimed "I am the law" in a juvenile delinquency case. Indeed, Hague reiterated that Jersey City rarely denied any speech or rally permits before November 29. It had to do so afterward, because new conditions threatened an "uprising," "disorder," and "disturbance." The CIO and ACLU may have proposed meetings just to discuss modification of Jersey City's (then valid) anti-leafletting ordinance, but their proposed list of speakers included subversives like Roger Baldwin and Morris Ernst, whose mere presence would cause an uproar in Jersey City. The same problem lay in subsequent requests by Representative Jerry O'Connell, Representative John Bernard, and socialist Norman Thomas. "Now, I have no desire to stop anybody from talking," Hague stated, "but in the face of this trouble I cannot surrender . . . and permit this invasion of these men." In reasoning that resonated with old conceptions of municipal power, he argued that Jersey City had a duty to deny speaking permits when that was necessary to preserve public safety. It was an ironic position that rhetorically affirmed speech rights on the one hand, but then effectually denied them in the name of public order on the other.[40]

Besides, radicals did not deserve free-speech rights, Hague contended. These people were communists and not "sincere Americans," he testified, because they endeavored "to deceive and overthrow the government." They widely talked about civil liberties and demanded free speech rights, but only as a "camouflage" to foment unrest. Whenever he heard an agitator discuss civil liberties and free-speech rights, consequently, Hague knew that such a person was secretly a communist insurrectionary: "you will find him with a Russian flag under his coat; you never miss." Hague did not, as often said nowadays, scoff at all speech rights: his point was that such rights should not extend to radicals whose public gatherings threatened "violence and bloodshed." Yet, what he gave to speech rights in principle, he took back when he denied them to so-called radicals. He even went so far as to say that communists should be driven from the country, perhaps placed in a "camp in Alaska" and "kept away from the American people." His reasoning resembled the Red scare ideology of the coming post–World War II McCarthy era, when even the courts treated communists as such an inherent national security threat that their rights were automatically denied. Such anticommunism was already emerging in Hague's own time. One fan letter cheered his proposal as a stroke of "genius."[41]

The plaintiffs' interrogation of Hague became testier as Ernst took over the questioning. Again, ranging far beyond the issues raised in the CIO complaint, the ACLU attorney probed Hague's political beliefs and knowledge to the point of ridicule. The ACLU lawyer first asked the mayor to define various "isms"—Nazism, fascism, socialism, and so forth—but the mayor declined to do so except to say that he regarded anarchists, socialists, and communists as pretty much alike. When the ACLU attorney next questioned Hague as to how he ascertained that Ernst himself was leader of the "movement," and the mayor responded that he studied people and learned from persons on the street, Ernst asked him to name one person and which street corners. Hague then rambled on to state that the ACLU's radical leadership made it an "undesirable" presence in Jersey City, but Ernst challenged that assertion by reading off names of distinguished ACLU national board members. Ernst continued by inquiring whether Hague, as a member of the Democratic National Committee, would advise Democratic political candidates to repudiate their support for the CIO, due to its alleged "Red" leadership, but withdrew the question after a drumfire of defense objections challenged its relevancy. As Darrow did with Bryan in the Scopes trial, Ernst tried to discredit Hague by showing him ignorant and contradictory.

The ACLU attorney applied a similar forensic approach to Jersey City's policy toward peaceful picketing. Reflecting the old 1920s view of the matter, Hague told Ernst that his administration did not allow mass picketing or walking the picket line with placards, but it permitted strikers to post three or four pickets at each entryway of a job site, while police stayed in contact with strike leaders to insure that pickets were orderly and caused no complaints. He explained that a state court of appeals decision had ruled that there was no legal right to picket where there was no legitimate labor dispute. Ernst, however, questioned Hague as to whether this policy was not now outdated under the Wagner NLRA. Had Hague's administration ever secured a legal opinion as to what new worker rights were protected under that law, he asked. Might picketing to organize a union now be covered? The mayor responded that Jersey City had not studied the NLRA. Again, this line of questioning by Ernst revealed Hague as out of touch.

The plaintiffs' lawyer continued to challenge the mayor's credibility by taunting him about other embarrassing issues. Wasn't the FBI's refusal to accept Jersey City's crime statistics a sign of the Hague administration's "dishonest and inaccurate" reporting on crime and police protection? Was Hague pleased that Nazi German newspapers praised his leadership? Wasn't the forcible "deportation" of persons out of Jersey City illegal under all circumstances? Hadn't Jersey City wrongly expelled socialist Norman Thomas to prevent his speaking there? Didn't Hague believe in free speech? On this last point, the mayor answered that yes, he did believe in free speech, even against the Constitution in favor of peaceful change of government, just so there was no general uprising. In a final zinger, however, he added that Jersey City would not allow Ernst to speak at Journal Square because mass protest would create uncontrollable commotion. Even Judge Clark raised doubts about the relevance of all of this.[42]

In his cross-examination, defense attorney John Matthews tried to salvage Hague's testimony from the plaintiffs' barrage by highlighting the mayor's fears about CIO disruption and the legal basis for the mayor's authority to thwart it. The defense counsel walked Hague through his determination that the CIO and ACLU were communist-inspired organizations, that midwestern sit-down strikes revealed the CIO's disruptive character, and that the CIO's so-called "invasion" of November 29 raised the reasonable expectation of violence in the Jersey community. In the midst of this interrogation, Hague sparked yet another courtroom uproar. After Judge Clark excluded his testimony insinuating Ernst's interference in a New York legislative investigation, the mayor took the story to news reporters in the hallway during a recess. When the hearing resumed, an outraged Ernst filed a motion to hold Hague in criminal contempt for trying illegally to influence courtroom proceedings. Only after apologizing did Hague continue his testimony. When he did resume, the mayor argued that Jersey City had a strong legal right to deny speaking rights to the whole line of CIO, ACLU, and socialist orators under the law of illegal assembly. Showing great familiarity with New Jersey court decisions by Judges Kalisch and Black, the mayor argued that Jersey City had good reason to expect that the utterances of various CIO supporters would cause the kind of breaches of peace that illegal assembly law prohibited.[43]

Contrary to the modern historical view, *New York Times* reporter Russell Porter decided at the time that Hague's courtroom performance had been a masterpiece, not the ordeal of a political boss on the run. Like many politicians, Porter wrote, the mayor looked, dressed, and behaved like a "consummate actor," captivating the courtroom in dramatic confrontations with the plaintiffs' attorneys, parrying criticisms with "humorous quips and sallies," and cheering the audience with heartwarming Americanisms. Like the playwright and lyricist George M. Cohan, Hague "'exited laughing,' leaving everyone in good humor." Most important, Mayor Hague defied sophisticated observers' expectations that the unlettered boss would make a fool out of himself by trying to evade charges against him. Instead, he took responsibility and admitted practically all of the accusations against him on the grounds that he was legally justified in doing what he did. According to Porter, Hague came across as thoroughly sincere in his belief that he was a champion of "100 percent Americanism" against a "real communist menace" that masqueraded behind the CIO, the ACLU, and other organizations. As the mayor of a city that had elected him every four years for a quarter of a century, Porter explained, Hague assumed that he had a moral duty to defend his constituents from "Reds" who aimed to overthrow government and organized religion by force and violence. He also assumed that the "Reds" had forfeited the protection of constitutional guarantees of free speech because they embraced the violent communist philosophy. Porter observed, however, that Hague's adversaries in the trial took the opposite position that all Americans, even communists, enjoyed the rights and protections of free speech and assembly. Behind all of the showmanship, he concluded, the trial boiled down to the serious legal issue of whether Hague's or his opponents' view of free speech would prevail.[44]

Porter was certainly correct that the trial represented serious legal business, not just a public exposé on the wrongdoings of a notorious city boss. On questions of law, the case revolved around whether Jersey City's suppression of leafletting, public meetings, and picketing by the CIO and its sympathizers constituted a violation of federally protected rights or whether it was a legitimate exercise of local police powers. Behind this legal quandary lay the question of whether federal or municipal authority prevailed. From the late-nineteenth-century *Davis* decision onward, courts and local officials had presumed that state and local governments held sway over the regulation of municipal order. That is why Jersey City police officers regularly informed agitators that it was their duty to enforce local court rulings and city ordinances rather than federal constitutional law. That is also why Jersey City public safety director Casey and Mayor Hague paid little attention to the newly enacted NLRA. Intervention by federal court decisions and national labor law on municipal policing was a new development in the late 1930s. How much this new federal authority could penetrate municipal affairs had to be decided.

On questions of fact, moreover, the trial inquired both into the motives and behavior of CIO organizers and their supporters and into the integrity of Jersey City's response to them. After the *Lovell* decision and Judge Clark removed alleged CIO violation of the anti-leafletting ordinance from the case, the hearing focused on the factual assessment of CIO motives. The plaintiffs' witnesses aimed to show that CIO organizers were innocent unionists simply trying to exercise their lawful rights, whereas the defendants' testimony attempted to prove that CIO operatives had communist leadership and a clear track record of violent disruption elsewhere in the country. Infamously, the defense tried to show in the vein of interwar anticommunism that the CIO and ACLU campaigns in Jersey City were part of a larger communist menace. That contention implicated the other main factual question as to whether Jersey City's prohibition of the CIO's allegedly subversive activities properly served the needs of public order. Outside of court, the CIO said absolutely not. The *CIO News* blasted Jersey City's charges as a "mythical red scare" that was "created by an entirely unscrupulous campaign of lies" and served as a pretext under which "labor unionists are manhandled, arrested and driven out of town" and their democratic rights were thoroughly suppressed.[45] That was rhetoric. Now, the matter appeared in a court of law and had to be decided by a federal judge. In light of legal and factual disagreements, the case of *CIO v. Hague* entailed far more than just a public judgment on Jersey City Mayor Hague's leadership.

* * *

Because of a three-month delay to complete research, Judge Clark did not render a decision in the case until October 27, 1938, much to the disappointment of plaintiff attorneys who wanted a quick ruling. During the interim, President Roosevelt offered his first public statement obliquely criticizing Jersey City's actions. Without naming names, he warned that "there can be no constitutional democracy" where there were "attempts to suppress individual liberty under the pretense of patriotism." FDR would not include Hague in his 1938 purge of untrustworthy Democrats, but his support for the mayor was slipping. Meanwhile, socialist Norman Thomas aggressively pursued legal relief for his April 30 deportation in both state and federal courts with help from Mayor Hague's arch Essex County foe, Republican lawyer and American Bar Association president Arthur T. Vanderbilt. On the state level,

Vanderbilt sought a mandamus ordering public safety director William Casey to issue Thomas a speaking permit, but New Jersey's conservative Supreme Court upheld Jersey City's public assembly ordinance and Casey's discretion under it to deny him a permit. On the federal level, a grand jury refused to indict the Hague regime for deporting Thomas in violation of the Lindbergh anti-kidnapping law, while the Department of Justice vacillated on investigating charges innovatively placed by Vanderbilt under Reconstruction-era Ku Klux Klan laws. Perhaps, to avoid antagonizing Hague as still a Roosevelt political ally, the justice department dropped the inquiry, but then under the fire of criticism restored it. Like the simultaneous justice department look into Harlan County, Kentucky, violations, Thomas's case signaled rising federal involvement in local civil-liberties abuses.[46] Hague's political fortunes seemed in decline.

In this evolving context, Judge Clark issued his sixty-page decision in *CIO v. Hague*. It first ruminated philosophically on the role of free speech and assembly in a democratic society and then ruled narrowly on the legal merits of the case. The broad perspective reflected not only Clark's personal flair for political science, but also widespread popular anxiety about the viability of liberal democracy in an age of economic depression and European dictatorship. Could democracy meet the exigencies of the time without succumbing to the allure of authoritarian government to suspend democratic rules in the name of social order?[47] Perhaps with an eye on that larger question, Clark contended that the Jersey case raised a question vital to the survival of all democracies: how could governments balance speech freedoms against the undesirable consequences of that liberty? In pursuit of an answer, he surveyed the history of speech in the Anglo-American tradition and the record of contemporary democratic and authoritarian countries before he turned to the legal questions. His ruling fit the foreboding political mood of the time as much as it considered law and facts in the Jersey case.

As he opened his decision on the case at hand, Clark recognized the Red scare atmosphere that surrounded the Jersey City controversy. In a medical analogy that never mentioned "communism," he characterized Jersey City's argument like this: its citizens were "allergic" to the CIO plaintiffs' political message and wanted to exclude the CIO from the city as a matter of "preventative medicine" to forestall the allergic reaction (a revolt by Jersey City residents) that its presence would cause. This did not entirely capture the city's reasoning. Jersey City argued that the CIO and its supporters were dangerous not only because their communist philosophy would spark a disruptive local response, but also because they aimed to stir up violence and disruption in the first place. In any case, Judge Clark admitted that he shared the "allergy" against those whose methods were "abhorrent to all true believers in democracy"—he too was an anticommunist—but he stopped short of evaluating evidence behind Jersey City's claim that the plaintiffs fell into that category. His opinion did not weigh testimony on prior CIO sit-down strikes, threats of "invasion," taunts of lawbreaking or communist influence in CIO ranks, but simply asserted that Jersey City offered "no proof" of radical influence or disruptive intent and affirmed CIO organizers' desire to move about the city and spread their ideas.[48] Crucially, then, Clark dismissed Jersey City's factual assertions as to why it had to suppress CIO activities to keep public order.

As Clark saw it, the case revolved around two legal questions: did the CIO-ACLU plaintiffs have legally enforceable speech rights, and did the actions of the Jersey City defendants impair those rights? To answer the first question, he turned to a long survey of western history, political philosophy, and law. From the work of political commentators like Francis Lieber and James Bryce, he ascertained that "all modern legal systems" recognized freedoms of locomotion, speech, and assembly, and from recent U.S. Supreme Court decisions, he determined that American courts had extended protection of those rights to the state level by incorporating the First Amendment into the "liberty" clause in the Fourteenth Amendment. The real question, then, according to Clark, was the extent of those rights. Quoting a long list of authorities from Aristotle to Walter Lippmann, he determined that speech was best allowed to roam free to accommodate human expression and facilitate the search for truth. From modern free-speech advocates like Theodore Schroeder and Zechariah Chafee, he added that Americans inherited uniquely strong libertarian tendencies from their revolutionary struggle for independence. Clark noted, however, that after Americans won independence, U.S. courts adopted Sir William Blackstone's common law definition of speech and press rights—that is, no prior governmental restraint on those liberties, although government might still punish speech or publications exhibiting licentious tendencies. The key problem for modern courts, according to Clark, was to distinguish between cases of truly dangerous speech and those in which innocent speech was wrongly repressed. Citing the familiar World War I cases of *Schenck v. U.S.*, *Frohwerk v. U.S.*, *Debs v. U.S.*, and *Abrams v. U.S.*, Judge Clark indicated that the U.S. Supreme Court had devised the "clear and present danger" standard to make that distinction.[49]

All of this reasoning applied to freedom of assembly as much as to freedom of speech, but with an important twist, according to Clark. Assemblies carried free-speech rights to their "ultimate and logical conclusion," he argued, but they also presented speech in "its most complicated and delicate phase."

Again quoting a long line of commentators through the ages, the judge inferred that public assemblies were a special form of speech—"free speech in particular circumstances"—and one that evoked the problem of properly balancing liberty against public safety. Tyrants regularly erred on the side of safety, since assemblies could mobilize the populace against them. That's why English King Charles II considered shutting down coffeehouses. That's why Italian dictator Benito Mussolini warned that the liberty to march in processions "must not be converted into license." Americans, according to Clark, had more openly accepted free speech and assembly. They were more inclined to let assembled speakers talk, imposing restraints characteristic of coercive regimes only in moments of alarm like the French war scare of the 1790s and the aftermath of President McKinley's assassination in the early 1900s.[50]

Drawing as much from history and political commentary as from law, then, Judge Clark turned to the case at bar and deduced that U.S. political and legal culture strongly recognized speech and assembly rights that CIO members and their supporters should have enjoyed in Jersey City. The judge ruled first that Jersey City's practice of deportation was illegal. While it might apply to enemy aliens, convicts, and persons likely to become a public charge, such banishment deprived CIO organizers of the ordinary right of locomotion at the discretionary fiat of police officers without benefit of a court trial. Equally, Jersey City's prohibition of literature distribution violated the constitutional right to communicate ideas to willing listeners. As confirmed by the *Lovell* decision, Clark maintained, anti-leafleting ordinances could not justify that practice, especially when mayors used regulations aimed at stopping litter or the clogging of sewers as a pretext for silencing unwanted messages. Moreover, the disruption of CIO efforts to rent private meeting halls might also have been a free-speech violation, but testimony in the case had not proven the city to be responsible.[51]

Alluding then to public rallies that CIO members, ACLU spokesmen, and speakers like Jerry O'Connell and Norman Thomas had requested, Clark determined that such orators had fundamental rights to meet in public space, though with limitations. Drawing an unprecedented distinction between streets and parks, he said that cities retained absolute control over streets and public squares, and might regulate or even exclude assemblies there, but only if they treated all groups equally. Cities could not ban meetings in parks, however, since parks' purpose was recreation, including recreation of the mind. Accepting the old-fashioned idea that municipalities had a proprietary interest over parks, the judge argued that cities still had to grant "easements of assemblage" for citizens to meet in those places. Cities might require that such easements be subject to a permit system, but they had to impose such regulation through proper procedures—something not done in Jersey City. Before refusing permits, Clark continued, city officials had to have "real proof" that speakers' previous orations or conduct had caused disruption. For such cases, he suggested a remarkable pre-censorship procedure by which municipal leaders could request advance copies of proposed speeches and prohibit them "in light of the reasonable apprehensions of disorder." Such apprehensions did not include potential disruption by listeners. Clark agreed with English precedents holding that "the speaker's own [past] conduct" should be the criterion on which to judge the danger of disruption. Otherwise, speakers "should be given the full protection consistent with the strength of the local guardians of public safety." He thus resisted restraint on public meetings, and expected clear evidence of potential disorder before restricting them—again, not provided by Jersey City. He wanted to avoid other nations' constraints like Nazi Germany's suspension of open-air gatherings.[52]

Clark admitted, however, that U.S. case law at that time leaned heavily against restrictions on municipal control over public gatherings such as Jersey City had done, largely because lower courts were obstructed by the legal barrier erected by the U.S. Supreme Court's 1897 *Davis v. Massachusetts* decision. Suggesting that its days were numbered, the judge argued that this ruling upholding Boston's exclusive control over speech in public parks was fatally flawed. The original Massachusetts Supreme Judicial Court decision by (then) state associate justice Oliver Wendell Holmes Jr., he said, was based on "dictum" about cities' proprietary rights over public property, and the U.S. Supreme Court accepted that groundless reasoning without much thought or scrutiny, as had other courts afterward. Importantly, Clark stressed, *Davis* was decided in the bygone era before the U.S. Supreme Court incorporated First Amendment civil liberties into the Fourteenth Amendment, and it still presumed that "free speech was not protected by action against the states." He thus portrayed *Davis* as outdated and poorly reasoned "double dictum," an impediment to "a reasonable easement of assemblage in public places." He predicted that cases favoring free assembly would flow freely once this relic of the legal past was overruled.[53]

In the end, the Republican judge from Essex County ruled firmly against the Democratic Jersey City defendants from Hudson County and in favor of the CIO-ACLU plaintiffs. Indeed, as the *New York Times* saw it, Judge Clark's decision marked a "sweeping victory" for the CIO, although it spoke to civil liberties, not labor organizing rights. It enjoined Jersey City from interfering with the plaintiffs' rights to move freely about the municipality (thereby ending the policy of "deportation"), to distribute leaflets and circulars, to address people at public meetings, and to display placards. The ruling cut most decisively against the police practice of deportation, since the judge found that procedure to be unconstitutional. Of course, the ruling sustained the principle of the U.S. Supreme Court's *Lovell* decision that cities could not interfere with handbill distribution on freedom of speech and press grounds. Most importantly, the decision adopted new Fourteenth Amendment jurisdiction that authorized federal judicial intervention in civil liberties questions on the state and local level, rejecting *Davis*'s presumption of local autonomy.

Reflecting the legal uncertainties of the time, however, the legal basis of Judge Clark's ban on Jersey City's interference with public meetings was vague. The judge did not apply the Reconstruction-era civil rights law to the case, and he chose not to pass judgment on the Wagner NLRA's applicability to this problem, explaining that interpretation of that law for the very same plaintiffs by Clark himself in the (then named) *Casey v. ACLU* case was still under review by the Third Circuit of the U.S. Court of Appeals.[54] Nor did he rule on the constitutionality of Jersey City's public meeting ordinance, but instead faulted Jersey City's implementation of that measure. His decision stated that Jersey City needed more proof that orators would be disruptive before denying them speaking permission. Jersey City took advantage of this. While labor leaders lauded the ruling and began planning an organizing drive in Jersey City, Mayor Hague and corporation James Hamill declared that the judge had treated the public meeting ordinance as constitutional. Consequently, they still vowed never to cower before "reds and radicals." Once again, Jersey City denied ACLU director Roger Baldwin and the NJCLU a speaking permit.[55]

Nonetheless, Judge Clark's remarks on the *Davis* case signaled a legal watershed that would restructure the constitutional world at Jersey City's expense and in the CIO-ACLU plaintiffs' favor. As Clark observed, *Davis* ruling took place in the era before the federal courts had extended First Amendment rights to states under the Fourteenth Amendment. This judicial posture had left cities insulated from federal intrusion into local police matters, and allowed the growth of heavy-handed municipal police practices in which Jersey City specialized. Yet, as *Stromberg*, *DeJonge*, *Lovell*, and other U.S. Supreme Court decisions of the budding civil-liberties revolution demonstrated, that era was passing. New constitutional interpretation increased federal judicial scrutiny over cities' treatment of civil liberties. In the long run, the ACLU and CIO were bound to win, and Jersey City was bound to lose.

The legal momentum favoring the CIO-ACLU plaintiffs accelerated when Judge Clark formulated his factual conclusions and final judgment. Rules of procedure allowed Clark to draw on the assistance of opposing attorneys, if he so chose, and plaintiff counselor Spaulding Frazer exploited the opportunity to suggest language for the judge's final decree that followed the plaintiffs' legal view of the case. In particular, Frazer requested elision of the "pre-censorship" process suggested by Clark's original decision, causing the judge to deny that he used such a term and then to adopt the plaintiffs' more libertarian outlook. For his part, Jersey City lawyer James Hamill testily objected to these proceedings, complaining that the defendants had neither received a copy of the plaintiffs' proposal nor been given sufficient time to respond. As far as he was concerned, the plaintiffs were still not entitled to relief.[56]

Hamill had good reason to worry. On November 7, 1938, after giving Hamill only forty-eight hours to reply to plaintiff suggestions, Clark issued a decree that was much tougher than his October 27 decision. It embraced nearly the whole CIO-ACLU civil libertarian position, taking little of Jersey City's case seriously. In regard to jurisdiction, Clark found that plaintiffs had clearly met the $3,000 statutory threshold of harm and had filed federal questions under both the Fourteenth Amendment and Reconstruction-era civil rights laws. On the latter point, significantly, Clark stepped beyond his October opinion and specifically cited sections of the U.S. Code originating in 1870–71 Ku Klux Klan Acts that forbid conspiracies against the exercise of civil rights. By doing so, he continued in the vein of his October decision by rejecting exclusive municipal control over speech in public places under the 1897 *Davis* ruling, and he asserted federal authority over that liberty in state and local affairs instead.

Regarding the purposes of the CIO and ACLU, Judge Clark ascertained that both groups aimed lawfully just to unionize workers and exercise speech rights, and that Jersey City offered "no competent proof" that either had violent intentions to disrupt U.S. or New Jersey government by force. In effect, the judge thoroughly dismissed the city's core communist allegations against the plaintiffs, showing that anticommunist rhetoric from the political arena earned little sympathy in a 1938 federal courtroom. In fact, stripping away Jersey City's anticommunist excuses, Clark determined that the city had "adopted and enforced" "a deliberate policy" of excluding the plaintiffs from municipal territory and preventing them from distributing circulars, raising placards, or holding meetings in public places, all in violation of constitutionally protected civil liberties. Likely in response to the CIO-ACLU lawyers' urging, Clark also removed legal ambiguities left in his October decision by declaring Jersey City's 1924 anti-leafletting, 1930 meeting permit, and 1935 placard ordinances all to be unconstitutional.[57]

His final judgment subsequently enjoined Jersey City from directly or indirectly interfering with the plaintiffs' efforts to communicate their thoughts on "public streets, highways, thoroughfares, parks and places" (except in accordance proper arrest procedures); obstructing their attempts to distribute handbills or carry placards in those areas; restraining the plaintiffs' ability to hold open-air assemblies in public parks, provided that plaintiffs sought timely permits that could be refused only for reasonable conflicts with park recreation; or restricting plaintiff street meetings, unless all street gatherings were banned. Indeed, Clark took the unprecedented position that the city had to protect the plaintiff gatherings from disruption by listeners, assuming that such protection was within the city's public safety capacity.[58]

The ACLU declared the decree to be "a clear-cut victory," and so it was in a broad way. Judge Clark moved beyond the merits of the case to discard traditional views of municipal policing and to embrace the broad rising modern theory of federally enforced civil liberties. First, Clark adopted the overall CIO-ACLU characterization of the Hague administration as a dictatorial enemy of civil liberties. His finding of "a deliberate policy" to thwart the activities of the CIO and its supporters underscored his view of Jersey City as an autocratic regime. In addition, Judge Clark's final decree enlarged his initial decision's protection of speech rights throughout the city. His order prohibited Jersey City's interference with the plaintiffs' effort to communicate their thoughts not just in or about city parks, but on any "public streets, highways, thoroughfares, parks and places," in essence turning all municipal space into a public forum. And the prohibition applied not only to public speaking and to the distribution of literature, but also to the display of placards, something that was little discussed at trial, as defense lawyers complained. Finally, the judge departed from old common law principles of illegal assembly and municipal power, endorsing new civil libertarian views that privileged public speech and assembly rights. Out went the common law presumption embedded in Jersey City's 1930 speaking permit ordinance that cities could deny permission to public speeches and gatherings that threatened riot or disorder. In came the new civil libertarian position that cities could refuse permits only when they had not been properly applied for or when proposed speeches and meetings conflicted with public parks' recreational purposes. Amplifying this libertarian outlook, Clark's final decree removed the precensorship process suggested in his original October decision, and it excised language treating public speeches and meetings as "easements" rather than full-fledged rights. Judge Clark's final decree forcefully embraced the rising civil liberation vision of speech and assembly rights.[59]

Jersey City hardly gave up the legal fight, however. The city's assistant corporation counsel quickly appealed Judge Clark's final judgment and decree to the Third Circuit of the U.S. Court of Appeals in Philadelphia. As that appellate panel prepared to hear the case, attorneys on both sides agreed to maintain the status quo until the court acted. The plaintiffs apparently chose not to test the Hague administration's compliance with Clark's order, instead waiting for the legal process to play itself out.[60]

Still, the situation remained tense. In a post-decree memo, Judge Clark expressed the hope that lawyers on both sides would persuade their clients to adopt "a reasonable modification of their conflicting points of view" while the appellate court did its work. "There can be no doubt but that the passions aroused by this sort of controversy are disruptive of democracy," he wrote. Yet, there was much to be passionate about. Not only did the civil liberties of the CIO and its supporters remain in question, and not only did Jersey City's police practices remain in doubt, but so also did the respective legal regimes that both sides represented—the CIO-ACLU constitutional vision of nationally protected rights versus Jersey City's traditional view of local municipal control and social order keeping.[61] The Third Circuit Court and ultimately the U.S. Supreme Court would determine whose rights and which vision would prevail.

# 5 The U.S. Supreme Court Decisions

## *"Time Out of Mind"?*

Looking back, modern observers regard the appeal of the case then known as *Hague v. CIO* to higher federal courts as an easy win, a slam dunk for civil liberties. Both the Third Circuit Court of Appeals and the U.S. Supreme Court found Jersey City's restraint on CIO members' speech and assembly rights to be unconstitutional, and in the process, constitutionalized the right of outdoor speaking in municipal public space for the first time. As Justice Owen Roberts asserted for the Supreme Court, citizens' use of streets, parks, and public places to assemble, communicate, and discuss public questions was "time out of mind" an ancient right, and part of the privileges and immunities granted to citizens of the United States under the Fourteenth Amendment. Such rights could not be "abridged or denied" under the "guise of regulation," as Jersey City had done.[1] Seemingly, this ruling confirmed fundamental U.S. civil liberties and rejected Mayor Hague's boss governance as outside of U.S. democratic traditions.

Yet, this longstanding image obscures the *Hague* case's tortuous path within federal appellate courts to reach the Supreme Court's final decision, as well as the complicated character of that ruling. At the time, federal court personnel, modern civil-liberties law, and modern labor law were all in flux. Judges nominated by President Franklin Roosevelt were just beginning to replace jurists appointed by presidents from Herbert Hoover back to Theodore Roosevelt, triggering some scandalous maneuvering on the Third Circuit Court of Appeals. Even the U.S. Supreme Court was in transition, reduced to seven justices out of nine, with remnants of the Hughes court under Hoover appointee Charles Evans Hughes still in charge, and Franklin Roosevelt's nominees not yet all having taken their seats. Simultaneously, federal appellate courts and the U.S. Supreme Court were only beginning to move beyond post-Reconstruction-era jurisprudence and to embrace the civil liberties and labor law "revolutions" of the time. This multifaceted federal judicial metamorphosis dominated *Hague*'s proceedings and outcome.

In federal appellate courts, *Hague* involved not just a fight between civil liberties and urban bossism, but also a battle between a fading post–Civil War legal-political regime and the rising New Deal legal and political order. Sidestepping labor issues, appellant and respondent attorneys fought over whether post–Civil War judicial analysis of federalism and municipal powers epitomized by the *Davis v. Massachusetts* case (1897) would persist, or whether new jurisprudence expanding federal judicial power over civil liberties under civil rights laws, the Fourteenth Amendment and the Wagner Act (NLRA) would prevail. As it turned out, a deeply divided U.S. Supreme Court produced only a fractured resolution of these constitutional questions in the *Hague* case, with five plurality, concurring, and dissenting opinions. Meanwhile, the contemporary specters of fascism and communism complicated public understanding of federal court proceedings. The popular hue and cry against Mayor Hague's "un-American" dictatorship, and the simultaneous popular movement against the ACLU's and CIO's alleged communism, obscured the public's, and our own, view of the complicated constitutional transformation taking place.

* * *

District court judge William Clark's October 27 decision and November 7, 1938, decree enjoining Jersey City from abridging CIO and ACLU speech and assembly rights triggered nasty wrangling in the *Hague* case's appeal. When Clark issued his final order, Jersey City lawyers Edward O'Mara and Charles Hershenstein asked him to stay its execution, complaining that it broadened the October ruling and hampered local law enforcement. Meanwhile, law school dean Spaulding Frazer for the CIO and ACLU requested enforcement of the injunction to stop the city's incursion on his clients' civil rights. Clark refused to grant a stay, and O'Mara and Hershenstein carried the case to the federal Third Circuit in Philadelphia, to which Clark had just been appointed by President Roosevelt during the previous summer.[2]

Proceedings before the Third Circuit featured tawdry efforts to manipulate the judicial process. Frazer and the CIO-ACLU's cocounsel Morris Ernst dutifully showed up in that court on the morning of November 9 to answer Jersey City's appeal before a regular three-judge panel, only to find that Jersey City counsel did not attend. Instead, when attorneys from both sides all appeared later in the afternoon, they were startled to face a five-member bench consisting of judges Albert Maris, John Biggs, and J. Warren Davis, along with retired judges Joseph Buffington and Joseph Thompson. With Davis presiding, the five-member panel heard O'Mara's motion for supersedeas (stay of the lower court's injunction) and then asked both sides to submit briefs. Stunned CIO-ACLU attorneys thought they saw "the spectral hand of Hague" at work, although differences in the judges' legal philosophy or fear of the CIO may have also prompted the strange lineup. Perhaps recalling President Roosevelt's ill-fated court-packing scheme of the year before, the CIO-ACLU lawyers charged that senior judge Davis had "packed" the unusual five-member bench with Hague sympathizers, even though the U.S. Judicial Code required a three-member court and excluded retired judges. They sought relief from Supreme Court Justice Owen Roberts, who presided administratively over the Third Circuit, and then appealed directly to the U.S. Supreme Court for an immediate hearing. Alluding to the stalled *Casey v. ACLU* case—involving another Jersey City supersedeas petition against a Judge Clark ruling that had languished before the Third Circuit for twenty months—they conjectured that the rigged five-member panel was preparing to stymie *Hague v. CIO* with a similar procedural delay. The Supreme Court refused to take the *Hague* case at this moment, but Buffington and Thompson suddenly withdrew, perhaps due to Roberts's influence at a regularly scheduled Third Circuit judges' conference on November 25–26, or perhaps due to Buffington's inept, disqualifying public remark that the CIO deserved a "prompt reprimand." With Buffington and Thompson gone, Davis, Biggs, and Maris were left to hear arguments for Jersey City's appeal on December 23. Curiously, in the interim, the Third Circuit Court resolved *Casey v. ACLU* in a decision by Judge Davis that dismissed the case on grounds that the end of labor disputes involved had eliminated the legal claims.[3] CIO-ACLU allegations of Hague tampering in Third Circuit proceedings seemed to embarrass the court, which was now eager to hear the *Hague* case promptly and hustle it along to the U.S. Supreme Court for a final disposition.

Still, the Third Circuit hearing of *Hague v. CIO* was as much a political show as it was a legal proceeding. In the process of addressing the central legal question—whether Judge Clark's November 7 injunction order should be sustained—rival attorneys presented contrasting images of Mayor Hague as either a "popular executive" defending his city from "riot and bloodshed" or a dictatorial "heresy hunter." On Jersey City's side, Edward O'Mara contended that the right of municipal "home rule" for cities to police their streets and maintain order was at stake. Clark's injunction was so sweeping, he said, that it would take that power away from city leaders and turn the district court into the city's governing authority. More important, Clark's order misinterpreted the Jersey City situation, O'Mara said. "Free speech" was not the issue: Jersey City supported free speech and had granted hundreds of public-assembly permits, even to communists. Instead, the issue was the danger created by the CIO and its ACLU allies, who aimed to stir up violence. Mayor Hague and Jersey City were not denying free speech and assembly, O'Mara said, but only asserting their authority to ban troublemakers. Corporation cocounsel Charles Hershenstein added that the federal courts did not even have jurisdiction in the case, since the plaintiffs had not met the statutory threshold of $3,000 in alleged harm. Jersey counselors concluded that the Third Circuit should stay Clark's order and dismiss the proceeding.

In reply, CIO-ACLU counselor Morris Ernst maintained that Mayor Hague and Jersey City flagrantly violated his clients' free-assembly rights, as well as interfered with their speech rights to distribute pamphlets and their freedom of locomotion to move about the city. The volatile local protests against the CIO and ACLU that city officials cited to justify their actions, he asserted, were actually fomented by the Hague administration itself. When it came to who was causing local disorder, Jersey City government was a

Figure 7. Rival attorneys Edward O'Mara of Jersey City, Morris Ernst for the American Civil Liberties Union, and Spaulding Frazer for the Committee for Industrial Organization at the Third Circuit, U.S. Court of Appeals, December 23, 1938. ACME/NEA press photograph.

"ring-around-the-rosy" proposition. Using antifascist language of the time, Ernst condemned Mayor Hague for acting like a dictator who had "adopted the ideologies of Stalin, Hitler and Mussolini." "Nothing will stop him but the firmest decree." The CIO-ACLU lawyers would let Judge Clark's injunction stand.[4]

A crucial development in Third Circuit hearing of *Hague v. CIO* was the American Bar Association's (ABA) submission of an amicus curiae brief in support of the CIO and ACLU, signaling the arrival of legal conservatives in the civil liberties movement. The brief originated in the ABA's brand-new Committee on the Bill of Rights. With outgoing ABA president Arthur T. Vanderbilt's approval, Wall Street lawyer Grenville Clark had championed the committee as a way for the ABA to improve its reactionary image against competition from its rising left-leaning rival, the National Lawyers Guild. At its first meeting in November 1938, hence, the committee decided to involve itself in the Jersey City dispute. Clark, with help from his young law office associate Louis Lusky and renowned civil liberties committee member Zechariah Chafee, wrote the committee brief to be submitted to the Third Circuit for the Jersey City case, adopting a posture much like the ACLU's emerging position that emphasized a principled neutral defense of civil liberties, regardless of the parties involved. Hailed by a *New York Times* editorial, the ABA brief focused on protecting what it treated as the bedrock democratic right of free assembly, a right that Jersey City seemed to violate with regularity. So vital was this right, the brief argued, that public authorities could not (as Jersey City did) use the threat of hostile public reaction as an excuse to deny it. In a democracy, government had the obligation to facilitate free public discussion.[5]

Although the brief emanated out of ABA's internal organizational impulses, it carried heavy political freight due to Arthur Vanderbilt's involvement. In addition to being the outgoing ABA president, he was a long-time Essex County Republican opponent of the Hudson County Democrat Frank Hague. From his Essex County spot, Vanderbilt had nurtured Republican Lester Clee's unsuccessful "clean government" gubernatorial campaign against Hague henchman Harry Moore in 1937, and then served as counselor for socialist Norman Thomas in his suit against Jersey City for being expelled in 1938.[6] Could Vanderbilt have been anything but happy to see the ABA committee take up the Jersey City cause?

Jersey City tried to block ABA intervention, however. At the bar association's January 1939 meeting in Chicago, Mayor Hague's Republican arch-rival Robert Carey, of all people, stood up to resolve against the ABA committee's jurisdiction over such matters, but was ruled out of order. Another delegate challenged bill of rights committee chair Grenville Clark's authority in the case, and too got voted down. Angered that the ABA committee had sided with the ACLU, Carey warned at a later meeting that the bar association was flirting too closely with radicals and was opening itself to controversy.[7] Although not a Hague ally, he seemingly spoke for conservative local political and business interests that bucked interference by outside groups affiliated with left-labor causes in the late New Deal era.

For his part, Mayor Hague tried to discredit the ABA brief by railing against his Essex County enemy Arthur Vanderbilt, whom he accused of being a communist pawn. The communist troika of Norman Thomas, Roger Baldwin, and Morris Ernst, Hague told the press, had "engineered" Vanderbilt to put up a "respectable front" for communists by filing the ABA's amicus brief in the Third Circuit. Such use of smears against political opponents was a stock Hague rhetorical tactic (earlier, he had denigrated his foes as perverts, corruptionists, racketeers, and so forth), but the mayor's deployment of communist accusations against Vanderbilt demonstrated once again how he strategically allied with the interwar anticommunist movement for his own purposes. The former ABA president, however, parried the charges as "ridiculous," adding that "Mr. Hague can't seem to understand that the issues of free press, free speech and lawful assembly are paramount. . . . Mr. Hague doesn't believe anyone who differs with him has such rights."[8] The Vanderbilt-Hague rivalry dramatized how the Jersey City fracas blended local politics with both the judicial battle over civil liberties and the political fight over communism.

Hague's far-fetched anticommunist rhetoric exposed the dubiousness of Jersey City's central legal argument in the Third Circuit Court case—that municipal authorities had the right and duty under local police powers to exclude the CIO and allies from public streets, because they were radicals who threatened public peace. The Third Circuit panel of Judges Davis, Biggs, and Maris that ultimately heard the case bluntly dismissed this Jersey City claim. In a transformative 2–1 decision, the Third Circuit Court registered a devastating critique of Jersey City's treatment of the CIO and supporters, disavowing the city's views of municipal power as thoroughly outdated, and articulating the protective modern view of speech and assembly rights on the municipal level. Generational change in court personnel produced this result. Had the original five-member court decided the case, a majority of old-school judges consisting of Buffington (appointed by President Theodore Roosevelt in 1906), Thompson (by Woodrow Wilson in 1914), and Davis (by Wilson in 1920) may well have affirmed Jersey City's theory of municipal police power. As it turned out, Franklin Roosevelt's appointees Biggs and

Maris on the three-judge panel embraced new jurisprudence and determined the Third Circuit's libertarian ruling.[9]

In his opinion for the Third Circuit majority consisting of himself, Maris, and Davis only in part, Judge John Biggs Jr., upheld Judge Clark's decree, dismissing Jersey City's charge that its breadth would convert the district court into the municipality's governing authority. Biggs framed his ruling squarely in terms of civil-liberties protection, stepping briskly away from old jurisprudence that treated assembly and speech rights as mere limitations on municipal powers. In a careful review of the trial record, Judge Biggs reiterated district court judge Clark's findings that CIO organizers and their supporters had entered Jersey City to carry out lawful activities rather than to cause disarray or violence, and that the municipality's allegations about threats of a mass CIO "invasion" and disruptive public meetings were all unsupported by evidence. If anything, said Biggs, the Hague administration itself spearheaded a movement to stir up local commotion "to keep the appellee labor groups out of Jersey City." "Reversing the usual procedure," Biggs observed sarcastically, Mayor Hague and his associates "troubled the waters in order to fish in them." Jersey City's treatment of the CIO and allies was thus one long record of illegal police misconduct and "gross violation of the civil rights of the persons concerned," particularly their liberty to movement physically about the city, their freedom to communicate by circulating handbills, setting up pickets or securing public meeting permits, and their rights to due process when faced with arrest or deportation from the city.

With transformational reasoning, moreover, Biggs held that there was no longer any legal basis for Jersey City to refuse CIO activists and their supporters the right to assemble and speak, but that there were strong constitutional grounds for requiring that municipality to defend those liberties. In particular, he ruled that the 1930 public-meeting permit ordinance under whose color the city denied CIO assembly and speech rights was unconstitutional on its face, as was the city's method of administering it. Jersey City had argued that it retained authority to pass and implement such an ordinance governing public speaking on highways or in parks following the theory of the U.S. Supreme Court's *Davis v. Massachusetts* decision. Biggs, however, distinguished the *Davis* case from Jersey City's situation (failure to apply for a permit, as compared to being denied a permit), and more importantly ruled that subsequent U.S. Supreme Court decisions had "modified" it. A long line of libertarian cases from *Gitlow v. New York* (1925) and *Near v. Minnesota* (1931) to *DeJonge v. Oregon* (1937) and *Lovell v. City of Griffin* (1938), he argued, had substituted "the modern doctrine of protection of liberty of speech and assembly against state and municipal restrictions," including those imposing "prior restraints" as Jersey City's ordinance did. Specifically, those latter cases "incorporated" First Amendment speech, press, and assembly freedoms into the Fourteenth Amendment and applied them against infringement by the states. Even if the Jersey City ordinance were considered valid, Biggs added, city officials administered it in a discriminatory and unconstitutional way, offering no evidence that there was actual need to suppress CIO violence, and deploying that law arbitrarily against the CIO and its allies, not against other groups.

In light of modern doctrine and practice, hence, Biggs rejected Jersey City's view of free speech and assembly as "shocking." The city claimed that it had to restrict exercise of those rights whenever public reaction to it threatened violence, but Biggs maintained that such a policy "places those rights in the hands of those who would destroy them" and would lead to "totalitarian government." Stating it more bluntly than Judge Clark's district court order had, he affirmed that legal priorities had shifted from protecting tranquility to protecting liberties. Under modern doctrine, "speakers may not be prohibited from speaking because they may say something that which will lead to disorder." As a result, rather than stopping orators from speaking to keep order, police should "preserve order while they speak."

In addition, Biggs confirmed the crucial point that federal courts had jurisdiction over the *Hague* case, in effect substituting emerging modern notions of national authority for Jersey City's old-fashioned view of limited national power. In the case, CIO and ACLU appellees had avowed national judicial jurisdiction under Reconstruction-era civil rights legislation that afforded federal protection to "rights, privileges and immunities secured by the Constitution and laws," including free speech, press, and assembly, and relief from unreasonable searches and seizures as enumerated in the Bill of Rights. Jersey City lawyers, however, countered with the preincorporation theory that the civil rights laws did not apply, because the specified rights predated and were not "secured" by the Bill of Rights, and applied only to the national government, not state governments. Biggs rejected the old view, arguing that the rights specified need not originate in the Bill of Rights to be "secured," and were protected under modern jurisprudence by the privileges-and-immunities and due process clauses of the Fourteenth Amendment. He also rebuffed Jersey City's technical contention that the case did not meet the statutory threshold of $3,000 in controversy to warrant the district court's jurisdiction, deferring to the district judge's determination that the threshold had been met. Clearly, the federal courts had jurisdiction.[10] Seemingly a sidelight, Biggs's jurisdictional ruling was important. It showed that *Hague* marked an effort to reshape the federal system and expand national authority over municipalities, as well as to defend civil liberties.

In a losing cause, Judge Davis reaffirmed the antiquated view of federal-state constitutional relations. While joining his majority colleagues in upholding the first part of Judge Clark's decree ordering Jersey City to refrain from deportations, unlawful searches and seizures, disruption of circular distribution, and interference with placard displays, he forcefully disagreed with the majority decision to sustain the second part denying the city's discretion to prevent public meetings. As Davis saw it, good law under New Jersey's home-rule act, the New Jersey case of *Harwood v. Trembly* (1921) and the U.S. Supreme Court decision in *Davis v. Massachusetts* still gave municipalities like Jersey City exclusive control over streets and parks to protect their cities from political violence. "Self-preservation is an inherent function of government," he declared. Most notably, Judge Davis rejected the majority's legal finding that *Davis* had been "modified" by libertarian Supreme Court decisions of the 1920s and 1930s, arguing that those rulings never explicitly mentioned *Davis* and could not be taken to modify it by implication. As a municipality, hence, Jersey City retained exclusive power to regulate streets and parks for public safety purposes, and to enact its public-meeting ordinance. And public safety director Daniel Casey in turn properly exercised his "ministerial" duty under that law to deny meeting permits to CIO and ACLU speakers, given the mass of evidence showing those orators' radical inclinations. The Third Circuit majority, Davis added, misrepresented the trial court record in finding that the Hague regime itself stirred up a volatile situation. Reiterating Jersey City's position almost verbatim, Davis asserted that "the issue here is not primarily free speech at all," although the CIO and ACLU were "seeking to make it such . . . [by] masquerading under the flag of free speech." As Davis defined it, the real issue in *Hague* was a municipality's right to use its legitimately exclusive power to regulate streets and parks to protect public safety without federal judicial interference, a right that Jersey City exercised properly in this case. Indeed, he concluded, the case should never have been in federal court in the first place, given that the $3,000 value of loss had never been substantiated, except by "bald statement."[11]

The Third Circuit ruling was thus not simply a libertarian rout of Boss Hague's dictatorial rule, as it is often portrayed, but critically also a reconceptualization of the role of civil liberties in the municipal arena. No doubt, the Third Circuit's unanimous endorsement of the district court's ruling on deportation, illegal searches, unlawful arrests, the disruption of leafletting, and the banning of placards delivered a rebuke to Jersey City. In doing so, the Third Circuit majority borrowed greatly from CIO-ACLU and ABA briefs and affirmed speech and assembly rights even more emphatically than Judge Clark's district court decree had done. Indeed, the Third Circuit majority broadened the affirmation of speech and assembly by removing the part of Judge Clark's decree that permitted Jersey City to ban the CIO-ACLU street meetings, if it banned all street gatherings. The Third Circuit wanted to facilitate speech by allowing all meetings.[12]

Moreover, as Judge Davis's dissent signaled, the Third Circuit majority's full-throated endorsement of civil liberties in Jersey City rested on the triumph of the New Deal era's rethinking of federal jurisdiction and municipal power. Indeed, had the *Hague* case come up to the Third Circuit just a year earlier, before the FDR appointees had taken their seats, Judge Davis may well have a written the decision and settled the case in Jersey City's favor on jurisdictional grounds. As it was, however, Judge Biggs's majority ruling fully absorbed the incorporation revolution's use of the Fourteenth Amendment to authorize federal courts to apply First Amendment rights on state and local levels, and it breathed new life into Reconstruction-era civil rights laws that also sanctioned federal intrusion into civil liberties in the states. One result was a new conception of city power. It could no longer be doubted, Judge Biggs argued, "that a city owns and its officials administer its streets and parks, not as private proprietors, but as trustees for the people." Under the new way of thinking, he said, public urban places should not just afford people the rights of travel and recreation, but also "must be open" for people to "exercise their rights of free speech and assembly."[13] Biggs's reasoning portended the end of the era of municipal autonomy that had long sheltered authoritarian local bosses like Frank Hague, and now brought cities into the emerging national constitutional regime that privileged civil liberties under federal judicial protection. Ascension of this new view was decisive for the CIO-ACLU victory and Mayor Hague's defeat in the Third Circuit.

Significantly left out, however, were claims for labor organizing that the CIO and ACLU had pressed in *Casey v. ACLU*. The Third Circuit decision on December 13, 1938, to dismiss that case had disabled those claims, much to the exasperation of CIO-ACLU attorneys who wanted to hold Hague accountable for "flagrant" labor violations. Morris Ernst subsequently filed a motion on behalf of the CIO to have Judge Clark broaden his November 7 decree in *Hague v. CIO* to include labor organizing issues, but *Hague* moved forward just as a civil-liberties case. Nonetheless, CIO counsel Lee Pressman hopefully saw the Third Circuit ruling as a victory for working people. Blurring the distinction between civil liberties and labor rights, he argued that workers had mobilized in Jersey City "to protect their democratic rights and to secure better living conditions through collective bargaining." Hague had tried "every trick in the anti-union repertoire to prevent this," he declared, but the circuit court had confirmed "that civil rights cannot be suppressed, even by mayors in control of corrupt city machines."[14]

* * *

As expected, Jersey City counselors Hamill, Mathews, O'Mara, and Hershenstein appealed the Third Circuit decision to the U.S. Supreme Court, repeating the city's legal defenses and asking the high court to vacate the Third Circuit ruling and district court decree. In their petition for certiorari, the Jersey City attorneys again asserted that federal courts lacked jurisdiction in the case, since the respondent CIO and ACLU had not met the $3,000 statutory threshold of harm and since violations claimed involved not federal but state rights. More importantly, the petition averred that the Third Circuit's affirmation of the district court decree conflicted with the U.S. Supreme Court's *Davis* decision and New Jersey precedents, all of which confirmed municipalities' absolute power to enact and administer ordinances that regulated speech and assembly in public places to preserve public order. Quoting Justice Edward White's opinion in *Davis*, the city reiterated that *Hague* centrally involved the exercise of municipal police powers, not speech rights. According to White, "the Fourteenth Amendment to the Constitution of the United States does not destroy the power of the states to enact police regulations . . . and does not have the effect of creating a particular and personal right in the citizen to use public property in defiance of the Constitution and the laws of the state." Jersey City contended that this precedent had never been overruled and thereby sanctioned the city's actions.[15]

Respondent CIO and ACLU attorneys Frazer and Ernst joined the petition for certiorari on grounds that used the contemporary rhetoric of antifascist Americanism as much as it relied on law. As they saw it, Judge Biggs's opinion sustaining the district court decree was "unanswerable in law, logic and policy" and compelled by the Supreme Court's own precedents. Jersey City's arguments, they insinuated, were hardly serious legal points, but mere "tactics" used to obscure "official suppression" of fundamental democratic rights. Such tactics had no place in the "American way of life," and the Supreme Court had to reject them "with the utmost clarity and finality." In a veiled reference to rising fascism in Europe, Frazer and Ernst added ominously, "the movement of world events places this Court under increased obligation to repulse attacks upon the civil liberties which lie at the base of the form of government under which we live." The court should not stop with a judgment on the narrow questions raised by the petitioners but should offer a "plenary review" of all of the issues raised by the Third Circuit case "without limitation." Under prevailing world conditions, the CIO and ACLU urged, the Supreme Court had to issue a full-fledged defense of free speech and assembly. The high court granted certiorari in early February 1939.[16]

When the U.S. Supreme Court agreed to hear *Hague v. CIO*, the case entered an evolving constitutional terrain that had great bearing on its outcome. The federal courts were momentously coming out of a long period of conservatism. Back in the Reconstruction era (1860s-1870s), section 1 of the Fourteenth Amendment and subsequent civil rights laws had planted the legal seeds for the federal courts to defend nationally designated rights against infringement by state action. Moreover, institutional reforms like the 1891 Evarts Act had strengthened federal circuit courts of appeal and expanded their potential as civil rights defenders. Nonetheless, that potential fell dormant through the late 1800s and early 1900s, as federal courts spurned the Reconstruction era's legal and constitutional revolution, particularly by declining to absorb the national speech, press, and assembly guarantees of the Bill of Rights into the Fourteenth Amendment for application on the state level. Thus, federal courts reneged on civil rights enforcement in *Plessy v. Ferguson* and other cases. Instead, their work shifted firmly to economic issues, where they narrowly construed federal regulatory power under the commerce clause, hampered worker agitation with labor injunctions, and restrained state protective laws by asserting "liberty of contract" rights under the Fourteenth Amendment's due process provision. Judges appointed in the Progressive era (early 1900s) remained overwhelmingly conservative (with some exceptions), including U.S. Supreme Court justices Willis Van Devanter and James McReynolds, who retained their seats into the 1930s. Through these years, Hoffer, Hoffer, and Hull conclude, "a robust Federalism (of the pre-Reconstruction sort) dictated deference to state courts."[17] Civil liberties persisted as a local issue under the authority of politicized state and local courts, allowing Jersey City and other municipalities to suppress labor activists, dissenters, and others in the name of keeping public peace. The bulwark of Jersey City's defense, the *Davis* decision, emerged from this environment.

Through the late nineteenth and early twentieth centuries, moreover, the judiciary remained quite hostile to free-speech claims, beginning to liberalize only in the post–World War I years. After Reconstruction, *U.S. v. Cruikshank* (1876) and other cases refused to find that the Fourteenth Amendment applied First Amendment rights to the states, *Davis v. Massachusetts* (1897) denied any implicit right to speak in public spaces controlled by municipalities, and *Patterson v. Colorado* (1907) limited speech rights to Sir William Blackstone's no prior restraint doctrine and "bad tendency" test. Even in the

Progressive era, the courts showed little sympathy for the free-expression rights advocated by libertarian radicals and the IWW. In post–World War I espionage cases like *Schenck v. U.S.* (1919), the U.S. Supreme Court enthroned Blackstone's "bad tendency" test in the "clear and present danger" doctrine when it interpreted the First Amendment for the first time. Only in the postwar years did the U.S. Supreme Court's outlook change. Starting with dissents in *Abrams v. U.S.* (1919), Justices Oliver Wendell Holmes and Louis Brandeis began defending a free market of ideas and the democratic value of speech rights. Then, *Gitlow v. New York* (1925) formally introduced the idea that the Fourteenth Amendment "incorporated" First Amendment protections. And Chief Justice William Howard Taft's administrative reforms of the federal judiciary along with the 1925 Judges' Bill increasingly focused federal courts' attention on "matters of national importance," including liberties protected by the Bill of Rights. The federal courts were slowly awakening to civil liberties, despite the Taft Court's conservative ascendancy through the 1920s.[18]

In the unprecedented conditions of the 1930s, the U.S. Supreme Court under Chief Justice Charles Evans Hughes (1930–41) finally unleashed the federal courts' latent potential for national civil libertarian stewardship. Under his leadership, the Hughes court tilted in a libertarian direction, even though conservative justices called the Four Horsemen (Pierce Butler, James McReynolds, Willis Van Devanter, and George Sutherland) continued to dominate the court during the first half of the decade. Moreover, the Great Depression and the New Deal administration of President Franklin Roosevelt put enormous pressure on the federal courts to revise traditional notions of federalism and judicial authority. After striking down state and federal anti-Depression economic measures in 1935 and 1936, the Supreme Court famously reversed course in 1937 and 1938, when the chief justice and Justice Owen Roberts revised their applications of the Fourteenth Amendment due process clause to uphold a state minimum wage law, and then reinterpreted the commerce and taxation clauses to validate the Wagner NLRA and social security legislation. Simultaneously, even before Roosevelt appointees took their seats, Hughes and his colleagues built on the 1925 *Gitlow* decision to incorporate First Amendment guarantees into the Fourteenth Amendment, thereby curbing local infringements on speech, press, and assembly.[19]

Meanwhile, organized labor's burgeoning political clout during and after the 1936 presidential election encouraged the federal courts to expand free speech and assembly rights for workers. Working-class constituencies led by the CIO surged during President Roosevelt's 1936 campaign, and they consolidated into a formidable political bloc in the immediate postelection years. They secured formation of the La Follette Congressional Committee on civil liberties, gained strong enforcement of labor laws by the National Labor Relation Board, and won favorable U.S. Supreme Court decisions. In the court rulings, the Supreme Court treated peaceful picketing as a form of protected communication (*Senn v. Tile Layers' Union*, 1937), sanctioned labor agitators' right to assemble peaceably (*DeJonge v. Oregon*, 1937), and allowed peaceful labor organizing by a communist (*Herndon v. Lowry*, 1937). Conceptually, the decisions intertwined labor rights with free-speech rights and regarded worker liberties as ordinarily to be respected, except under circumstances that served the public good.[20]

The *Hague* case, hence, arrived at the U.S. Supreme Court at a transformative legal juncture, when the courts were expanding civil liberties and the rights of labor. In this context, Jersey City seemed bound to lose and the CIO-ACLU team seemed bound to win. The direction of legal and political change, not just the merits of the case, inclined the Court in *Hague v. CIO* toward a libertarian outcome.

* * *

Arguments before the U.S. Supreme Court in *Hague v. CIO* exhibited a showdown over conflicting notions of constitutional power, as well as a battle over civil liberties. Given less attention from modern scholars that it deserves, the Jersey City petitioners' brief notably defended the old constitutional order. The case was really about municipal power, not civil liberties, Jersey City said. Moreover, the facts of the CIO controversy showed that municipal officials acted responsibly. Most importantly, the federal courts lacked jurisdiction in the case. It was a fundamental principle, Jersey's brief asserted, that municipalities had police powers to control and regulate streets and public places for the public convenience. New Jersey statutes delegated power to every city government to preserve peace and order in public places, and to enact ordinances that established rules for the time, manner, and usage of public streets, parks, and waterfronts. Repeated state and federal court decisions, especially *Davis v. Massachusetts*, upheld the municipal duty to keep public order and to exercise absolute authority over speaking in public places. Jersey City's 1930 speaking-permit ordinance was thus perfectly legal.[21]

According to the Jersey City petitioners, consequently, the free-speech and assembly cases cited by the CIO and ACLU respondents were not applicable to *Hague* litigation. *Near v. Minnesota* was not relevant because it involved prior restraint of a publication. *DeJonge v. Oregon* was beside the point since it entailed speech in a private place. And *Lovell v. Griffin* was not relevant here, as it was about an overly broad city ordinance that interfered with house-to-house leafletting, not street speaking or distribution of literature on the streets. Jersey City's brief particularly objected to an alleged new right that respondents attributed to the *Lovell* ruling: the "right to self-expression in the public streets." No court had ever recognized such a "catch-all, cover-all phrase." If, according to Jersey City,

> that right [of free speech] is sought to be exercised in public streets and places in conflict with the right of the public at large to free and untrammelled use of such places, and in contravention of public officials entrusted with their administration, the right is necessarily disrupted; not because it is any the less intrinsically a fundamental right, but because, under the circumstances, its exercise becomes a perversion of the right and an invasion of the rights of the community generally. The "liberty" referred to in the Fourteenth Amendment is, in the language of Mr. Justice Cardozo in *Palko v. Connecticut*, "a concept of ordered liberty."

According to this reasoning, Jersey City asserted, the district court decree exaggerated the respondents' speech rights and unreasonably "shackled" city officers in the exercise of legitimate police functions.[22]

Under their construction of the facts, moreover, Jersey City lawyers found that Mayor Hague and his assistants had acted responsibly through the whole CIO ordeal. During his long career, the attorneys argued, Hague's police had kept a "moral and clean city" with little labor unrest until 1937, when alleged communist Harry Bridges instigated a maritime strike, when ACLU attorney Arthur Garfield Hays showed up to defend the dissidents, and then when CIO operatives invaded the city to distribute leaflets in defiance of local ordinances. Before this, the city's public safety directors rarely had to deny speaking permits, but the new onslaught left them with no choice but to refuse those permissions to the CIO, ACLU, Norman Thomas, and others in order to maintain public peace and order. Midwestern sit-down strikes revealed the CIO's disruptive proclivities, and communist associations exposed the ACLU's own violent intentions. A broad array of Jersey City residents led by veterans portended an uproar if CIO or ACLU street protests were allowed. Public safety director Daniel Casey thus reasonably and fairly exercised his discretion when he rejected speaking permits to these groups and individuals, because that prevented just what city ordinances rightfully forbid—riots, disturbances, and disorderly assemblages.[23]

Most important, Jersey City attorneys attacked the CIO's and ACLU's claim that federal courts had jurisdiction in the case. The Jersey lawyers contended that the U.S. district court could not assume jurisdiction under Federal Judicial Code sections 24(1) and 24(14), because the case involved neither a minimum loss of $3,000 in damages nor the deprivation of rights "secured by the U.S. Constitution" or "secured by any law of the United States providing for equal protection." This latter contention rested on a narrow, old-fashioned interpretation of Reconstruction-era civil rights laws, forerunners of today's U.S. Code section 1983, which is now a bulwark of civil liberties protection. In line with the 1930s civil liberties revolution, the CIO and ACLU maintained that this legislation affirmed national rights that Jersey City had denied, but Jersey lawyers reached back to the U.S. Supreme Court's post-Reconstruction interpretation of these laws to curtail federal involvement in local civil liberties issues.[24]

With significant—if antiquated—reasoning soon forsaken by the U.S. Supreme Court, Jersey City attorneys urged strict construction of the Judicial Code phrase "secured by the Constitution and laws" to gut national civil liberties protections. In the *Slaughterhouse Cases* (1873), they argued, the U.S. Supreme Court rendered its essential interpretation of the Fourteenth Amendment, determining not only that the rights protected under the amendment's "privileges and immunities" clause pertained to just a few limited national citizenship rights predating the Constitution, but holding also that the "due process" and "equal protection" clauses created no new rights but merely established a mechanism by which rights already recognized on the state level could be protected from detrimental state action.[25] This view created an opening for Jersey City to claim that the Fourteenth Amendment and Reconstruction-era civil rights laws did not "secure" or "create rights in the first instance" that justified federal judicial involvement under section 24(14). *Cruikshank*, they added, confirmed that the First and Fourteenth Amendments created few rights anew but sustained rights presumed already to belong to a free people, such as the right of the people to assemble peacefully for lawful purposes. Under section 24(14), Jersey City lawyers concluded, people had to look to state, not national, government for protection of this preexisting fundamental right. According to *Cruikshank*, "the right was not created by the amendment; neither was it continued and guaranteed, except as against congressional interference. For their protection in its enjoyment, therefore, the people must look to the States. The power for that purpose was originally placed there, and it has never been surrendered to the United States."[26] Certainly, Jersey City wanted to affirm this declaration of state and local autonomy against national interference.

Nowadays, the distinction between rights "created," "secured," or "granted" by the Constitution and those that are "preexisting" or "fundamental" might seem trivial. At the time of *Slaughterhouse* and *Cruikshank*, however, it sustained the nineteenth-century boundary between state and federal power and kept authority over civil liberties on the state level. As Justice Samuel Miller stated in *Slaughterhouse*, Congress did not mean to "transfer the security and protection of . . . civil rights . . . from the States to the Federal government" when it passed the Fourteenth Amendment. Such a transfer would "fetter and degrade the State governments by subjecting them to the control of Congress"—a radical change in "the whole theory of relations of the State and Federal governments" that Congress hardly intended. In effect, *Slaughterhouse* and *Cruikshank* established a framework of jurisprudence that kept civil liberties enforcement out of federal courts until the 1930s. As late as *U.S. v. Wheeler* (1920), a landmark interpretation of the U.S. Constitution's Article IV "privileges and immunities" clause, the U.S. Supreme Court continued to reject federal protection of "fundamental" rights, leaving it exclusively to the states.[27]

In its brief, Jersey City drew on this analysis to dismiss the federal district court's jurisdiction in the *Hague* case and to perpetuate a view of the U.S. federal system that kept municipal police practices insulated from national legal scrutiny. Strictly reading the Judicial Code's section 24(14) in light of U.S. Supreme Court decisions running from *Slaughterhouse* to *Wheeler*, Jersey attorneys denied that any rights claimed by the CIO and ACLU—whether peaceable assembly, free speech, freedom of the press, peaceful picketing, practicing one's calling (as a labor organizer), or even freedom from removal ("deportation")—belonged in federal court, because none of them was "secured" or "created in the first instance" by the U.S. Constitution or its amendments according to section 24(14)'s meaning. And while the respondents may have cited many court cases to support their federal claims, they provided no citations that used the term "secured" properly, and they offered "not an iota of authority" to show that *Cruikshank*'s line of analysis had ever been overruled. As Jersey attorneys saw it, the *Hague* case should have been tossed out of federal court, and the CIO, ACLU, and Jersey City should have continued to live together in a constitutional world wherein virtually no national enforcement of civil rights prevailed. Jersey City would regulate civil liberties as it saw fit, and Mayor Hague's police would crack down on CIO demonstrations and ACLU speeches as they deemed necessary. As far as Jersey lawyers were concerned, the district court's decree and injunction should be reversed.[28]

* * *

The respondents' brief for the CIO and ACLU not only rebutted Jersey City's arguments, but also articulated the emerging new constitutional philosophy of the 1930s that was replacing nineteenth-century doctrines rehearsed by Jersey City. For one thing, the respondent lawyers offered a much slimmer conception of municipal power than Jersey attorneys affirmed, so that civil liberties, not city authority, became the focal point of the case. Jersey's bedrock legal precedent *Davis v. Massachusetts*, they argued, was not really analogous to the Jersey City situation. More significantly, it was no longer good law. Subsequent to that 1897 ruling, they observed, the U.S. Supreme Court had brought speech and assembly rights under Fourteenth Amendment protection, so that municipal actions had to be weighed newly against these guarantees. Cities were no longer "private proprietors" that presided over public places to keep order; they were now "trustees" for the people and their civil rights.[29]

The respondents devoted most of their brief to cataloging Jersey City's many abuses of newly recognized rights. The city violated "liberty of persons" by deporting CIO labor organizers across state lines, tailing their cars, and subjecting them to unreasonable searches and arrests. Jersey authorities also violated CIO organizers' constitutional privilege to move freely about, and disrupted their speech and press rights by banning pickets, placards, and literature distribution on the streets. Most important, Jersey City's 1930 speaking permit ordinance allowed officials to use an unconstitutionally vague standard—to prevent "riots, disturbances or disorderly assemblage"—to refuse permits. That vagueness invited "police pre-censorship" by safety director Daniel Casey to silence CIO members and supporters.[30]

In the most searing part of their brief, the respondent lawyers excoriated the Hague regime for acting irresponsibly and for concocting a "deliberate policy" for the "total obliteration of civil rights" of CIO and ACLU members. Echoing antifascist portrayals of Hague, the respondents' brief mocked his claims to good leadership, declaring that he instead headed an "arrogant" regime that strove for "dictatorship" and "total power" over all of Hudson County. Moreover, according to the respondents, the Hague administration's contention that it faced imminent public disorder from CIO organizers and their supporters was not reasonably supported by the facts. All of Jersey's ominous warnings about disruption—amplified by Mayor Hague's erroneous descriptions of the respondents as "undesirables," "Reds," and "communists"—were simply a "subterfuge" to obscure the Hague administration's suppression of groups with which it disagreed. And the protests by veterans and other Jersey City groups against CIO members and their supporters did not truly threaten public disruption either, because those events were orchestrated by the Hague administration itself. As in any other city, Jersey City's police could easily have contained any disturbances that confronted speakers, its first duty, according to respondents. Yet, rather than responsibly calm the waters of city politics, Hague's administration did what the Court of Appeals imputed—"troubled the waters in order to fish in them."[31] Suppression of the rights of CIO members and their supporters was the purpose.

Finally, in its most important legal argument, the respondent brief rejected Jersey City's contention that federal courts lacked jurisdiction in the case, dismissing that argument as a "johnny-come-lately" plea manufactured to save Jersey City's losing case. The district court, the respondents asserted, had correctly found jurisdiction in Judicial Code section 24(1)'s $3,000 threshold in controversy, section 24(12)'s prohibition of conspiracies to deny civil rights, and section 24(14)'s ban on state infringements of rights secured by the Constitution and federal laws. They added that Jersey lawyers' reliance on *Slaughterhouse*'s and *Cruikshank*'s distinction between "guaranteed" and "secured" rights had been superseded by numerous U.S. Supreme Court rulings beginning with the 1925 *Gitlow* case, which assumed that First Amendment speech and assembly rights now applied to the states through the Fourteenth Amendment's due process clause. And the respondents were correct: following *Gitlow*, the high court regularly used the terms "fundamental," "protected," and "secured" interchangeably when interpreting Fourteenth Amendment guarantees. As Chief Justice Charles Evans Hughes wrote in *Near v. Minnesota* (1931), "it is no longer open to doubt that the liberty of the press, and of speech, is within the liberty safeguarded by the due process clause of the Fourteenth Amendment from invasion by state action. It was found impossible to conclude that this essential personal liberty of the citizen was unprotected by the general guaranty of fundamental rights of persons and property."[32] Free speech, a free press, and peaceable assembly were now nationally protected rights that federal courts recognized and that states and cities had to obey.

The CIO and ACLU attorneys thus concluded that their clients not only satisfied section 24(1)'s $3,000 minimum of damages from Jersey City, but also suffered infringements under the Fourteenth Amendment "privileges and immunities," "due process," and "equal protection" clauses, all now covered under section 24(14) rights "secured by the Constitution." Clearly a state actor, Jersey City had impaired these rights by denying the respondents free passage across state lines; physical freedom from arbitrary arrest; relief from unreasonable searches; free exercise of speech, press, and peaceable assembly; and equal treatment under the law. Since Jersey City continued these violations, the respondents asked the Supreme Court to affirm the district court decree and to enjoin the city's illegal practices permanently.[33]

By doing so, the respondents not only called Jersey City to account for its abuses, but also urged the high court to bring that municipality into the new constitution scheme that was emerging in the mid-twentieth-century civil-liberties revolution. As respondents saw it, federal and state courts alike were recognizing freedom of speech, press, and assembly as an "integral part of American democracy."[34] In effect, the CIO and ACLU lawyers encouraged the U.S. Supreme Court to bolster democracy by nationalizing First Amendment civil liberties and applying them to political fiefdoms like Jersey City that had previously been insulated from their enforcement by the states' rights emphasis of the nineteenth-century federalism. For Jersey City, and for other isolated counties and municipalities with quasi-authoritarian local governments, such federal intrusion threatened a revolution in the local structure of political power. The respondents were advancing a large constitutional vision with high political stakes.

* * *

The ABA amicus brief—like its original submission to the Third Circuit Court—affirmed the emerging modern views of civil liberties and municipal power even more pointedly than the respondents' brief did. Asserting again that the ABA intervened purely to serve that organization's interest in defending "fundamental rights and immunities" "secured" to citizens by the Bill of Rights, the brief moved past prevailing labor and anticommunist rhetoric, ignored jurisdictional questions, and focused on civil libertarian principles that the U.S. Supreme Court had yet to rule on. The ABA brief singled out freedom of assembly as the fundamental right most needing articulation in the Jersey City case. According to the brief, that freedom was "an essential element of the American democratic system," a point that surely resonated in the global political atmosphere of 1939, when democracy seemed imperiled by rising fascism.[35] The ABA framed the case as a fight for democracy as well as a struggle for CIO liberties.

The ABA brief centrally argued that peaceable assembly was a vital democratic right that Jersey City officials wantonly violated. The right to assemble peacefully was essential to democracy, the brief contended, because it facilitated face-to-face discussion in ways not fulfilled by other media like newspapers or radio, particularly for unpopular causes. Yet, Jersey City impaired that freedom when it came to CIO members and their supporters by arbitrarily administering its arguably unconstitutional 1930 speaking-permit ordinance. Like the CIO-ACLU respondents, the ABA maintained that the ordinance established an unconstitutional standard for refusing permits, allowing the city's public safety commissioner discretion beyond municipal traffic and recreational needs to deny permits to prevent "riot, disturbances and disorderly assemblage." Indeed, the ABA asserted, Jersey City's safety commissioner Daniel Casey abused that discretion by denying permits to the CIO and its allies while allowing them to favored groups. Jersey City's claim that it refused the CIO permits to ward off violence was simply not persuasive in fact or law. CIO organizers, ACLU speakers, and others acted in a peaceful and lawful way. Moreover, the ABA emphasized again, Jersey City could not allow opponents' or hecklers' threats of violence to silence speakers. It was a municipality's duty to deploy the police to defend speakers' rights against such threats. A flaw in Jersey's speaking-permit ordinance was its failure to require the safety commissioner to assess police capabilities to contain disorder before deciding to issue or deny a permit.[36]

The ABA brief especially rejected Jersey's analysis regarding municipal authority. Instead, it affirmed the rising new view of the relationship between municipalities and civil liberties. For that, the brief took special aim at *Davis v. Massachusetts*, the main legal precedent in Jersey City's defense of its actions. According to the ABA, *Davis* did not control the *Hague* case, because it rested on a different factual situation—speaking without seeking a permit, rather than being refused a permit—and because it reflected out-of-date law. On the latter point, the brief stated, U.S. courts no longer held that cities had comprehensive power to close streets and parks to remove expressive activity. Rather, in the years after *Davis* through the 1920s and 1930s, the "whole trend" of jurisprudence was to sustain speech and assembly in public places. Public policy had shifted from keeping municipal order to facilitating discussion. Perhaps conceding to New Deal–era conservatives who feared government-owned enterprises, also, the ABA, like the CIO-ACLU respondents, dismissed *Davis*'s view that cities were street and park "owners" that could forbid all expressive activity there, and adopted the new philosophy that streets and parks were "public utilities" to be administered for public purposes, "one of the most important of which is the right of free assembly therein for public discussion at reasonable times and places." The ABA concluded that the U.S. Supreme Court should uphold the district court injunction and decree against Jersey City. It also supported the Third Circuit's modification of that order to require that Jersey City not only refrain from discriminating against CIO and ACLU speakers, but also keep streets and parks open for all speakers.[37]

Widely lauded by the press and later well-regarded in U.S. Supreme Court chambers, the ABA brief contributed legal clarity to the central freedom-of-assembly principle in the *Hague* case without the political distractions. According to legal historian Laura Weinrib, ABA bill of rights committee assistant Louis Lusky's contribution was central. He drew on his earlier experience as a clerk helping Supreme Court justice Harlan Fiske Stone draft his famous footnote 4 affirming basic freedoms.[38] The ABA's *Hague* brief thus encouraged the Supreme Court's own internal movement to revise jurisprudence that addressed competing claims of government powers and civil liberties. The brief served to upend Jersey City's constitutional vision inherited from the nineteenth century that preserved municipal power and its safe harbor in old-fashioned federalism, embracing instead a new constitutional view of nationalized civil rights that placed the CIO and its supporters under federal protection.

The politics of the *Hague* case became starkly evident during three hours of oral arguments before the U.S. Supreme Court on February 27 and 28, 1939. As reported by the *New York Times*, Charles Hershenstein appeared for Jersey City and stressed "the duty of city officials to protect citizens from violence." He questioned the jurisdiction of federal courts to intervene in the case, affirmed the constitutionality of the city's speaking-permit ordinance, and defended the discretion of the public safety director to refuse public meeting permits when he feared that disorder might result. By contrast, according to the *Times*, CIO-ACLU lawyers emphasized the way in which Mayor Hague's administration had assumed "absolute power" from "extra-legal" sources to suppress CIO and ACLU operatives from meeting and speaking about union rights and civil liberties in streets and parks. As the *Times* saw it, the oral argument boiled down to a debate between Jersey City's claims to legitimate municipal governance and the CIO-ACLU complaint that city officials had brazenly denied basic speech and assembly rights.[39]

* * *

When it heard oral arguments in *Hague v. CIO*, the U.S. Supreme Court itself was in the grip of change. Only seven of the nine justices heard the case: William Douglas had yet to be confirmed to fill the seat of the retiring Louis Brandeis, and FDR appointee Felix Frankfurter recused himself due to his ACLU membership.[40] This left a fragmented court with one foot each in old and new eras. James McReynolds and Pierce Butler remained from the ultraconservative Four Horsemen appointed by Presidents Taft, Wilson, and Harding, while Coolidge and Hoover appointees Harlan Fiske Stone, Owen Roberts, and Chief Justice Charles Evans Hughes occupied the central part of the court's philosophical spectrum, and only two nominees by President Franklin Roosevelt sat in on the case, Hugo Black and Stanley Reed. In a generational sense, then, the seven-justice panel that heard *Hague* consisted of the remnants of the 1930s Hughes court before the Roosevelt court of the 1940s crystallized. Centrists Roberts, Hughes, and Stone dominated deliberations in *Hague*, while McReynolds and Butler asserted only a fading voice of constitutional conservatism, and Black and Reed exerted little influence as of yet. Previously a Progressive Republican governor, associate Supreme Court justice, presidential candidate, and diplomat, Chief Justice Hughes exercised a moderating influence in this complicated situation. The Depression and New Deal put enormous pressure on the changing court to make constitutional adjustments, but he guided it according to his convictions that "delicate balances" undergirded the U.S. constitutional system, and that the court's job was, as legal historian G. Edward White explains, "to adapt this system of balance to an industrial, urbanized, polyglot society without essentially disturbing the equilibrium."[41]

The Hughes court is famous for its switch from fierce resistance to easy acceptance of New Deal–era economic legislation, such as state minimum-wage laws, the NLRA, and Social Security. Yet, the court simultaneously advanced the "civil liberties revolution." Indeed, the two trends intertwined. The court's accommodation to New Deal economic measures accentuated its increasing activism for civil liberties and labor rights. Yet, while the court's shift on economic matters was abrupt and dramatic, its transformation of civil liberties proceeded through low-key "absent-minded incrementalism." The constitutional mechanism was the "incorporation doctrine," holding that the Fourteenth Amendment's due process clause absorbed fundamental liberties enumerated in the Bill of Rights and applied them against disparaging state action. Although the U.S. Supreme Court had long sustained the rule of *Barron v. Baltimore* (1833) that the Bill of Rights did not pertain to the states, Justice Edward Sanford suddenly endorsed incorporation with little debate in the 1925 *Gitlow* case by declaring parenthetically that the Fourteenth Amendment embraced First Amendment speech and press guarantees. Then, without much discussion again in 1931, Chief Justice Hughes formalized the doctrine in *Stromberg v. California* (Butler and McReynolds dissenting) and *Near v. Minnesota* (all Four Horsemen in dissent), holding that "it has been determined" and "it is no longer open to doubt" that the Fourteenth Amendment due process clause covered free speech and press. Conservatives Butler and McReynolds resisted this approach on old-fashioned federalism grounds. They still regarded state governments as the bodies most appropriate to regulate citizens' welfare and civil rights. Thus, in his *Near* dissent, Butler recognized that *Stromberg* and *Near* had formally incorporated free speech and press into the Fourteenth Amendment and bound states to protect those rights, but he still dissented for the reason that states remained the best forum for enjoining scurrilous speech. Nonetheless, he later joined the Hughes court's "incorporation revolution" in the 8–0 *DeJonge* ruling that extended incorporated protections to freedom of assembly.[42]

By the late 1930s, hence, the Hughes court had cultivated a new constitutional vision to replace the conservative jurisprudence that had prevailed from the 1870s to 1920s. Legal doctrines that had allowed federal courts to restrain local labor legislation and confine the management of civil liberties to states and localities gave way to judicial deference to economic legislation, including New Deal labor laws, but activism toward civil rights. Indeed, the Hughes court articulated a hierarchy of rights deserving special federal judicial scrutiny in *Palko v. Connecticut* (1937) and Justice Stone's footnote 4 in *U. S. v. Carolene Products* (1938). In those decisions, the court developed a new "double standard" that tolerated economic measures while calling for "more searching judicial inquiry" of state laws affecting "political processes ordinarily to be relied upon to protect minorities." *Cruikshank*'s nineteenth-century theory of dual federalism that had long insulated abusive municipalities like Jersey City from federal oversight fell by the wayside as a new nationalistic view of civil liberties took hold.[43]

This subtle ideological drift was fundamental to the work of the Hughes court, but not one appreciated by Jersey City lawyers. In strict legal logic, Jersey attorneys argued correctly that the U.S. Supreme Court had never overruled *Cruikshank*'s distinction between "fundamental" and "secured" rights that had kept federal courts out of civil-liberties regulation on the local level, but they failed to grasp (or to acknowledge) incremental changes in the Hughes court's constitutional interpretation that had abandoned the old jurisprudence and had nationalized civil liberties instead. By comparison, the CIO-ACLU lawyers had a much firmer understanding of, and in fact helped to promote, the new tenor of the Hughes court's constitutional thinking. Given the flagrant civil-liberties violations that pervaded Jersey City's political life in the late 1930s, perhaps Jersey lawyers had no choice but to seek refuge in the fading old constitutionalism. Or perhaps, at the time, Jersey attorneys might not have seen their position as so hopeless, and the CIO-ACLU posture as so sure, as we see it today.

As the U.S. Supreme Court took up *Hague v. CIO*, letters to Justice Black reaffirmed the public's view of the case as a showdown between fascist dictatorship and democracy. On February 9, 1939, R. G. Wolfe of Joplin, Missouri, advised Black that Mayor Hague had "overstepped his jurisdiction" and "overridden the Constitution" when he refused to let union men into his city to discuss the improvement of working conditions. Jersey City's American Legion post only worsened matters when it threatened to drive "invading" CIO and ACLU members out of the city. If the Supreme Court were to allow Hague and veterans to "dictate as Hitler," Wolfe warned, then

American democracy would be gone. A couple of months later, beleaguered Hague opponent John Longo sent Black a letter attaching a magazine article describing his ordeal of arrest and detention by "the Law" (Mayor Hague) on trumped-up election fraud charges, and suggested that Black ought to take a stand against Hague because he and Longo were both fighting against demagogues. Alluding to Black's own struggle against critics who had tried to scuttle his appointment due to his Ku Klux Klan membership, Longo observed that he had spoken out on Black's behalf and was gratified that Black was now on the court to confront civil liberties abuses.[44]

Subsequently, on June 5, 1939, the U.S. Supreme Court handed down its *Hague* decision in a 5–2 ruling in favor of the CIO-ACLU respondents, but deep divisions over constitutional reasoning belied public perception then and today that this was a clear-cut exoneration of civil liberties. Five of the seven justices wrote at least short opinions, and Justice Roberts writing for the court did not command a majority for his constitutional analysis. Indeed, it was odd that Chief Justice Hughes assigned the opinion to Roberts, given that Roberts's constitutional thinking drew the support of just himself and Justice Black, while Justice Stone's concurrence attracted three votes, including that of the chief justice himself. Personal affinities may have influenced the assignment. Roberts was socially close to Hughes, whereas Stone and the chief had grown disaffected. In a handwritten internal memorandum to Stone praising his *Hague* concurrence, Justice Frankfurter (sitting out of the *Hague* deliberations) confirmed such an estrangement when he confided that he "appreciated even more intimately what [Stone's] problems on the court are."[45] Personal chemistry seemingly caused Hughes to steer *Hague* to Roberts's desk, producing a narrower and muddier ruling than Stone would have written.

A controversial justice who staked out a moderate, if unsteady position on the court during the 1930s, Owen Roberts wrote a decision in *Hague* that seemed to fall in line with the court's string of civil libertarian rulings, but on the basis of rather eccentric reasoning. Rather than rely on the incorporation doctrine's Fourteenth Amendment due process clause analysis to reach his libertarian result, Roberts cited the Fourteenth Amendment privileges and immunities clause, deploying logic closely resembling old "limits of power" analysis that defined speech rights in terms of properly limiting the exercise of state (or municipal) powers. According to legal scholar Charles Pfohl, Roberts's reasoning constituted a "Rosetta Stone" that translated nineteenth-century principles of public speech into the twentieth-century language of rights. In the 1930s, however, such logic seemed muddled. Its fuzziness comported with Roberts's reputation for wavering on economic issues, wherein

Figure 8. Justice Owen Roberts. Library of Congress, Prints and Photographs Division, LC-DIG-hec-20949.

he first sided with the Four Horsemen against New Deal legislation, then abruptly reversed course in 1937 to uphold such laws, but then retreated from wholesale endorsement of New Deal measures after 1938. Critics charged him with a lack of judicial courage, vacillating according to political pressures rather than following the law. Still, he voted consistently in favor of civil liberties, and in fact upheld them in his *Herndon v. Lowry* (1937) and *Schneider v. New Jersey* (1939) opinions, although he did not leave a firm doctrinal legacy.[46]

Roberts opened his *Hague* decision with a long review of the lower-court record that condemned Jersey City and exonerated the CIO and its sympathizers. He summarized the CIO-ACLU complaint that Jersey City had launched an unlawful, deliberate plan to deny CIO organizers and their associates their constitutional rights to free speech and peaceable assembly. He also acknowledged Jersey City's claim that CIO organizers were undesirable in the municipality as communists, but he accepted the district court's factual rebuttal that there was "no competent proof" that CIO speakers had ever stirred up trouble before or had any intentions other than to meet and discuss worker rights peacefully. Roberts further accepted the lower-court finding that Jersey City deployed police with "force and violence" to carry out a deliberate policy of "forbidding the respondents and their associates from communicating their views respecting the National Labor Relations Act to the citizens of Jersey City by holding meetings or assemblies in the open air and at public places."[47] He framed the facts narrowly by ignoring Jersey City's concerns about circumstances under which the CIO confrontation took place, with the seamen's strike, the sit-down strikes, the rhetorical threats of "invasion," and alleged willful lawbreaking. Instead, he construed the case as one simply about workers' rights to assemble and speak about labor rights, and determined that the factual record left no doubt about Jersey City's bad behavior. The real question before the Supreme Court, Roberts decided, was jurisdictional: whether CIO-ACLU respondents had a cause of action against Jersey City under federal law, and if so, whether the district court injunction and decree provided the proper remedy.

Roberts broke down his jurisdictional analysis into three parts: whether the CIO and ACLU had a cause of action in federal courts; whether Jersey City could restrict speech and assembly under municipal police powers; and whether the district court decree was valid. In regard to the cause of action, lower courts had recognized jurisdiction under sections 24(1), 24(12), and 24(14) of the Federal Judicial Code, but Roberts sharply qualified it. He rejected jurisdiction under section 24(1) on grounds that nothing in the record valuated $3,000 in controversy, ignored section 24(12) banning conspiracies, but acknowledged jurisdiction under section 24(14) on the basis of the Fourteenth Amendment privileges and immunities clause. Section 24(14) created a federal cause of action for alleged deprivation under color of law of "any right, privilege or immunity secured by the Constitution" or "any right secured by any law of the United States providing for equal rights of citizens of the United States." According to Roberts, the natural-born CIO respondents in the case, though not the ACLU as an artificial organization, enjoyed national citizenship rights under the Fourteenth Amendment privileges and immunities clause that qualified under section 24(14). Those rights included meeting and discussing a federal law like NLRA, as he said that CIO members proposed to do. True, he admitted, the Reconstruction-era *Slaughterhouse* and *Cruikshank* cases had ruled that the Fourteenth Amendment had created no new rights, but he added that those cases still recognized peaceable assembly as a fundamental right of national citizenship, overlooking *Cruikshank*'s distinction between the national right to lobby congress and the not-covered right of meeting for other lawful purposes. Arguably, the efforts of CIO members to rally in Jersey City fell under the latter uncovered category. Nonetheless, Roberts ignored the difference and assumed that CIO members were clothed with the assembly rights of national citizenship. Such citizenship would mean nothing, Roberts argued, "if it did not carry with it the right to discuss national legislation and the benefits, advantages, and opportunities to accrue to citizens therefrom."[48]

Roberts's privileges and immunities analysis offered an innovative approach to securing rights under the Fourteenth Amendment, a more pointed theory than he gave contemporaneously in his vaguer *Herndon* and *Schneider* decisions. It was expansive in the sense that it used *Slaughterhouse*'s and *Cruikshank*'s references to the right of travel to accommodate labor organizers' need to move about, but it was very narrow in the sense that it sanctioned assembly rights only for citizens' discussion of national legislation. Yet, all of this operated outside of the U.S. Supreme Court's "incorporation revolution" that utilized the due process clause, and it won only Justice Black's support. In a May 1939 internal court memorandum, Justice Stone warned Roberts that his approach was constitutionally untenable. Were the court to adopt Roberts's interpretation, Stone contended, "we run the risk in unnecessarily giving an entirely new trend to the privileges and immunities clause." He reminded Roberts that, at the time that they were decided, the *Slaughterhouse* and *Cruikshank* rulings had both determined that neither the privileges and immunities nor the due process clauses of the Fourteenth Amendment covered the Bill of Rights. Moreover, the Supreme Court later ruled again and again that the privileges and immunities clause had not absorbed those freedoms. Stone added, however, that judicial decisions had by 1939 decided that many of the bill's liberties were after all secured by due process. It followed, then, that Jersey City violated CIO speech and assembly freedoms guaranteed by that clause, thereby establishing the CIO's cause of action under section 24(14). This became Stone's argument in a concurring opinion.[49]

Having decided that CIO members had federally recognized speech and assembly rights under the privileges and immunities clause, Roberts then inquired as to whether Jersey City could encroach on those rights by virtue of municipal police powers. Blurring the distinction between streets and parks, he confronted and rejected Jersey City's contention that the 1897 *Davis* decision gave cities ownership of those areas and absolute authority to exclude expressive use of them. Distinguishing rather than passing judgment on it, Roberts asserted that *Davis* involved a different kind of ordinance (a general regulation of parks) than the Jersey City litigation did (permission to assemble), and thus that it did not apply to the *Hague* case. More importantly, he decided that whatever its title to streets and parks, Jersey City had to recognize the fundamental and ancient right of citizens to use them for expressive purposes. Streets and parks, he declared famously, "have immemorially been held in trust for the use of the public, and, time out of mind, have been used for the purposes of assembly, communicating thoughts between citizens and discussing public questions." From ancient times, he said, streets and parks had been "a part of the privileges, immunities and rights of citizens." His argument was conservative, appealing not to the First Amendment or universal speech rights, but to traditional limits on municipal power. Still, he reconceived municipal authority in a critical way. Roberts indicated that cities were trustees, not just owners of public property, and thus had a duty—later called the public forum doctrine—to respect citizen use of public space for democratic processes. Municipalities might regulate that space for public convenience and safety, but could not abridge the people's right to public expression there in the guise of regulation.

Abuse regulatory power is just what Jersey City did, according to Roberts. The city's 1930 speaking-permit ordinance was "void upon its face" because it allowed the public safety director to refuse a permit on "his mere opinion" that meetings and speeches posed a threat of "riots, disturbance, or disorderly assemblage." Moreover, Jersey City's administration of the ordinance exhibited "uncontrollable official suppression" of citizens' privilege to meet and speak in public places. This was a watershed moment. The Roberts ruling in effect lifted the legal shield that had insulated abusive and politically motivated municipal police practices from national constitutional scrutiny since the 1800s. Now, Jersey City and other municipalities had to adhere to the principle that they were trustees for the people's right to rally and express themselves in public places, a right that extended to CIO labor organizers and everyone else.[50]

Having decided that the CIO respondents did enjoy nationally protected rights and that Jersey City as a municipality could not unilaterally interfere with them, Roberts then addressed and upheld the district court decree, although he modified it. Brushing aside Jersey City's objection that it was too vague to enforce, he found the decree's section A ("liberty of person") forbidding exclusion or removal of CIO respondents, except in cases of valid arrest, search, or seizure, to be valid. He also confirmed most of section B ("liberty of the mind") but decided that some of it "goes too far." He found the part enjoining Jersey City from interfering with CIO members and associates from peacefully communicating their views on the streets as "unassailable," but determined that this section improperly tried to specify the conditions for distributing literature and securing speaking permits, and should have stopped just at declaring Jersey City's anti-leafletting and meeting permit ordinances to be invalid and unenforceable. That left CIO members free to circulate handbills as they wanted, or "to hold meetings without a permit and without regard to the void ordinance."[51] Altogether, Roberts narrowed the district court injunction down to a simple proscription of Jersey City's unconstitutional ordinances and actions in regard to deportation, literature distribution, and public meetings, leaving CIO members and those acting with them to move freely about the city, circulate handbills, and organize public rallies. The change was momentous. At the very least, Roberts's decision ratified the district court's devastating blow to Mayor Hague's Jersey City police regime. In regard to municipal governance and civil liberties, moreover, it marked the end of one constitutional era and the start of a new one.

The constitutional basis of this change remained very much in doubt, however. Justice Stone, joined by Justice Reed, wrote a concurring opinion that laid out a much broader legal foundation for CIO speech and assembly rights. A Republican and former law school dean appointed by President Coolidge in 1925, Stone gradually cultivated a social utilitarian approach to judging that blossomed in the Supreme Court's 1930s civil liberties revolution. As reflected by his footnote 4, he urged varying standards of judicial review for cases involving different social interests, particularly strict scrutiny of state actions affecting political rights and powerless minorities. In his *Hague* concurrence, consequently, Stone joined with Roberts to affirm the district court decree against Jersey City, though on different constitutional grounds. As forecasted in his May memorandum, he rejected the Fourteenth Amendment privileges and immunities clause as the source of CIO freedoms to be protected. According to Stone, that passage included only peaceable assembly in the form of petitioning Congress; the CIO-ACLU respondents had never asserted citizenship rights under privileges and immunities, and lower courts had found little evidence (aside from the November 29 flyer) that CIO members tried to discuss the Wagner NLRA on Jersey City streets, a prerequisite for showing violation of national citizenship rights. Overall, Stone complained that privileges and immunities proffered a "novel constitutional doctrine" and construed the case too narrowly. It was CIO members' right to meet and converse for any lawful purpose that was at stake, not just their right to meet and discuss subjects relevant to national citizens.

The real subject of the *Hague* case was, according to Stone, the freedom of speech and assembly guaranteed to all persons regardless of citizenship under the Fourteenth Amendment due process clause: "nor shall any State deprive any persons of life, liberty, or property, without due process of law." And that, he agreed with Roberts, meant "natural," not "artificial" (i.e., organizations like the ACLU), persons. The case consequently did not rest on the respondents' citizenship status or on their efforts to exercise national citizenship rights like discussing the federal Wagner NLRA. Instead, "it is enough that [Jersey City has] prevented respondents from holding meetings and disseminating information whether for the organization of labor or for any other lawful purpose." Such a violation of due process by state action, he added, qualified as a deprivation of a right "secured by the Constitution" that warranted review by the federal courts under section 24(14) of the Judicial Code. True, *Slaughterhouse* and *Cruikshank* "at the[ir] time" had not extended the due process clause to cover speech and assembly, but "later expansion by judicial decision" had incorporated those rights into the clause. True also, section 24(14) used the term "secured by the Constitution" rather than "protected," but any distinction between those two terms was "not persuasive." By 1939, Stone concluded, the Supreme Court regarded speech and assembly to be protected by the Fourteenth Amendment due process clause, an alleged deprivation that gave federal courts jurisdiction under section 24(14), regardless of the $3,000 threshold under section 24(1). It was on due process grounds, he said, that the court should sustain the district court injunction and decree. He did not interpret due process to affirm a positive right of access to public space, but avowed that it prohibited "interference" with meetings and distributing information there "in the broadest terms."[52]

Chief Justice Hughes's succinct concurrence illuminated the divide within the Supreme Court majority over how to approach federal judicial jurisdiction

Figure 9. Justice Harlan Fiske Stone. Library of Congress, Prints and Photographs Division, LC-USZ62-137254.

over speech and assembly freedoms. He agreed with both Roberts and Stone to affirm the lower courts' judgment in favor of an injunction and decree against Jersey City, but he split the difference on the constitutional issues. On one hand, he endorsed Roberts's opinion that discussing the NLRA was a protected privilege of U.S. citizenship. On the other hand, he concurred with Stone that the record did not show that CIO members were in fact denied that specific right by Jersey City, and consequently that federal jurisdiction for CIO members' speech and assembly rights lay on other grounds, presumably the due process clause.[53] Hughes thus reinforced the court's sanction against Jersey City for its abuses, and by doing so he solidified federal judicial support of civil liberties. Nonetheless, he left the constitutional rationale uncertain.

Even such an ambiguous endorsement of federal judicial authority did not get unanimous support. The two remaining Four Horsemen on the court, Justices McReynolds and Butler, each wrote short dissenting opinions that rejected federal judicial involvement in the case and called for vacating the district court decree that had restrained Jersey City. In an old-fashioned way, McReynolds decided that the district court should not have enjoined "the essential right of the municipality to control its own parks and streets." It was beyond the capacity of federal courts to manage such local affairs, which were best left to local officials. Besides, he said, the CIO-ACLU respondents should have pursued their claims in state courts, bringing them to the federal level only if national questions arose. Butler chimed in on grounds that the rule of *Davis v. Massachusetts* should have controlled the *Hague* case. In principle, he argued, the permit ordinance upheld in *Davis* was just like the meeting permit ordinance in *Hague*. He would not have voided the Jersey ordinance as Roberts had done. Together, he and McReynolds sought to sustain the old conservative jurisprudence articulated in Butler's *Near* dissent that federal courts should defer to state governments as the most appropriate bodies tending to the welfare of citizens, including the regulation of speech.[54] That McReynolds and Butler were outvoted in the *Hague* case, however, showed how the constitutional tide was turning. Changing law and court personnel supplanted their nineteenth-century view of federalism and advanced the rising twentieth-century philosophy that national courts should intervene on the state and local level as guardians of civil freedoms.

* * *

Given five opinions in *Hague v. CIO*, the U.S. Supreme Court sent a confusing message as to what the case actually decided. One thing was clear, as was seen at the time and is remembered today: the court reprimanded Mayor Hague's Jersey City and approved restraints on its abusive practices.

By a five-to-two margin, the court declared that Jersey City's meeting permit ordinance was unconstitutional, that the city had trampled on the rights of CIO members and their supporters, and consequently that those individuals were entitled to the protection of the U.S. district court's injunction and decree as modified by appellate courts. The court thus affirmed district court orders to stop Jersey City's "deportation" policy, enjoin its interference with the distribution of circulars and display of placards, and bar its enforcement of its unconstitutional meeting permit ordinance. The Supreme Court majority also upheld Third Circuit modification that proscribed Jersey City from preventing CIO gatherings by banning all meetings, in effect opening the city up to all public rallies held under reasonable conditions. And the high court excised those parts of the decree that spelled out terms of distributing flyers and securing meeting permits, thereby giving CIO members and their associates freedom to circulate handbills and organize peaceable rallies as they saw fit. The Supreme Court thus vindicated CIO members' public assembly and speech rights, subjecting those freedoms only to the restriction of lawful traffic regulations and arrest procedures. The decision delivered Jersey City a sharp political defeat and the CIO-ACLU respondents a clear victory.

Beyond this judgment, however, the Supreme Court's constitutional ruling in *Hague* was murky. As John A. McIntire and Charles S. Rhyne of the National Institute of Municipal Law Officers observed in 1939, the divergent *Hague* opinions contained "sharp differences in approach to the fundamental problems" of free speech and assembly, and consequently "made impossible [the] recognition of any one opinion as the authoritative pronouncement of the Court." On one hand, the two urbanologists asserted, Justice Roberts chose the narrow strategy of not overruling *Davis*'s view of a city's absolute proprietary ownership of public streets and parks, and only affirmed that cities' absolute authority was limited by citizens' privilege to assemble for discussion of national legislation. In effect, McIntire and Rhyne recognized that Roberts still adhered to old limits of municipal power analysis and had not fully embraced the modern understanding of civil liberties. On the other hand, the urbanologists acknowledged Justice Stone's broader view. Rather than rest speech and assembly rights on citizens' privileges and immunities, Stone placed the matter under the due process clause that guaranteed speech and assembly to all natural persons against state encroachment.[55] As they saw it, this division left in doubt both the constitutional extent of municipal power and the status of civil liberties.

Despite its doctrinal obliqueness, *Hague* gained a reputation as an important legal change. Modern legal observers have decided that *Hague* overruled *Davis* in substance, if not in name, sharply diminishing municipal power over public places, and liberating outdoor expressive rights. Indeed, modern scholars like Timothy Zick see *Hague* as notable for abandoning *Davis*'s conception of municipal ownership of public places and adopting the "trusteeship" view of public civil liberties instead. Moreover, commentators have concluded that Stone's *Hague* concurrence reinforced the jurisprudence of his *Carolene Products* footnote 4 and advanced the Supreme Court's "civil liberties revolution." In *Hague*, he used the due process clause to heighten judicial scrutiny over rights that needed safeguarding for democratic processes. This did not, however, expand labor rights. The *Hague* decision upheld CIO unionists' right to rally and speak in public places, but as citizens or persons rather than as labor organizers. It also set a precedent for using litigation to advance worker liberties but did not follow other contemporaneous labor cases that equated labor picketing with speech rights, addressed private, nongovernmental infringement on worker liberties, or most importantly, endorsed collective bargaining.[56] Legally, *Hague*'s legacy was complex. Yet, after the long, bitter, tumultuous street battle and court fight, observers then and today most remember the decision as a victory over Mayor Hague's authoritarian leadership and a validation of assembly and speech rights for workers and sympathizers.

# Epilogue

## *Aftermath and Legacy*

A few days after the U.S. Supreme Court announced its *Hague v. CIO* ruling, the *CIO News* published an editorial cartoon titled "Old Tanglefoot" capturing the newly renamed Congress of Industrial Organizations' (CIO) view of the case. The cartoon portrays an exasperated Frank Hague unsuccessfully trying to detach his feet from sticky flypaper labeled "Supreme Court Decision" and "Bill of Rights," while a gleeful CIO worker looks on.[1] The drawing inferred that the court's application of the Bill of Rights to the Jersey City situation had immobilized the lawless Hague and exonerated rights of CIO workers. It capsulized what would become the historical reputation of the *Hague* decision: the case affirmed basic American speech and assembly freedoms under the Bill of Rights and put the autocratic Mayor Hague squarely in his place. Democracy won; dictatorship lost.

"Old Tanglefoot" was good publicity but doubtful constitutional and political history. *Hague*'s legacy was more complicated than the drawing suggested. In a legal sense, the decision was certainly important for diminishing municipal police powers over urban streets and parks, and establishing a constitutional right to speak and assemble in public places—the so-called public-forum doctrine. Yet, the cartoon obscured the fact that Justice Owen Roberts's plurality opinion in *Hague* relied not on the Bill of Rights (the first ten amendments to the U.S. Constitution, especially the First Amendment), but on the privileges and immunities clause of the Fourteenth Amendment. It also obscured the fact that Roberts's plurality reasoning did not establish the modern constitutional basis for outdoor expressive rights, which later shifted to the First Amendment as incorporated into the Fourteenth Amendment due process clause, much as Justice Stone argued in his concurring opinion.

Figure 10. "Old Tanglefoot," partially inaccurate editorial cartoon celebrating the *Hague v. CIO* decision in the *CIO News*, June 12, 1939. Reproduced with permission from Special Collections and University Archives, University of Maryland Libraries.

Moreover, the *Hague* ruling did not affect the victors evenly. In the immediate aftermath of the decision, the CIO and its partners in the ACLU and the ABA appraised the meaning of *Hague* in their own separate ways, finding that the decision affected each group differently. Contrary to the implications of the "Old Tanglefoot" cartoon, *Hague* did not benefit worker rights to picket, organize, and bargain collectively—which courts partitioned off into a separate area of law—nearly as much as it helped popular movements to rally and speak in public places. *Hague*'s great legacy was for popular protest.

Most ironically, the *Hague* ruling had remarkably little effect on the target of the case, Mayor Frank Hague. Contrary to historical reputation, the *Hague* decision did not strike directly at Hague's political power and did not produce his immediate demise. Rather than dethroning the would-be autocrat, *Hague* caused the mayor to adapt to the new constitutional parameters of outdoor meetings, and to accept the CIO's presence in Jersey City. He persisted as Hudson County's Democratic boss until a new political coalition finally defeated his regime in 1949.

*Hague*'s complex impact quickly became apparent in its own time. Soon after the ruling, the *New York Times* assessed its ramifications for citizen rights, but not for organized labor. The *Times* detailed the Supreme Court's main holdings that Jersey City's meeting permit ordinance was unconstitutional and that the municipality might regulate outdoor rallies, but not absolutely prohibit use of streets and parks for public meetings. The *Times* also confirmed that the court plurality did not invoke the First Amendment to reach these conclusions, instead extending the Fourteenth Amendment for a second time (after *DeJonge*) to freedom of peaceable assembly. By doing so, a *Times* columnist explained, the Supreme Court affirmed Anglo-Saxon common law and U.S. constitutional principle. The public's right to speak in streets and parks, he quoted Justice Roberts as saying, was "immemorable," ignoring as Roberts did that cities had widely disparaged that right until the 1930s.[2]

Among the litigants, the decision's firsthand effect was to bring contrition from Jersey City and diverse forms of jubilation from the CIO, the ACLU, and the ABA. In Jersey City, counselor Charles Hershenstein issued a statement for Mayor Hague that recognized the U.S. Supreme Court decision as the final word on the matter, and promised full compliance with the ruling, although he confessed some uncertainty as to what the "numerous opinions" in the case meant. Meanwhile, CIO regional director William Carney characterized the decision politically as a "victory for the people" over fascism, declaring that "this decision is the opening gun in the fight to rid New Jersey of Hagueism." CIO-ACLU cocounsel Spaulding Frazer reacted in a more lawyerly way by stressing the Supreme Court's annulment of Jersey City's meeting permit ordinance, but his partner Morris Ernst echoed Carney's political remarks with typical flamboyance by asserting that the decision sent a warning to "little petty dictators" who occasionally "bobbed up" in America. In more measured tones, the ABA saw the decision as an opportunity to extend civil liberties. ABA Bill of Rights Committee chair Grenville Clark reacted to *Hague* by calling for the establishment of "Hyde Parks" in U.S. cities—that is, outdoor venues specially designated for public debate. Not everyone could rent a hall, he said, but anyone could mount a soapbox.[3]

Plotting by the CIO-ACLU respondents to exploit a favorable Supreme Court ruling dated back to April 1939. In the spirit of CIO-ACLU collaboration, ACLU counselor Ernst lunched with CIO president John L. Lewis to discuss plans to "capitalize on a victory" and consider "steps to be taken in case of defeat." Assuming victory, Lewis promised to "lay his hands on a couple of thousand of dollars" to support activities after the Supreme Court ruling, and Ernst agreed to draw up a detailed program. Still anticipating ACLU cooperation with labor groups, Ernst's ambitious plan envisioned a large campaign to test Jersey City's respect for civil liberties: mass circulation of literature on the streets, service of 25,000 copies of the federal court decree on Jersey City employers, radio broadcasts, meetings in rented halls and outdoor locations, relocation of the CIO's regional office from Newark to Jersey City, a robust union organizing drive, and a dramatic presentation of the federal court decree to city hall.[4]

Even in celebration, however, the ACLU and CIO soon went their separate ways. The immediate product of Ernst's advance planning was a mass outdoor meeting sponsored by the ACLU at Journal Square in Jersey City on June 12, 1939. Expressing its own libertarian version of Americanism, an ACLU press release described the rally as a demonstration that civil liberties were "at last established" in Jersey City and contended that such an event was "fundamental Americanism," not "radicalism or foreign doctrines" as the Hague administration had previously smeared it. As a sign of changing times, public safety director Daniel Casey courteously promised full cooperation when the ACLU and the NJCLU reached out to make arrangements.[5]

The ACLU's June 12 "monster public meeting" came off without a hitch with five thousand observers in attendance. Its speakers included nearly every prominent man (no women) harassed by Jersey City officials or police during the previous seven months, although neither CIO representatives nor Mayor Hague's Republican opponents showed up. The gathering signaled, as legal historian Laura Weinrib explains, that the ACLU would break away from its former labor allies in the aftermath of the *Hague* ruling. This was an ACLU rally celebrating the benefits of an impartial defense of free speech, although orators made a few last references to the labor struggle. ACLU attorney Arthur Garfield Hays stated that the U.S. Supreme Court decision marked a triumph for democracy by showing that "no one, not even the Mayor of Jersey City, is above the law." ACLU director Roger Baldwin followed by linking the free-speech issue explicitly to labor organizing, declaring that the real issue in the Jersey City struggle was not the right of communists to speak but the right of independent unions like the CIO to operate in the municipality. Socialist Norman Thomas then remarked that the monster meeting itself was a victory for speech and democracy, since Jersey City residents now had their rights "more firmly established."

Diverse speakers amplified these themes. The *Catholic Worker* editor William Callahan praised the victory over Mayor Hague's regime as a product of enlightened groups "sticking together," and he boldly urged the audience to use the triumph as a springboard for addressing other injustices in the United States, such as those suffered by immigrants and African Americans. Jersey City attorney Ashley Carrick mocked the "tranquility" that the city administration claimed to be defending, arguing that genuine free speech always generated some commotion. NJCLU chair Reverend Archey Ball characterized the Jersey City victory as a triumph for Christian values, since they could prevail only where discussion was open. WDL secretary Morris Milgram lauded the court decision as a victory for labor unions over Mayor Hague's effort to suppress them. Rabbi Benjamin Plotkin stated that the controversy left Jersey residents "fed up" with their notoriety, and he encouraged them to seize the occasion of the Supreme Court ruling to establish better community relations.[6]

Despite the victory celebration, legal gains remained limited, as Norman Thomas found out. Back in February 1939, Thomas had filed suit in New Jersey courts to secure a writ of mandamus ordering Director of Public Safety Daniel Casey to grant him a speaking permit under the Jersey City's 1930 ordinance. The New Jersey Supreme Court had refused to issue the writ, and then in the wake of the U.S. Supreme Court's *Hague* decision, the New Jersey Court of Errors and Appeals affirmed the lower court denial. Since the U.S. Supreme Court had voided the 1930 ordinance in *Hague*, the Court of Errors reasoned, there was no longer any valid law requiring Thomas to seek a permit.[7] *Hague* secured Thomas's speaking rights in Jersey City just as it did for everyone else, but it undercut his effort to get judicial relief specifically for himself.

Meanwhile, the CIO and its legal counsel Lee Pressman interpreted the implications of the *Hague* ruling very differently for organized labor. CIO press releases and articles in the *CIO News* agreed with the ACLU that the U.S. Supreme Court decision debarred Jersey City from a host of civil-liberties violations when it affirmed Judge Clark's district court decree. Far more impressive to the CIO and Pressman, however, were new federal legal remedies that the ruling created to protect union organizers from abuse on state and local levels. CIO leaders stressed that the Supreme Court upheld the jurisdiction of the federal courts to hear cases involving violations of workers' speech, press, and assembly rights, as well as rights to organize under the Wagner Act (NLRA), by virtue of the federal Civil Rights (Ku Klux Klan) Acts of 1870 and 1871. New forms of relief were available under those laws.

Workers could now seek federal court injunctions, file actions for damages, submit both civil and criminal charges, and seek help of U.S. district attorneys against abusive local officials. From the CIO perspective, *Hague* did not just defend civil liberties, but also improved labor organizers' legal standing to pursue their collective rights. *Hague* abetted the CIO's larger legal strategy to defend labor organizing by protecting worker civil liberties, an argument made in *Carlson v. California* (1940) to treat picketing as protected speech.[8]

CIO leaders argued, hence, that the *Hague* ruling had great implications for the labor movement. As Pressman saw it, *Hague* assured workers that they had "definite legal recourse to check the tyrannies by which [Mayor Hague] and other petty Hitlers have attempted to destroy the civil rights of American workers." Other "petty Hitlers" did emerge. Just the summer before *Hague* was decided, CIO operatives tried to enter New Orleans to organize workers as they had done in Jersey City, only—as in Jersey City—to meet a barrage of opposition from city police, employers, and local AFL unions. Employers signed closed-shop agreements with AFL unions, and then "lawless" police raided CIO headquarters, seized records, and then jailed eighty-four union members, including six female CIO office workers. Meanwhile, AFL "goon squads" lay in wait to harass and beat up CIO organizers, and police arrested others, promptly deporting them out of town. Arriving on the scene to assess the situation, Lee Pressman observed that "the situation smells strongly of similar tactics used by Mayor Frank Hague." A *CIO News* editorial cartoon portrayed a dark shadow cast over New Orleans by a vulture labeled "Spirit of Hague." Eventually, the National Labor Relations Board intervened in the struggle and staged a vote to determine union representation in New Orleans. The case showed that other antiunion trouble spots mirrored Jersey City's situation, but that union organizers could now seek federal remedies to break local antiunion resistance.[9]

Back in Jersey City, the CIO planned to take advantage of the Supreme Court's *Hague* decision. Vowing that the fight "has just started," regional director William Carney relocated CIO offices to Jersey City and announced a massive union organizing drive there with no particular reference to immigrant or black workers. There would, however, be no "mass invasion" as alleged in November 1937 to give "Hague stooges" a pretext to interfere. Moreover, Carney indicated plans to target the Hague regime politically, a standard CIO tactic to improve the political environment for union organizing. The CIO would team up with LNPL to beat Hague at the polls just as it beat him in court, and it would gather information to help the U.S. Justice Department's new Civil Liberties Unit to file criminal charges against the Hague administration for violating civil liberties. Meanwhile, Jersey CIO leaders warned that the *Hague* decision might push the mayor's operation "underground," so that surrogates like veterans could keep his regime's antiunion policy going.[10] Deep mistrust festered.

To kick off its campaign, the CIO staged its own rally at Jersey City's Pershing Field on June 27, 1939, with themes quite different from those at the earlier ACLU meeting. The event attracted between five thousand and eight thousand city residents—all without a permit, since the city's permit ordinance had been nullified. And while Jersey City assigned sixty police officers to patrol the gathering, four hundred CIO ushers easily kept order. Most important, CIO notables rather than civil libertarians appeared as speakers, although again they were all men, given the CIO's presumption of male leadership. With nary a mention of communist class struggle or racial justice, speakers urged the importance of the labor movement and the need for unions to eliminate Jersey City's "sweatshop menace." CIO vice president John Brophy offered the most scorching oration. He accused the Hague administration for serving as a mouthpiece for "labor-hating captains of finance," contending that the Supreme Court decision marked a victory over such antiunion forces as much as it marked a triumph for civil liberties. Now, with Hague beaten, he asserted, workers in Jersey could seek union recognition and better working conditions. Council member Leonard Goldsmith followed by contrasting the night's peaceful mass meeting to the police violence that greeted CIO organizers when they first arrived a few years before. Transport workers union president Michael Quill then characterized Jersey City as one of the last strongholds of antiunion employers that was finally giving way to enlightened labor relations. Regional director William Carney concluded with a pledge to bring CIO organization to Jersey City workers and, with that, "decent working conditions" at last. He closed the meeting by thanking Jersey City police officers who had been standing by quietly for their "cooperation." The crowd cheered as the officers escorted speakers safely to their cars.[11] The CIO event came off as the model of a peaceful, and constitutionally protected, labor rally.

Over time, however, *Hague* supported labor rights far less than it promoted popular civil liberties. CIO legal counselor Lee Pressman's expectation that Reconstruction-era civil rights laws would become a powerful tool for protecting labor organizers from local harassment did not materialize. Particularly, *Hague* suggested potential for section 1 of the 1871 Ku Klux Klan Act covering rights "secured" by federal law, which eventually became section 1983 in Title 42 of the U.S. Code, to give workers civil remedies for local officials' abuse of their civil rights. Shortly before the *Hague* ruling, the U.S. Justice Department's newly created Civil Rights Unit started enforcing that old measure, and after *Hague*, the CIO embraced it. Yet, the law had limited effect until the 1960s, when judicial reinterpretation reinvigorated it, though not for labor cases. In harbingers of change, the U.S. Supreme Court judged that Louisiana election officials' fraudulent ballot count was an infraction covered by the statute in *United States v. Classic* (1941), and decided that a Georgia sheriff's fatal beating of a black prisoner was so too in *Screws v. United States* (1945). Then in 1961, Justice William Douglas determined in *Monroe v. Pape* that police officers' warrantless entry into a Chicago home and physical abuse of its black residents constituted a section 1983 violation of constitutional rights. *Monroe* vastly expanded civil rights protection of racial minorities, prisoners, public employees, property owners, and others—though not labor organizers—from local police misconduct.[12]

Indeed, whatever promise that *Hague*-era jurisprudence held out for "labor speech," it fizzled in the long run. For a while after Franklin Roosevelt's landslide reelection as president in 1936, New Deal politics heightened the association of labor rights with free speech. Congress enacted, and the U.S. Supreme Court upheld, the NLRA sanctioning workers' right of self-organization, including rights to communicate in picketing, strikes, and collective bargaining. Congress also set up the La Follette Civil Rights Committee to investigate employer infringement on workers' expressive freedoms. Side by side these developments, the Supreme Court recognized speech components in peaceful labor picketing, breaking away from the historic view of *Truax v. Corrigan* (1921) that picketing was a kind of legal tort and a form of economic coercion. In *Thornhill v. Alabama* (1940), decided in tandem with the *Carlson* case, the court agreed that government could regulate picketing to serve economic stability, but it could not ban or interfere with picketing's speech elements unless they posed "a clear danger of some substantive evil." Nonetheless, with help of the conservative 1947 Taft-Hartley law, the court soon backtracked and limited its treatment of picketing as speech, nullifying picketing laced with violence, infused with intentions to influence third parties, or prone to unlawful purposes. In subsequent shopping mall cases, moreover, the court narrowed labor protestors' outdoor expressive rights on commercial property. In *Amalgamated Food Employees v. Logan Valley* (1968), it upheld picketing in a private plaza only because that area functioned as a public "community business block," and then in *Lechmere v. NLRB* (1992) it denied nonemployee union organizers' right to circulate handbills in a retail store's private parking lot. In the long run, the Supreme Court relegated public labor speech to the lowest rung of protection, retaining the view that it was primarily commercial and economic.[13]

While confining "labor speech," the U.S. Supreme Court simultaneously followed in the vein of the ACLU's and ABA's *Hague* arguments by broadening the public-expression rights of other groups whose speech was seemingly more political, beginning with Jehovah's Witnesses. In *Cantwell v. Connecticut* (1940), the court reversed Newton Cantwell's conviction for disturbing the peace when he proselytized his religion door-to-door and on the streets of New Haven, Connecticut, without first securing a license from city officials as required by state law. According to Justice Owen Roberts, the state statute's licensing requirement and its local administration violated Cantwell's First Amendment religious freedoms as embraced by the "liberty" concept in the Fourteenth Amendment's due process clause. Then, in *Cox v. New Hampshire* (1941), the Supreme Court faced the threshold question as to whether municipalities still retained the power to require permits, a kind of "prior restraint" for Jehovah's Witnesses who conducted an "information march" along a city street in Manchester, New Hampshire. Distinguishing it from Jersey City's meeting permit ordinance, which allowed the public safety director to deny permits for vague concerns about "riots, disturbances or disorderly assemblage," Chief Justice Charles Evans Hughes upheld a state statute here that allowed cities to require permits that imposed time, place, and manner regulations, so long as those regulations did not infringe on speakers' messages. Then, more like *Cantwell* in *Niemotko v. Maryland* (1951), new chief justice Fred Vinson ruled for a unanimous Supreme Court that a Havre de Grace, Maryland, park commissioner's refusal to issue a permit for the Jehovah's Witnesses to conduct Bible talks in public parks infringed on their First Amendment religious freedom rights as incorporated into the Fourteenth Amendment. Justice Felix Frankfurter's concurrence in *Niemotko* outlined circumstances (such as traffic or the mode of communication) under which cities might legitimately impose regulations. In the Jehovah's Witnesses cases, hence, the Supreme Court sustained *Hague*'s idea of an "immemorial" right to speak and meet in urban public spaces, now squarely basing it on the Fourteenth Amendment due process clause.[14] Labor rights were not involved.

In his *Cox v. New Hampshire* ruling, Chief Justice Hughes articulated the new philosophy according to which the U.S. Supreme Court recalibrated the reach of municipal powers to regulate public speech and assembly after *Hague*. Hughes demonstrated that the Court had hardly dismissed cities' need to carry out certain order-keeping functions, but now searched for a new balance between reduced city police powers and increased recognition of civil liberties. While acknowledging the people's constitutional right to speak and assemble in public places, Hughes contended that such a right depended on "the existence of an organized society maintaining public order." Control of city traffic, for instance, was a familiar way that municipalities kept order. The question for cases involving street parades, processions, or other expressive uses of public space, he concluded, was whether control by local officers "is exerted so as not to deny or unwarrantedly abridge the right of assembly and the opportunities for the communication of thought and the discussion of public questions immemorally associated with the resort to public places."[15] Assembly rights were presumed; regulation needed justification.

The balance between speech and assembly rights versus municipalities' legitimate order-keeping functions—the central issue in *Hague*—persisted in civil rights cases during the 1960s, again with *Hague*'s labor dimensions long forgotten. In *Edwards v. South Carolina* (1963), Justice Potter Stewart for the U.S. Supreme Court struck down the Palmetto state's arrest, conviction, and punishment of African American civil rights protestors who demonstrated peacefully on state capitol grounds as an infringement of their rights of speech, assembly, and petition under the First and Fourteenth Amendments. Eerily like *Hague*, authorities in this case argued that the demonstrators threatened to provoke a breach of peace, requiring state intervention, but Stewart determined that facts did not show provocations warranting an exception to protestors' right to express themselves on public property. Similarly in *Cox v. Louisiana* (1965), Justice Arthur Goldberg decided that black civil rights advocate Elton Cox's arrest and conviction for leading a demonstration across the street from a Baton Rouge courthouse was also an encroachment of free speech and assembly rights under the First and Fourteenth Amendments. While reiterating Hughes's *Cox v. New Hampshire* language that the guarantee of liberty implies "the existence of an organized society maintaining public order," Goldberg still determined that Louisiana's breach of peace statute was overly broad and Cox's group showed no evidence of disorder. Only in *Adderly v. Florida* (1966) did a divided Supreme Court draw the line. In this case, Justice Hugo Black for a narrow 5–4 majority determined that protest on the premises of a jail constituted a trespass on county property under the state's trespass law, and consequently that the rights to free speech and assembly did not apply at that location. Jail property was not like the public grounds outside of a state capitol or city courthouse.[16] Perhaps, as some commentators observe, Black's ruling and slim majority in *Adderly* marked the court's backlash against the civil rights movement's "excessive civil disorder," but his opinion here as well as those in *Edwards* and *Cox v. Louisiana* show that the Supreme Court still labored to balance city police powers and civil liberties in public places.

Beyond the civil rights era, the American public protest tradition continued to challenge courts and municipal authorities to implement the *Hague* policy—that is, to reconcile the municipal duty to provide public safety with the popular right to assemble and speak in public places. Liberal civil rights, anti–Vietnam War, women's rights, gay rights, and environmental protests of the 1960s and early 1970s gave way to conservative antitax, antibusing, antiabortion, and indeed neo-Nazi and "alt-right" demonstrations through the late 1900s into the early 2000s. The same old legal dilemmas persisted. And both courts and lawmakers, according to law professor Timothy Zick, expanded regulation of public space in the wake of social change. The U.S. Supreme Court gradually circumscribed the definition of public places, encompassing streets, parks, and sidewalks but ruling out airports and private shopping malls. Moreover, courts accepted cities' authority to require assembly and parade permits, request general liability bonds, impose clean-up fees, and apply "time, place, and manner" restrictions. The threshold question always remained as to when officials could interfere with presumed public-assembly rights to prevent violence. In the notorious August 2017 "Unite the Right" demonstration in Charlottesville, Virginia, for instance, White Nationalists properly secured a meeting permit (upheld in court) to protest removal of a Confederate statue, but they arrived conspicuously armed and chanting provocative slogans. An ugly melee followed.[17] Had these marchers exceeded the bounds of the fundamental right of outdoor expression? The legal shadow of *Hague* still hangs over modern social activism.

Paradoxically, the *Hague* decision had least long-term effect on its most visible aspect—politics. The decision did not deliver the crushing political blow to Mayor Hague that the CIO and ACLU had desired. Demonstrating urban bosses' typical adaptability—had not Chicago boss Edward Kelly reversed his stand in favor of organized labor after the 1937 Memorial Day Massacre?—Hague accommodated CIO leaders, much as he had mended relations with presidential candidate Franklin Roosevelt back in 1932 after initially opposing FDR's nomination. In early August 1939, at the request of CIO representative Albert Smith, Hague officials brought astonished CIO leaders to city hall for cordial discussions. Escorted to Hague's inner sanctum on the second floor, they were greeted by the mayor's nephew Frank Hague Eggers with warm handshakes and by Deputy Mayor John Malone with the promise that "the doors of City Hall are always open to you." Smith and electrical workers union head Thomas Niels then asked Hague officials to assist in resolving a local labor dispute. And they did. Local 421 of the United Electrical, Radio and Machine Workers had threatened a strike over a H. Goodwin and Sons wage cut, but under orders from Mayor Hague, public safety director Daniel Casey brought the two sides together to negotiate. His mediation forestalled a strike and deferred a wage reduction.[18]

CIO leaders reasoned that this unexpected overture was good politics on both sides. With the 1940 presidential election coming up, CIO officials speculated that Hague had decided to get on the CIO's good side to secure political support for his faction of the Democratic party. More important, CIO leaders recognized that Republicans who had supported them during the Hague controversy were not really their friends, given the Republican Party's antilabor national platform. The CIO would rather work with local Democrats, even with the Hague administration. The rapprochement made political sense, like Hague's earlier alliance with AFL unions in the 1920s.[19] Could it happen again?

So it seemed. In July 1939, Jersey City enacted a new public-meeting ordinance that the ABA praised as "a model municipal enactment." Even the ACLU agreed that "'Jersey City [was] Open to Free Assembly.'" In addition, Mayor Hague incorporated the CIO into his political coalition, naming as "labor advisor" none other than Morris Isserman, brother of Newark labor law attorney Abraham Isserman, whom Hague had earlier lambasted as the "Red counsel." Hague's actions typified his practice of "penetration and permeation," as political scientist Richard Connors called it, wherein the mayor "penetrat[ed] the formal and informal institutions of the community, and either [tied] them to his regime as satellites or neutraliz[ed] them as political forces." Indeed, when Hague ran for reelection, the CIO endorsed his candidacy. Seemingly a turnabout, these developments showed that the *Hague v. CIO* controversy had never been just a front for business hostility to industrial unionism and civil liberties, but was instead a conflict about urban political power. Hague adapted to new power realities in his customary way.[20]

In the new political and legal environment, the CIO made progress toward "converting Hague's Jersey City into a union town," even though Jersey's diversified economy of small manufacturers was not entirely hospitable to industrial unionism. While the accommodation with Hague eventually caused the CIO to forgo its political activities with the LNPL, CIO operatives organized a dye company, gypsum works, cosmetics factories, and the Westinghouse Elevator plant, among other firms, and notably won strikes and established unions at several notorious runaway sweatshops at Harborside. Moreover, the New Jersey CIO moved offices to Jersey City, and the state CIO council, shipbuilder unions, and steel worker unions held annual conventions there. So entrenched did the CIO become in Jersey City that its state council sponsored a big World War II–era war bond rally there in 1943, a display of "working-class Americanism" in what had earlier been Hague's exclusive lair of ethnic politics.[21]

Meanwhile, Hague's administration prospered for a time, but then disintegrated for reasons largely unrelated to the CIO drive. At the presidential level, Jersey City's ugly battle with the CIO eroded FDR's respect for Hague, leading the president to quietly back Democratic former Secretary of the Navy Charles Edison for governor in 1940. Governor Edison turned out to be an implacable Hague foe, depriving the mayor of his former influence in state politics, but Roosevelt never opposed Hague openly and the mayor survived as he always had on his local organization's muscle. Yet, even here, Hague's power dwindled. A more diverse and cosmopolitan wartime generation of Jersey City voters came of age in the 1940s, while Mayor Hague's previous mastery of ethnic politics stagnated. Relying on Irish loyalists to the end, the mayor did not refresh his machine's ranks with younger people, failed adequately to nurture ethnic outsiders, let city services deteriorate, and became an absentee mayor doing business by telephone from the Jersey shore and Florida vacation spots. After he relegated the mayoralty to his able nephew Frank Hague Eggers in 1947, Hague's regime collapsed in 1949 when dissident Second Ward Irishman John Kenny assembled a rival coalition of disaffected Democrats, Republicans, Italians, and Poles—but still not black voters—and ousted Hague's slate from power.[22]

*Hague v. CIO*'s legacy thus differs from its reputation. Shaped by politics of the late 1930s, especially the debate between anticommunist and antifascist partisans of the time, reputation recalls the Hague-CIO affair as a political battle between the champions of democratic civil liberties and a homegrown practitioner of tyranny, a battle that Mayor Hague lost decisively. Actually, Hague endured politically even as CIO workers triumphed in Jersey City. And the *Hague* ruling did little for labor rights per se. What the *Hague* case changed most was the constitutional structure of power surrounding municipalities' regulation of public expression. Gone were old principles of the pre–*Hague* era that allowed cities draconian authority to police outdoor activities in the name of public order. After *Hague*, urban power was reduced to trusteeship for the people's speech and assembly rights that were now protected by federal courts. Mayor Hague's regime carried on, but the *Hague* decision bequeathed a new era of legally protected civil liberties in public urban settings for workers and everyone else.

# Notes

## *Abbreviations*

| | |
|---|---|
| ACLU Papers | American Civil Liberties Union Records, Public Policy Papers, Department of Rare Books and Collections, Princeton University Library, Princeton, NJ. |
| AFL-CIO Records | George Meany Memorial AFL-CIO Archives, Special Collections and University Archives, University of Maryland Libraries, College Park, MD. |
| Frank Hague Collection | Frank Hague Collection. New Jersey Room, Jersey City Free Public Library, Jersey City, NJ. |
| *Hague* case file | Frank Hague et al. v. Committee for Industrial Organization, et al., Supreme Court of the United States, Case File, October Term 1938, No. 651. |
| Jersey City Commission Minutes | Jersey City Board of Commissioners Minutes New Jersey Room, Jersey City Free Public Library, Jersey City, NJ. |
| National (Wickersham) Commission | National Commission on Law Enforcement and Observance. Montclair, NJ: Patterson Smith Publishing Corporation, 1968, originally published by the U.S. Government Printing Office, 1931. Various reports. |
| TR | Transcript of record in *Hague* case file. |
| Vanderbilt Papers | Arthur T. Vanderbilt Political, Professional and Judicial Papers, Special Collections and Archives, Olin Library, Wesleyan University, Middletown, CT. |

## *Introduction*

1. Testimony of Jules Nydes, TR 1, 346–48; testimony of Morris Milgram, TR 1, 403–4, 412; testimony of David Clendennin, TR 1, 217–19; testimony of Aaron Gilmartin, TR 1, 358–59; testimony of Samuel Macri, TR 2, 917–19, all in *Hague* case file.

2. Macri testimony, TR 2, 918; testimony of Dan Foley, TR 1, 178–82; Gilmartin testimony, TR 1, 360; testimony of Nancy Cox, TR 1, 310; testimony of James Sweeney, TR 1, 287; Clendennin testimony, TR 1, 219; Plaintiffs' exhibit P-1, TR 4, 1, all in *Hague* case file.

3. Sweeney testimony, TR 1, 287; Foley testimony, TR 1, 182–83; Nydes testimony, TR 1, 348; "Labor March on Jersey City Ends without Disorder," *Jersey Observer*, November 29, 1937, 1, 12.

4. Sweeney testimony, TR 1, 287–91; Foley testimony, TR 1, 182–85; Morris Milgram testimony, TR 1, 403–4; Gilmartin testimony, TR 1, 360–62; Cox testimony, TR 1, 311; Clendennin testimony, TR 1, 220–23.

5. Clendennin testimony, TR 1, 223–26; Sweeney testimony, TR 1, 291–95; Cox testimony, TR 1, 311–12; Gilmartin testimony, TR 1, 363–65; testimony of Grace Milgram, TR 1, 414–16, *Hague* case file; Foley testimony, TR 1, 187–90; "Labor March," 12.

6. Hague v. CIO, 307 U.S. 496 (1939).

7. On *Hague* and the public-forum doctrine, see Zick, *Speech Out of Doors*, 184–86.

8. Hall, *American Patriotism, American Protest*; Lumsden, *Rampant Women*; Rabban, *Free Speech in Its Forgotten Years*, 77–128; Zick, *Speech Out of Doors*, 36–51. Although the ACLU led litigation, this book uses the acronym "CIO-ACLU" to indicate CIO and ACLU partnership in the *Hague* case.

9. The basis for Hague scholarship remains McKean, *The Boss*. See also Casebeer, "Public . . . Since Time Immemorial"; Connors, *A Cycle of Power*; Fisher, *On the Irish Waterfront*, ch. 3; Gibbons, "*Hague v. CIO*"; Dorsett, *Franklin D. Roosevelt and the City Bosses*, 84–93; Fleming, "The Political Machine II"; Hart, *The Last Three Miles*, 75–85, 148–151, and *American Dictators*; Isserman, "CIO v. Hague"; Kaplan, "The Great Civil Rights Case of *Hague v. CIO*"; N. Johnson, *Battleground New Jersey*; Steinberg, *The Bosses*, 10–58; Vernon, *The Life & Times of Jersey City Mayor Frank Hague*, 10–19; Weinrib, *The Taming of Free Speech*, 226–69. On mayoral reputations, see Holli, *The American Mayor*, 12–13.

10. Strum, *When Nazis Came to Skokie*, 36–46; Zick, *Speech Out of Doors*, 144–81; Delgado and Stefancic, *Must We Defend Nazis?*, 1–18.

11. Finan, *From the Palmer Raids to the Patriot Act*, 27–33, 112–15; P. Hoffer, W. Hoffer, and Hull, *The Federal Courts*, 196–200, 240–53; Leuchtenburg, *The Supreme Court Reborn*, 237–43; Pfohl, "*Hague v. CIO* and the Roots of the Public Forum Doctrine"; Rabban, *Free Speech*, 14–19, 77–128, 165–68; Zick, *Speech Out of Doors*, 183–86. The *Herald-Tribune* is quoted from Weinrib, *Taming*, 228.

12. Callow, *The City Boss in America*, 10–11, 51–55; Colburn and Pozzetta, "Bosses and Machines"; Chudacoff and Smith, *The Evolution of Urban Society*, 157–64; Miller, *The Urbanization of Modern America*, 99–105; Mohl, *The New City*, 85–90, 100–7; Stave, *The New Deal and the Last Hurrah*, 3–9; Stave et al., "A Reassessment of the Urban Political Boss."

13. Barrett, *The Irish Way*, 26–31, 196–224; Boyer, *Urban Masses and Moral Order in America, 1820–1920*, 197–99, 282; Porter, *Mary Norton of New Jersey*, 10–11; Callow, *City Boss*, 9; Chudacoff and Smith, *Evolution*, 174–88; Connors, *Cycle of Power*, 35,

55–56, 72–74; Erie, *Rainbow's End*, 6–23; McKean, *Boss*, 202; Miller, *Urbanization*, 105–7.

14. Fogelson, *Big-City Police*, 151–71; Hart, *American Dictators*, 118–19; Hart, *Last Three Miles*, 80; M. Johnson, *Street Justice*, 119–48; Vernon, *Life & Times*, 59; Walker, *Popular Justice*, 173–77.

15. Abernathy, *The Right of Assembly and Association*, 27–53; Leuchtenburg, *Supreme Court Reborn*, 243–46; Rabban, *Free Speech*, 342–71; Walker, *In Defense of American Liberties*, 51–55, 68–70, 77–81; Gitlow v. New York, 268 U.S. 652 (1925); Whitney v. California, Justice Brandeis concurring, 274 U.S. 357 (1927); Weinrib, *Taming*, 1, 80–81, 83–84, 105–45.

16. Hart, *American Dictators*, 47, 114–18; Hart, *Last Three Miles*, 76, 83–85; N. Johnson, *Battleground New Jersey*, 86–92; McKean, *The Boss*, 69–71.

17. Morris Milgram testimony, TR 1, 421–22.

18. Bernstein, *The Lean Years*, 83–173, 335–53; Bernstein, *Turbulent Years*, 37–170; Casebeer, "Public," 150; L. Cohen, *Making a New Deal*, 323–24, 346–47; Connors, *Cycle of Power*, 93, 99–100; Gerstle, *Working-Class Americanism*, 5, 155, 166–75; Varacalli, "Ethnic Politics in Jersey City," 8–9; Troy, *Organized Labor in New Jersey*, 69–124; Zieger, *The CIO, 1935–1955*, 22–59, 66–81.

19. See Barrett, *Irish Way*, 230–31; Fischer, *Spider Web*, xv–xvii, 26–27, 80–94; Heale, "Citizens versus Outsiders," 46–63, Goodall, "Red Herrings?," 77–102, Pearson, "Fighting the 'Red Danger,'" 135–60, Ruotsila, "Leftward Ramparts," 165–93, and the introduction, all in Goldstein, *Little "Red Scares"*; Luff, *Commonsense Anticommunism*, 129–51; Schrecker, *Many Are the Crimes*, 4–15, 61–84.

20. Finan, *From the Palmer Raids*, 27–37; Leuchtenburg, *Supreme Court Reborn*, 237–45; Rabban, *Free Speech*; Walker, *In Defense*, 79–81.

21. Finan, *From the Palmer Raids*, 38–50, 109–15; Forbath, *Law and the Shaping of the American Labor Movement*, 98–127; Walker, *In Defense*, 51–55; Weinrib, *Taming*, 129–37; Weinrib, "Against Intolerance," 13–18.

22. Finan, *From the Palmer Raids*, 115–30, Walker, *In Defense*, 72–92; Weinrib, *Taming*, 183–225, and "Against Intolerance," 22–23; Cottrell, *Roger Nash Baldwin and the American Civil Liberties Union*, 167–68.

23. Franczak, "The Fascist Game"; Klehr, *The Heyday of American Communism*, 210–11; J. Ross, *The Socialist Party of America*, 328–87; Swanberg, *Norman Thomas*, 190–224; Vials, *Haunted by Hitler*, 3–6, 33–58; Weinrib, *Taming*, 244–51.

24. Connors, *Cycle of Power*, 87; N. Johnson, *Battleground New Jersey*, 99–104.

25. See Larson, *Summer for the Gods*, 170–93.

26. Pfohl, "*Hague v. CIO*," 560–66. Abernathy, *Right of Assembly*, 115–28; Berman, "A New Deal for Speech"; Bernstein, *Turbulent Years*, 671–78; Casebeer, "Public," 174–77; Cortner, *The Supreme Court and the Second Bill of Rights*, 83–96; P. Hoffer, W. Hoffer, and Hull, *Federal Courts*, 291–98; Kaplan, "Great Civil Rights Case," 921–23, 929–31; Leuchtenburg, *Supreme Court Reborn*, 245–52; Parrish, *The Hughes Court*, 43–45; McIntire and Rhyne, "Civil Liberties and Municipal Powers"; Pfohl, "*Hague v. CIO*," 560–66; W. Ross, *The Chief Justiceship of Charles Evans Hughes*, 172–95; Walker,

*In Defense*, 106–7; Weinrib, *Taming*, 262–65; Zick, *Speech Out of Doors*, 185–86; U.S. v. Carolene Products Co., 304 U.S. 144, 152 (1938).

27. Rollin Kirby cartoon in *Judge Clark's Injunction against Mayor Hague* (ACLU pamphlet), November 1938, in Frank Hague Collection; Weinrib, *Taming*, 267–69; Walker, *In Defense*, 110–11.

28. "Jersey City's Mayor Hague," 45.

## *Chapter 1. The Rise of Boss Hague: Municipal Politics and Civil Liberties in the Old Era*

1. "Powers of Police Limited by Court," *Trenton Evening News*, August 2, 1920, 1; "Powers of Police," *Trenton Evening News*, August 5, 1920, 2; "In the Field of Labor," *Iron Age*, August 26, 1920, 529; Collins v. Cody, 95 N.J.L. 65, 67–68 (1920).

2. Isserman, "CIO v. Hague," 14–15.

3. Table 14, "Population of the 100 Largest Urban Places: 1910," in Gibson, *Population of the 100 Largest Cities and Other Urban Places in the United States*, www.census.gov/population/www/documentation/twps0027/tab14.txt, accessed July 30, 2015; table 39, "Comparative Summary for 1914, 1909 and 1904," in U.S. Department of Commerce, *Census of Manufacturers*, 928; Vernon, *The Life & Times of Jersey City Mayor Frank Hague*, 28–30; Fisher, ch. 2 of *On the Irish Waterfront*; Hart, *The Last Three Miles*, 33–34, 37.

4. Vernon, *Life & Times*, 26–28; Hart, *Last Three Miles*, 36–37; Barrett, *The Irish Way*, 197–202, 205; Varacalli, "Ethnic Politics in Jersey City," 6–8; table 5, "Composition and Characteristics of the Population for Ward and Cities of 50,000 or More," U.S. Department of Commerce, *Thirteenth Census (1910)*, Statistics for New Jersey, 602.

5. Chudacoff and Smith, *The Evolution of Urban Society*, 157–64; Erie, *Rainbow's End*, 7–14; Mohl, *The New City*, 83–84, 106–7; Callow, *The City Boss in America*, 51–55; Miller, *The Urbanization of Modern America*, 99–105; Stave, *The New Deal and the Last Hurrah*, 3–12. Steinberg, *The Bosses*, 10.

6. Barrett, *Irish Way*, 26–30; Erie, *Rainbow's End*, 11, 19–22; McKean, *The Boss*, 5–7, 16–19, 27–29; Hart, *Last Three Miles*, 38–43; Hart, *American Dictators*, 12–23; Dorsett, "Frank Hague, Franklin Roosevelt, and the Politics of the New Deal," 24–25; Vernon, *Life & Times*, 37–51.

7. Dorsett, "Frank Hague," 25–26; Foster, "The Early Career of Frank Hague," 4, 73–78; Holli, *The American Mayor*, 55–56; Vernon, *Life & Times*, 51–52; Chiles, *The Revolution of '28*, 11–32.

8. Mohl, *New City*, 118–19; Grundy, *The History of Jersey City*, 51; Hart, *Last Three Miles*, 14–15; Hart, *American Dictators*, 23–26; Connors, *A Cycle of Power*, 29–33; Vernon, *Life & Times*, 51–55.

9. M. Flanagan, *America Reformed*, 81–86; Miller, *Urbanization*, 105–7; Chudacoff and Smith, *Evolution*, 174–78; Mohl, *New City*, 115–33; Boyer, *Urban Masses and Moral Order in America, 1820–1920*, 197–99, 282; front cover, *Jersey City Commission Minutes*, 1913–14.

10. DiGaetano, "Urban Political Reform," 41–44; Callow, *City Boss*, 55, 71–73, 75; Connors, *Cycle of Power*, 94–97; Fleming, "The Political Machine II," 37; Hart, *Last Three Miles*, 76; Holli, *American Mayor*, 41–42, 97–100; L. Cohen, *Making a New Deal*, 259–60; table 12, "Foreign White Stock, by Nationality," 136, and table 5, "Composition and Characteristics of the Population for Wards of Cities of Cities of 50,000 or More," 152, both in U.S. Department of Commerce, *Thirteenth Census*, vol. 3, *Population*; table 8, "Nativity and Parentage of the Foreign Stock," in U.S. Department of Commerce, *Sixteenth Census (1940), Population, Nativity and Parentage*, 77; table C-35, "Age by Race and Sex for Jersey City," in U.S. Department of Commerce, *Sixteenth Census (1940), Population*, vol. 2, *Characteristics of the Population*, 917.

11. Fogelson, *Big-City Police*, 17–34, 42–60, 110–14; Walker, *Popular Justice*, 56–65, 133–60.

12. *Jersey City Commission Minutes*, June 17, 1913, 15–16; KcKean, *The Boss*, 38–40; Foster, "Early Career," 87–95; Hart, *Last Three Miles*, 45; Steinberg, *Bosses*, 26–28; Vernon, *Life & Times*, 56–61.

13. "Monahan Put Back as Chief of Police," *New York Times*, May 25, 1915, 7; "New Charges by Hague in Monahan Case," *Jersey Journal*, June 3, 1915, 1; "To Settle Who 'Framed-Up' in Monahan Case," *Jersey Journal*, June 4, 1915, 1, 2; editorial, "Trial of Patrolman Butler," *Jersey Journal*, June 4, 1915, 4; *Jersey City Commission Minutes*, June 25, 1915, 66–67, October 16, 1916, 167; "Hague Bans Chief Monahan as Candidate," *Jersey Journal*, October 11, 1916, 1, 10.

14. "Hague Hotly Defies PBA," *Jersey Journal*, May 1, 1917, 4; Connors, *Cycle of Power*, 38–39; McKean, *The Boss*, 40; Steinberg, *Bosses*, 26–28; "Moran, Favored by Witnesses, Records, Guilty," *Jersey Journal*, October 14, 1916, 1, 3; "Lieut. Moran Reduced to Rank of Patrolman," *Jersey Journal*, October 19, 1916, 1, 3; editorial, "Commissioner Hague's Mistake," *Jersey Journal*, October 19, 1916, 4; Editorial, "The Moran Case," *Jersey Journal*, October 21, 1916, 4?; "Precinct Captains Must Now Join in 'Gumshoe' Work," *Jersey Journal*, June 8, 1915, 1. The Jersey City Commission repeatedly sought review of police officer applications for retirement on disability. See, e.g., *Jersey City Commission Minutes*, December 9, 1915, 461–62; Vernon, *Life & Times*, 59.

15. *Jersey City Commission Minutes*, September 9, 1915, 287; "Ziegener Again Asks Hague as to $14,000 Fund," *Jersey Journal*, September 4, 1915, 1, 3; "Cops Want Right to Hit Back at Superiors," *Jersey Journal*, September 10, 1915, 1,4; editorial, "Probing the Police Funds," *Jersey Journal*, September 10, 1915, 6; "PBA Selects This City for Convention," *Jersey Journal*, September 23, 1915, 9.

16. Ad, "Let the People of Jersey City Look Facts Squarely in the Face," *Jersey Journal*, May 2, 1917, 6; "Hague Hotly Defies PBA"; ad, "The Real Issue," *Jersey Journal*, May 3, 1917, 6.

17. Walker, *Popular Justice*, 167–69; "Cops Here in Move to Form Labor Union," *Jersey Journal*, July 31, 1919, 1; ad, "Real Issue"; Fisher, *Irish Waterfront*, ch. 2; Vernon, *Life & Times*, 61–64; "Average Majority Hague Ticket, 42,008," *Jersey Journal*, May 11, 1921, 1; editorial, "A Big Vote of Confidence," *Jersey Journal*, May 11, 1921, 6; *Jersey City Commission Minutes*, May 15, 1917, 602.

18. On varying assessments of Hague's early politics, see Foster, "Early Career," 4; Steinberg, *Bosses*, 26–38; Hart, *Last Three Miles*, 47; Grundy, *History*, 53–55. On the historiography of city bossism, consult Mohl, *New City*, 85–90; Stave et al. "A Reassessment of the Urban Political Boss," esp. 301–3; Colburn and Pozzetta, "Bosses and Machines."

19. Erie, *Rainbow's End*, 83–84; Connors, *Cycle of Power*, 46–48, 58–60; ad, "Efficiency and Progressiveness Are the Things that Count in Municipal Affairs," *Jersey Journal*, May 7, 1921, 8; *Jersey City Commission Minutes*, May 17, 1921, 728; edited typescript, "Mayor Hague's Address at Wildwood, October 26 1934," 1, Frank Hague Collection.

20. Boyer, *Urban Masses*, 170–71, 176–79, 197–99; Hart, *Last Three Miles*, 45–46, 78–80; Hart, *American Dictators*, 33–38; Grundy, *History*, 52; Connors, *Cycle of Power*, 56; ad, "Real Issue."

21. Barrett, *Irish Way*, 62; Connors, *Cycle of Power*, 35, 56–60, 72–74, 83–86; McKean, *The Boss*, 159–63; Porter, *Mary Norton of New Jersey*, 9–11; J. Owen Grundy to Richard J. Connors, February 17, 1965, Frank Hague Collection; Steinberg, *Bosses*, 46; Hart, *American Dictators*, 37–38; Fisher, *Irish Waterfront*, ch. 2; Varacalli, "Ethnic Politics," 7; "Mayor Hague's Address," 1, 7.

22. Rabban, *Free Speech in its Forgotten Years*, 5, 129–76; Pfohl, "*Hague v. CIO* and the Roots of the Public Forum Doctrine," 533–55.

23. Zick, *Speech Out of Doors*, 26–33; Rabban, *Free Speech*, 23–128; ch. 239, *Acts of the One Hundred and Twenty-Second Legislature of the State of New Jersey*, 1898; Lumsden, *Rampant Women*, 23–51.

24. Davis v. Massachusetts, 167 U.S. 43, 43–48 (1897); Zick, *Speech Out of Doors*, 34–35; Rabban, *Free Speech*, 165–67.

25. Pfohl, "*Hague v. CIO*," 538–44, 546–52, quotations on 540–41 and 538.

26. Zick, *Speech Out of Doors*, 43–44; Rabban, *Free Speech*, 77–128; Dubofsky, *We Shall Be All*, 173–97; Wertheimer, "Free Speech Fights," 133–237; Haywood v. Ryan, 85 N.J.L. 116, 116–19 (1913).

27. Rabban, *Free Speech*, 110–16; *Jersey City Commission Minutes*, January 22, 1924, 473.

28. Rabban, *Free Speech*, 126–28.

29. Ibid., 98, 116–25.

30. State v. Scott, 86 N.J.L. 133, 133–39 (1914); State v. Quinlan, 86 N.J.L. 120, 124–26 (1914); State v. Boyd, 86 N.J.L. 75, 76–78 (1914); Rabban, *Free Speech*, 119–21; State v. Tony Tachin and Fred Fedodoff, 92 N.J.L. 269, 270–77 (1919).

31. Abernathy, *The Right of Assembly and Association*, 19–27; Harwood v. Trembley, 97 N.J.L. 173, 174–77 (1921).

32. State v. John C. Butterworth, et al., 104 N.J.L. 43, 44–47 (1927); State v. Butterworth, et al., 104 N.J.L. 579, 581–90 (1928); Abernathy, *Right of Assembly*, 27–40; N. Johnson, *Battleground New Jersey*, 48–51.

33. *Jersey City Commission Minutes*, January 21, 1920, 452, April 15, 1930, 579–80.

34. Tanenhaus, "Picketing as Free Speech," 400–402; Forbath, *Law and the Shaping of the American Labor Movement*, 108–9; American Steel Foundries v. Tri-City Trades

Council, 257 U.S. 184, 204–7 (1921); Truax v. Corrigan, 257 U.S. 312, 328–29, 337 (1921); Troy, *Organized Labor in New Jersey*, 95–96; "Hoffman Ignores Peaceful Sit-Ins," *New York Times*, March 18, 1937, 2; Plaintiffs' exhibit P-38, TR 4, 45, in *Hague* case file.

35. Grundy to Connors, 11; Grundy, *History*, 55; McKean, *The Boss*, 163, 216–17; Connors, *Cycle of Power*, 72–73, 74, 77; Hart, *Last Three Miles*, 46, 79; Holli, *American Mayor*, 68.

36. Fogelson, *Big-City Police*, 111–12; Fleming, "Political Machine," 35; Hart, *Last Three Miles*, 80; M. Johnson, *Street Justice*, 109–11.

37. Barrett, *Irish Way*, 201, 209–10; Fogelson, *Big-City Police*, 20, McKean, *The Boss*, 40; Connors, *Cycle of Power*, 119–22; J. Owen Grundy, "Before 1949: Thirty Years War on Hagueism," undated and unpublished manuscript, 5–7, Frank Hague Collection.

38. Boyer, *Urban Masses*, 287–88; Walker, *Popular Justice*, 170–84; National (Wickersham) Commission, *Report No. 14, Report on Police*, 140.

39. Finan, *From the Palmer Raids to the Patriot Act*, 113; "Hoboken Police Cited," *New York Times*, May 11, 1937, 7; "Crempa Case Rally Banned in Elizabeth," *New York Times*, October 6, 1935, 42; "Rout 300 Pickets at Passaic Mills," *New York Times*, September 19, 1934, 3.

40. U.S. Department of Commerce, *Fourteenth Census (1920)*, vol. 9, *Manufacturers*, 946–49; McKean, *The Boss*, 203–9; Fogelson, *Big-City Police*, 124–25; "Gets Biggest Police Chief Pay," *New York Times*, November 19, 1935, 6; M. Johnson, *Street Justice*, 172.

41. McKean, *The Boss*, 202; Charles Francis Coe, "Call a Cop," *Police Reporter* 2, no. 1 (March 1934): 6–7; William V. McLaughlin, "The Policeman and the Citizen," *Police Reporter* 2, no. 6 (August 1934): 18. The ACLU claimed that the *Reporter* was a Hague organization newsletter produced to extend its political influence. See "Hague Machine's Racket with the Church and the Police," memo January 1, 1938, reel 165, vol 2040, ACLU Papers.

42. "Overheard in the Precincts," *Police Reporter* 4, no. 2 (April 1936): 19; "Jersey City Police Department Safety League," *Police Reporter* 4, no. 2 (April 1936): 15.

43. Albert Thierfelder, "Proficient Policemen Physically 'Phit,'" *Police Reporter* 4, no. 4 (September 1936): 4–5; William V. McLaughlin, "Policeman-Poseur," *Police Reporter* 4, no. 2 (April 1936): 8. After the statue was vandalized in 1961 and 1976, the city moved it to a lot behind city hall at the Montgomery Street and Marin Boulevard intersection.

44. "Do You Remember?," *Police Reporter* 4, no. 4 (September 1936): 18.

45. National (Wickersham) Commission, *Report No. 11, Report on Lawlessness in Law Enforcement*, 19–23, 38–159, 238–61; M. Johnson, *Street Justice*, 133–38; Walker, *Popular Justice*, 172–74.

46. M. Johnson, *Street Justice*, 133; Walker, *Popular Justice*, 175.

47. Richardson, *Urban Police in the United States*, 159; M. Johnson, *Street Justice*, 149–179; National (Wickersham) Commission, *Report No. 11*, 83–90; Finan, *From the Palmer Raids*, 109–11; "Police Brutality" and "New York" files, ACLU Papers.

48. Goodall, "Red Herrings?," 93–95; "New Jersey Rallies Quiet," *New York Times*, March 7, 1930, 2; "Red Group Causes Brief House Flurry," *New York Times*, February 11, 1931, 3.

49. Ch. 280, *Acts of the One Hundred and Fifty-Seventh Legislature of the State of New Jersey*, 1933, superseded by ch. 133, *Acts of the One Hundred and Fifty-Eighth Legislature of the State of New Jersey*, 1934, amended by ch. 166, *Acts of the One Hundred and Sixtieth Legislature of the State of New Jersey*, 1936; "New Disorderly Persons Act," *Police Reporter* 2, no. 6 (August 1934): 20; "Chief Casey Defends Disorderly Persons Act," *Police Reporter* 3, no. 2 (March 1935): 21; "An Important Legal Decision," *Police Reporter* 2, no. 1 (March 1934): 20; "New Jersey Disorderly Persons Act," in *Report on the Denial of Labor and Civil Rights in Hudson County, New Jersey*, published by the National Committee for the Defense of Political Prisoners, February 1937, 8–9, reel 165, vol. 2040, ACLU Papers; McKean, *The Boss*, 190.

50. Typescript, *Report of the American Civil Liberties Union and the New Jersey Civil Liberties Union to the Attorney General of the United States*, November 7, 1938, cover letter and esp. pp. 5–6, 45–46, reel 165, vol. 2041, ACLU Papers. See also McKean, *The Boss*, 210–17, for the general pattern of Jersey police activity in the 1930s.

51. Fleming, "Political Machine," 37; *Report of the American Civil Liberties Union*, 2–3.

52. *Report of the American Civil Liberties Union*.

53. Ibid., 9–10, 37; Isserman, "CIO v. Hague," 19–20; "Picketing to be Tested," *New York Times*, June 19, 1934, 13; "Corliss Lamont Seized as Picket," *New York Times*, June 28, 1934, 3; "Bingham Receives 30-Day Jail Term," *New York Times*, June 29, 1934, 15; "Anti-Picketing Drive Upheld in Jersey City," *New York Times*, July 1, 1934, 19; "Lamont Opposes Delay in Trial," *New York Times*, July 6, 1934, 9; "AFofL Enters Jersey City Fight," *New York Times*, July 12, 1934, 8; "Jersey City Lifts Ban on Picketing," *New York Times*, July 13, 1934, 10; "Politics a Factor in Jersey City Row," *New York Times*, July 22, 1934, E7; "Picket Injunction Voided in New York," *New York Times*, July 24, 1934, 5; "Lamont, Bingham Tell of Picketing," *New York Times*, August 1, 1934, 15; "Jersey City Case Won by Pickets," *New York Times*, September 12, 1934, 4; "N.J. Mayor Railroads Pickets," *Daily Worker*, July 2, 1934, sec. 2, pp. 1, 4; "Six Week Fight Wins Right to Picket in Mayor Hague's City," *Daily Worker*, July 23, 1934, sec. 2, p. 1.

## *Chapter 2. Workers in Transition: Remaking Labor Unionism in a Boss-Run Town*

1. Hart, *The Last Three Miles*, 87–95; "W. J. Carney, CIO, Stricken in Street," *New York Times*, November 12, 1940, 30. The Committee for Industrial Organization became the Congress of Industrial Organizations after breaking from the American Federation of Labor in 1938.

2. Weinrib, *The Taming of Free Speech*, 226. See also McKean, *The Boss*, 183–94; Hart, *American Dictators*, 122–23; Steinberg, *The Bosses*, 53–55; Troy, *Organized Labor in New Jersey*, 183.

3. U.S. Department of Commerce, *Fourteenth Census (1920)*, vol. 9, *Manufacturers*, 946–49; U.S. Department of Commerce, *Fifteenth Census (1930)*, vol 6, *Occupations*, 1033–1039. On Chicago, see L. Cohen, *Making a New Deal*, 11–38.

4. Bernstein, *The Lean Years*, 83–89; Dubofsky, *The State and Labor in Modern America*, 86–89, 97–102; Forbath, *Law and the Shaping of the American Labor Move-

*ment*, 157–59; Duplex Printing Press Company v. Deering, 254 U.S. 443 (1921); American Steel Foundries v. Tri-City Trades Council, 257 U.S. 184 (1921); Truax v. Corrigan, 257 U.S. 312 (1921); Greene, "Growth of New Jersey Equity," 54–58; "What Constitutes Lawful Picketing in New Jersey."

5. Bernstein, *Lean Years*, 89–91; A. Cohen, *The Racketeer's Progress*, 1–9, 254–56.

6. Troy, *Organized Labor*, 69–76, 87–98; McKean, *The Boss*, 183; Connors, *A Cycle of Power*, 99–100; Fisher, *On the Irish Waterfront*, ch. 2.

7. Troy, *Organized Labor*, 68–70, 181; "Rail Shop Strike at Deadlock Here," *New York Times*, July 9, 1922, 2; "'No Violence,' Says Rail Strike Chief," *New York Times*," July 13, 1922, 2; "Meat Strike Here Cuts City's Supply," *New York Times*, December 13, 1921, 21; "Jersey Union Men Eject Radicals," *New York Times*, May 17, 1920, 30; "Labor's Policy in Politics," *New York Times*, May 23, 1920, 1; "Pickets Serenade Jersey Dye Plant," *New York Times*, March 10, 1926, 10; "No Hudson County Strike," *New York Times*, August 7, 1927, 3; "Union Endorses Davis," *New York Times*, August 29, 1924, 3; "New Jersey Labor Endorses Smith," *New York Times*, September 8, 1928, 2; "Labor Plans Test in Highest Court," *New York Times*, October 4, 1921, 2; "Want Judges Elected," *New York Times*, February 11, 1932, 21; "Says Stone Unions Delayed Schools," *New York Times*, August 12, 1927, 19; "Stone Union Trial Nearing Its Close," *New York Times*, September 23, 1927, 28; "Union Leaders Indicted," *New York Times*, June 24, 1920, 17; "Bridge Bids Unfair, Union Head Charges," *New York Times*, September 9, 1926, 12; "Builders in Jersey under Federal Fire," *New York Times*, May 10, 1930, 40; Bedford Cut Stone Co. v. Journeymen Stone Cutters' Association, 274 U.S. 37 (1927).

8. Troy, *Organized Labor*, 90–92, 181–82; Hart, *Last Three Miles*, 87–92; McKean, *The Boss*, 184–85; Vernon, *The Life & Times of Jersey City Mayor Frank Hague*, 98; "Labor Leader Joins Employers' Group," *New York Times*, February 23, 1928, 11; "Labor Bank Opens New Building," *New York Times*, August 2, 1928, 21; "Brandle Indicted as Evader of Taxes," *New York Times*, November 27, 1930, 27.

9. Connors, *Cycle of Power*, 98–99; "'Open Shop' Upheld in Jersey City Vote," *New York Times*, July 8, 1920, 30; Fisher, *On the Irish Waterfront*, ch. 2; "Longshore Strike Nearing the End," *New York Times*, November 1, 1919, 3; "'No Violence,' Says Rail Strike Chief"; "Hague Fails to End Jersey Taxi Lockout," *New York Times*, October 13, 1927, 42; "Labor Plans Test in Highest Court," *New York Times*, October 4, 1921, 2; Troy, *Organized Labor*, 181–82; "Union Endorses Davis"; "New Jersey Labor Endorses Smith"; "Burkitt Arrested in Campaign Row," *New York Times*, April 30, 1929, 15; "30 Meetings Mark Final Hague Fight," *New York Times*, May 12, 1929, 19.

10. McKean, *The Boss*, 46–71; Vernon, *Life & Times*, 15–16; N. Johnson, *Battleground New Jersey*, 86–91; "Hague's Man Beats Larson Man," *New York Times*, November 7, 1929, 22.

11. Troy, *Organized Labor*, 70–71; Gerstle, *Working-Class Americanism*, 230–58; L. Cohen, *Making a New Deal*, 21–148, 324, 333–49.

12. Bernstein, *Lean Years*, 338–40; Kessler-Harris, *Out to Work*, 259–60; Connors, *Cycle of Power*, 100; A. Cohen, *Racketeer's Progress*, 266–68.

13. Hart, *Last Three Miles*, 94–95; Vernon, *Life & Times*, 98.

14. Hart, *Last Three Miles*, 98–148; Vernon, *Life & Times*, 99; McKean, *The Boss*, 186; Fisher, *On the Irish Waterfront*, ch. 2; "Firm Paid $289,462 to Keep Open Shop," *New York Times*, March 4, 1937, clipping, reel 146, vol. 994, ACLU Papers.

15. McKean, *The Boss*, 186–90; Steinberg, *Bosses*, 53–55; Connors, *Cycle of Power*, 100; Hart, *Last Three Miles*, 143–47; Vernon, *Life & Times*, 99; "Hague Urges Fight to Oust Gangsters," *New York Times*, December 11, 1932, 25; "Jersey Labor Unit under Receivership," *New York Times*, January 18, 1933, 6; "Hague Orders War on Labor Rackets," *New York Times*, May 2, 1934, 7; testimony of Frank Hague, TR 3, 1161–66, in *Hague* case file. Without mentioning Depression-era conditions, labor attorney Abraham Isserman remembered that construction unions had "substantial treasuries" that were "frittered away' when Hague induced receivership proceedings. See Isserman, "CIO v. Hague," 17.

16. On the classic view of Hague's shifting attitude toward labor, see Weinrib, *Taming*, 226, and Hart, *American Dictators*, 121–22. On Hague's characterization of labor racketeers, see "Hague Urges Fight to Oust Gangsters."

17. Bernstein, *Lean Years*, 416–427; Teaford, *The Twentieth-Century American City*, 82; "Whalen Is Assailed for Drive on Reds," *New York Times*, March 12, 1930, 3; M. Johnson, *Street Justice*, 152–62; Finan, *From the Palmer Raids to the Patriot Act*, 109–14, 125–28.

18. "Ready to Curb Red Rally," *New York Times*, March 6, 1930, 10; "New Jersey Rallies Quiet," *New York Times*, March 7, 1930, 2; "Elizabeth Reds Routed," *New York Times*, March 16, 1930, 28; "Jobless Reds Fight with Newark Police," *New York Times*, January 8, 1931, 20; "Police Halt Rally of Reds in Newark," *New York Times*, January 29, 1931, 16; "35 Silk Strikers Held in Paterson," *New York Times*, July 30, 1931, 2; "Silk Strikers Win 1,500 More to Ranks," *New York Times*, August 4, 1931, 22; *Report of the American Civil Liberties Union and the New Jersey Civil Liberties Union to the Attorney General of the United States*, November 7, 1938, pp. 2–3, 13, and 16–17, ACLU Papers; Isserman, "CIO v. Hague," 16–17.

19. Troy, *Organized Labor*, 91–92; Bernstein, *Turbulent Years*, 30, 37–317; Dubofsky, *State and Labor*, 111–19.

20. *Report of the ACLU to the Attorney General*, 12, 19, 28–29, 30; National Committee for the Defense of Political Prisoners, *Report on the Denial of Labor and Civil Rights in Hudson Country* (pamphlet), New Jersey, 1937, pp. 13–14, 34, reel 165, vol. 2040, ACLU Papers; "Jersey City Ousts 36 Strike-Breakers," *New York Times*, August 8, 1934, 15.

21. *Report of the ACLU to the Attorney General*, 9–10; Isserman, "CIO v. Hague," 19–20; "Anti-Picketing Drive Upheld in Jersey City," *New York Times*, July 1, 1934, 19; "Politics a Factor in Jersey City Row," *New York Times*, July 22, 1934, E7.

22. "Picketing to Be Tested," *New York Times*, June 19, 1934, 13; "Corliss Lamont Seized as Picket," *New York Times*, June 28, 1934, 3; "Bingham Receives 30-Day Jail Term," *New York Times*, June 29, 1934, 15; "AFofL Enters Jersey City Fight," *New York Times*, July 12, 1934, 8; "Jersey City Lifts Ban on Picketing," *New York Times*, July 13, 1934, 10; "Politics a Factor"; "Lamont, Bingham Tell of Picketing," *New York Times*,

August 1, 1934, 15; "Jersey City Case Won by Pickets," *New York Times*, September 12, 1934, 4; "Bingham Verdict Upset," *New York Times*, December 23, 1934, 8; Max Perlow, "Six Week Fight Wins Right to Picket in Mayor Hague's City," *Daily Worker*, July 23, 1934, sec. 2, p. 1; Cottrell, *Roger Nash Baldwin and the American Civil Liberties Union*, 202–3; Laura M. Weinrib, "Civil Liberties Outside the Courts," 309–10; Weinrib, *Taming*, 227.

23. J. Owen Grundy to Richard Connors, February 17, 1965, Frank Hague Collection; Teaford, *Twentieth-Century American City*, 56–62, 75–82.

24. Teaford, *Twentieth-Century American City*, 83–90; R. Flanagan, "Roosevelt, Mayors, and the New Deal Regime," 430, 434–35; Dorsett, *Franklin D. Roosevelt and the City Bosses*, 15–30, 54–60, 70–81, 84–92, 108–9; Stave, *The New Deal and the Last Hurrah*, 16; Grundy to Connors; Vernon, *Life & Times*, 87–96. Fleming, "The Political Machine II," 40.

25. Bernstein, *Turbulent Years*, 326–27, 348–49, 352–634; Zieger, *The CIO, 1935–1955*, 1–2, 22–79, 86; Auerbach, *Labor and Liberty*, 6, 52–53; Klehr, *The Communist Experience in America*, 83–85; Meyer, *Manhood on the Line*, 82–86; L. Cohen, *Making a New Deal*, 333–48; Kessler-Harris, *Out to Work*, 268–69.

26. International City Mangers' Association, *The City's Role in Strikes: A New Outlook and Suggested Techniques* (booklet), 1937, reel 146, vol. 998, ACLU Papers.

27. Bernstein, *Turbulent Years*, 400–431, 683–99; Zieger, *CIO*, 22–41.

28. Zieger, *CIO*, 66–71; Troy, *Organized Labor*, 105–15; "Notes for CIO Speakers," memo, reel 1, and "Report of Director John Brophy to the Meeting of the Committee for Industrial Organization in Atlantic City, October 11, 1937," reel 2, RG1–037 Office of the President, the CIO Files of John L. Lewis, Part 2: General Files of the CIO and AFL, AFL-CIO Records; testimony of Thomas Cometa, TR 1, 500, and testimony of Samuel Macri, TR 2, 891, *Hague* case file.

29. Macri testimony, TR 2, 892–95, 958–60, 997–98, 1013–14, and testimony of Jules Nydes, TR 1, 343–44, 348, both in *Hague* case file; Russell Porter, "Hague Subpoenas all CIO Records," *New York Times*, June 10, 1938, 2; "CIO Strikes in Jersey City," *CIO News*, February 5, 1938, 3.

30. Troy, *Organized Labor*, 116–18; William Green to Vincent J. Murphy, June 17, 1937, reel 30, and William Green to Fred Scriven, June 17, 1937, reel 33, RG1–001, American Federation of Labor Records: The Samuel Gompers Era, Office of the President, in AFL-CIO Records.

31. Fischer, *Spider Web*, esp. 71–79, 93–94; Goldstein, *Little "Red Scares"*, xiv–xv; Luff, *Commonsense Anticommunism*, 136–41; Cottrell, *Roger Nash Baldwin*, 204–7, 255; Schrecker, *Many Are the Crimes*, 48–64.

32. Schrecker, *Many Are the Crimes*, 66–69; Luff, *Commonsense Anticommunism*, 142–68; Heale, "Citizens versus Outsiders," 46–48; Klehr, *Communist Experience*, 88–89, 117.

33. Bernstein, *Turbulent Years*, 580–84.

34. National Committee for the Defense of Political Prisoners, "Report," 20–24; Connors, *Cycle of Power*, 98; "Ship Strike Ties Up All Dollar Lines," *New York Times*,

December 30, 1936, 2; "Picketing Seamen Routed by Police," *New York Times*, December 31, 1936, 2; "Jersey City Police Oust Ship Strikers," *New York Times*, January 1, 1937, 9; Jay T. Wright, typescript, Report by the New Jersey Civil Liberties Union (NJCLU), December 1936–January 1937, pp. 2–4, reel 153, vol. 1051, ACLU Papers.

35. "Striking Seamen Held for Assault," *New York Times*, January 6, 1937, 15; J. Owen Grundy to Mr. (Roger) Baldwin, January 11, 1937, and J. Owen Grundy to "Friend Baldwin," March 19, 1937, reel 153, vol. 1051, ACLU Papers; "Harvey Says Reds Sway Rule of City," *New York Times*, May 17, 1937, 11; "Big Jersey Plant Signs with CIO," *New York Times*, March 19, 1937, 9.

36. News clipping, "Ask La Follette to Probe N.J. Labor Suppression," *Daily Worker*, March 9, 1936, reel 146, vol. 994, ACLU Papers; National Committee for the Defense of Political Prisoners, *Report*; Lucille B. Milne to A. J. Isserman, January 26, 1936; typewritten lists of NJCLU state committee and board members, undated (May 1936?); Jay Wright to Friends, undated circular letter (May 1936?); Abraham J. Isserman to Mr. Baldwin, October 5, 1936, all on reel 139, vol. 944, ACLU Papers. ACLU memo on telephone call with Jay Wright, January 7, 1937; Wright typescript; ACLU Board of Directors, minutes, point 14, May 3, 1937; ACLU press release, September 4, 1937; "Labor in Jersey to War on Hague," *New York Times*, January 11, 1937, 8; J. Owen Grundy to Mr. Baldwin, January 11, 1937; Grundy to Baldwin, March 19, 1937; J. Owen Grundy to "Friend Baldwin," December 31, 1936, all on reel 153, vol. 1051, ACLU Papers.

37. Grover, *Nazis in Newark*, 195, 248n74, 254, 297n8, 339.

38. Trial transcript, ACLU v. Casey, March 5, 1937, pp. 527–31, 534–38, 548, reel 153, vol. 1051, ACLU Papers; Weinrib, "The Liberal Compromise," 347–48; and Weinrib, *Taming*, 229–30.

39. ACLU v. Casey transcript, 541–42, 549, 554–55, 566–67; Weinrib, *Taming*, 229–30.

40. "Hays to Test Right to 'Get Arrested,'" *New York Times*, February 1, 1937, 7; "Court Likens the Police of Jersey City to Hitler," *New York Times*, March 6, 1937, 34; "Wright Officials Accused by Union," *New York Times*, March 16, 1937, 6; "Hoffman Ignores Peaceful Sit-Ins," *New York Times*, March 18, 1937, 2; Casey v. American Civil Liberties Union, 100 F. 2d 354 (1938); Weinrib, "Liberal Compromise," 348–51.

41. Vials, *Haunted by Hitler*, 3–6, 33–35, 46–58; Franczak, "The Fascist Game," 576.

42. J. Ross, *The Socialist Party in America*, 339–86; Swanberg, *Norman Thomas*, 180–82, 190–200; McAlister Coleman, "Jersey Hitler," *Socialist Call*, May 9, 1937, reel 146, vol. 995, ACLU Papers.

43. "Oil Men May Unionize," *New York Times*, January 18, 1937, 2; "Labor Drive Planned," *New York Times*, February 15, 1937, 12; "CIO Spreads in New Jersey," *New York Times*, March 1, 1937, 4; "CIO Begins Drive in Textiles Today," *New York Times*, March 19, 1937, 3; "CIO Maps Plans for Jersey Drive," *New York Times*, March 21, 1937, 2; "Big Jersey Plant Signs with CIO"; "CIO Council Formed," *New York Times*, July 24, 1937.

44. "Hoffman Presses His Attack on CIO," *New York Times*, February 23, 1937, 9; "CIO Agents Defy Hoffman to Fight," *New York Times*, February 22, 1937, 2; "Ban

on Circulars Voted," *New York Times*, March 25, 1937, 15; "CIO Postal Cards Barred Mails," *New York Times*, June 13, 1937, 3; "AFofL in Jersey Ousts CIO Unions," *New York Times*, September, 1937, 5; Troy, *Organized Labor*, 100–101.

45. "Hague Is Inducted for His Sixth Term," *New York Times*, May 19, 1937, 17; "In Jersey City, the Sun Shines on All Alike," flyer, reel 165, vol. 2040, ACLU Papers. List of officers and directors of the Jersey City Chamber of Commerce, vol. 22, no. 8 (September 1937): 4; C. Bertram Planter, "Jersey City: An Ideal Industrial Center," vol. 22, no. 6 (June 1937): 1; "Amend, Supplement or Repeal the Wagner Act," vol. 22, no. 8 (September 1937): 4; "Anti-Injunction Bill a Matter of Concern," vol. 22, no. 3 (March 1937): 13–14; all in *Jersey City*. McKean, *The Boss*, 189–90; Weinrib, *Taming*, 229; "Charges Campaign to Curb Labor Act," *New York Times*, June 20,1937, 5.

46. Testimony of Thomas Cometa, TR 1, 500–504, 509–10, Macri testimony, TR 2, 890–916, "CIO Prepared for Invasion," *Newark Evening News*, November 23, 1937, TR 4, 67, all in *Hague* case file.

47. "Moore Is Backed by Jersey Labor," *New York Times*, September 16, 1937, 3; "New Jersey Vote," *Daily Messenger*, November 2, 1937, 1; Arthur Krock, "In the Nation: National Bearing of the Result in New Jersey," *New York Times*, November 5, 1937, 22; N. Johnson, *Battleground New Jersey*, 99.

48. "144 Election Aids Accused in Jersey," *New York Times*, October 24, 1937, 19; "Clee Assails Court over Vote Warrants," *New York Times*, October 27, 1937, 18; "Pugilists to Guard 'Honest' Jersey Vote," *New York Times*, November 2, 1937, 7; "U.S. Senator Defeats Minister Opponent," *Middletown (NY) Times Herald*, November 3, 1937, 1; "Moore Elected by Scant Vote in New Jersey," *Brooklyn Daily Eagle*," November 3, 1937, 4; "Hague Votes Win for Moore in New Jersey," *Daily Worker*, November 4, 1937, 5; "32 Jersey Ballots Laid to One Voter," *New York Times*, December 7, 1937, 17; "Dead Were Voted, Senator Clee Says," *New York Times*, January 5,1937, 9; "Jersey Recount to Be Demanded," *New York Times*, November 5, 1937, 8; "To Ask Legislative Action," *New York Times*, November 5, 1937, 8; editorial, "A Jersey Recount," *Middletown (NY) Times Herald*, November 5, 1937, 4; Krock, "In the Nation"; "Move to Recount in Jersey Defied," *New York Times*, November 7, 1937, 7; "Clee Will Ask for Jersey Recount Today," *New York Times*, November 13, 1937, 2; "Recount in Hudson Granted to Clee," *New York Times*, November 14, 1937, 5; N. Johnson, *Battleground New Jersey*, 100–101.

49. "I Am the Law," *Brooklyn Daily Eagle*, November 14, 1937, 24; Paul Gallico, "Hague Sells Self to Gallico in Interview," *Jersey Observer*, January 14, 1938, 1; McKean, *The Boss*, 224–25; Vernon, *Life & Times*, 18–19; Teaford, *Twentieth-Century American City*, 51.

50. "Files Charges against I-Am-the-Law Hague," *Brooklyn Daily Eagle*, November 17, 1937, 2; "CIO Unit Here Plans Invasion of Jersey City," *Newark Sunday Call*, November 21, 1937, in TR 4, 47, and "CIO Prepared for Invasion," *Newark Evening News*, November 23, 1937, in TR 4, 67, *Hague* case file; "CIO Girds for a Fight with Hague," *Jersey Observer*, November 24, 1937, 1; Ordinance to Regulate Distribution of Newspapers, etc., in TR 4, 139–40, *Hague* case file; "Jersey City Drive Opening," *New York Times*, November 28, 1937, 8.

51. "CIO Tests Hague's Ban on Distribution of Labor Handbills," *Dunkirk Evening Observer*, November 29, 1937, 13. Testimony of Daniel Casey, TR 2, 757–60, testimony of David Silverstein, TR 1, 251–57, 264–66, Macri testimony, TR 2, 917–29, testimony of Dan Foley, TR 1, 172–77, 192–93, 197, testimony of Morris Milgram, TR 1, 402–4, testimony of Grace Milgram, TR 1, 415, testimony of Daniel Clendennin, TR 1, 215–16, 241–42, testimony of Harry Ahern, TR 1, 374–76, testimony of Bella Kussy, TR 1, 382–87, testimony of Nancy Cox, TR 1, 310–11, testimony of Aaron Gilmartin, TR 1, 359–62, all in *Hague* case file.

52. Ahern testimony, TR 1, 376, Grace Milgram testimony, TR 1, 415, testimony of Sol Chernofsky, TR 1, 388–89, Kussy testimony, TR 1, 384, Clendennin testimony, TR 1, 220–26, Gilmartin testimony, TR 1, 363–65, testimony of James Sweeney, TR 1, 287–91, Cox testimony, TR 1, 310–12, all in *Hague* case file; Grover, *Nazis in Newark*, 248.

53. "Labor March on Jersey City Ends without Disorder," *Jersey Observer*, November 29, 1937, 1; "Court Holds 6 Under Bail to the Jury," *Jersey Observer*, November 30, 1937, 1; "Ride CIO Men to City Limits," *Brooklyn Daily Eagle*, November 29, 1937, 1, 3; Cox testimony, TR 1, 313; Kussy testimony, TR 1, 385; Grace Milgram testimony, TR 1, 416; unofficial trial transcript, November 29, 1937, TR 4, 3, *Hague* case file.

54. "Laud Hague for His CIO Stand," *Jersey Observer*, December 1, 1937, 1.

## *Chapter 3. Street Fight and Media Fight: The Battle for Jersey City*

1. "Dictatorship Is Proclaimed in Jersey City," *CIO News*, December 7, 1937, 2; "Hague's C.I.O. Fight Hailed by Chamber," *New York Times*, December 23, 1937, 9.

2. On interwar anticommunism in the United States, see Fischer, *Spider Web*, esp. chs. 5, 9, and 10; Luff, *Commonsense Anticommunism*, 133–36; Goldstein, *Little "Red Scares"*; Heale, "Citizen versus Outsiders," 61–63.

3. Feldman, *Free Expression and Democracy in America*, 3.

4. Katznelson, *Fear Itself*, 98–99, 117–27; Vials, *Haunted by Hitler*, 3–6, 33–58; McAlister Coleman, "Jersey Hitler," *Socialist Call*, May 7, 1937, reel 146, vol. 995, ACLU Papers; Norman Thomas, *Hagueism Is Fascism*" (pamphlet), published by the WDL, ca. 1938, Frank Hague Collection.

5. Feldman, *Free Expression*, 3.

6. On the historiographical image of Hague, see Weinrib, *The Taming of Free Speech*, 226–28; N. Johnson, *Battleground New Jersey*, 2–6, 76, 108–10, 112–26; Hart, *American Dictators*; Vernon, *Life & Times*, 10–11; Hart, *The Last Three Miles*, 75–81, 137, 169–70; Finan, *From the Palmer Raids to the Patriot Act*, 130–32; Dorsett, "Frank Hague," 33; Steinberg, *The Bosses*, 10–12, 39–40, 43–44, 46–47, 53–55; Connors, *A Cycle of Power*, 55–56, 58, 72–73, 76–78, 98–99; McKean, *The Boss*, 228–31, 239–41.

7. See Dorsett, *Franklin D. Roosevelt and the City Bosses*.

8. "Will Ask Writ of Certiorari for CIO Men," *Jersey Observer*, December 2, 1937, 1, 4.

9. "Laud Hague for His CIO Stand," *Jersey Observer*, December 1, 1937, 1; "Refers CIO to Court Appeals," *Jersey Observer*, December 4, 1937, 1; "Federation Is Backing Hague," *Jersey Observer*, December 6, 1937, 1, 16; "Executive Board of Central Labor Union Backs CIO Stand," *Jersey Observer*, December 8, 1937, 1; "Second Labor Union

Backs Mayor's Fight against CIO's Picketing Methods," *Jersey Observer*, December 9, 1937, 1; "Labor Union Lauds Hague in CIO Fight," *Jersey Observer*, December 15, 1937, 1; exhibit P-19, TR 4, 18–19, *Hague* case file. For depictions of Hague as antilabor, see McKean, *The Boss*, 187–96; N. Johnson, *Battleground New Jersey*, 108. On the significance of the split between the AFL and CIO in Jersey City, see Weinrib, *Taming*, 234–35.

10. "Lawyers Fight to Free Union Men from Jail," *Middletown (NY) Times Herald*, November 30, 1937, 12; Flow Chart of Organizational Structure of CIO's Jersey City Drive, reel 153, vol. 1051, ACLU Papers; CIO press release, December 2, 1937, Information Department, AFL-CIO Press Releases, 1937–1995, AFL-CIO Records; "CIO Maps Battle on Jersey City Ban," *New York Times*, December 3, 1937, 5; JMB (Jerome Britchey) to RNB (Roger Baldwin), memo December 17, 1937, reel 153, vol. 1051, ACLU Papers; ACLU Board of Directors Minutes, December 20, 1937, reel 153, vol. 1051, ACLU Papers; ACLU press release, December 20, 1937, reel 153, vol. 1051, ACLU Papers. On CIO counselor Lee Pressman's view of litigation in the *Hague* case, see Gall, *Pursuing Justice*, 105–8.

11. "Reveals the Forces Back of CIO Here," *Jersey Observer*, December 8, 1937, 24; "Hague Shows Ernst Record as a Radical," *Jersey Observer*, December 13, 1937, 1; "Rebuke to CIO Pleases Hague," *Jersey Observer*, December 17, 1937, 1; "Hague Says Isserman Is Red Counsel," *Jersey Observer*, December 20, 1937, 1.

12. J. Owen Grundy to Mr. [Roger] Baldwin, January 11, 1937, reel 153, vol. 1051, ACLU Papers; J. Owen Grundy to "Friend [Roger] Baldwin, March 19, 1937, reel 153, vol. 1051, ACLU Papers; Fischer, *Spider Web*, 80–94; Luff, *Commonsense Anticommunism*, 2012), 133–34, 149–50; Cottrell, *Roger Nash Baldwin and the American Civil Liberties Union*, 207, 255; Heale, "Citizens versus Outsiders," 61–63; Schrecker, *Many Are the Crimes*, 61–69; Pearson, "Fighting the 'Red Danger,'" 156–60; Seaton, *Catholics and Radicals*, 18–22, 49; Franczak, "The Fascist Game," 571–76; "Communistic Trend in CIO Deplored by Truth Society President in Forum Address," *Jersey Observer*, December 10, 1937; 3; "Declares Unions Have Right to Strike but Condemns Law-Breaking in 'Invasion' Here," *Jersey Observer*, December 13, 1937, 3.

13. CIO press release, December 2, 1937; "CIO Maps Battle"; "CIO to Organize City Labor Council," *New York Times*, December 6, 1937, 15; "Dictatorship Proclaimed"; Franczak, "Fascist Game," 576; Denning, *The Cultural Front*, xvi–xviii.

14. "Topics of the Times," *New York Times*, December 18, 1937, 18; Editorial, "'I Am the Law,'" *New York Times*, December 17, 1937, 24; "Baldwin Accuses Hague of Tyranny," *New York Times*, December 15, 1937, 3; ACLU press release, December 20, 1937.

15. "Clear Plant after Threat of Force," *Jersey Observer*, December 7, 1937, 1; "Hoffman Ignores Peaceful Sit-In," *New York Times*, March 18, 1937, 2; "Baldwin Accuses Hague of Tyranny"; testimony of Francis Hunter, TR 1, 486, *Hague* case file; "Hague and CIO Deadlocked," *New York Times*, December 26, 1937, 48.

16. "Hague Fails to Ban Meeting for Foes," *New York Times*, December 22, 1937, 23.

17. "State AFL Fights State Labor Party," *New York Times*, November 28, 1937, 8; "Jersey Labor Party Formed," *Jersey Observer*, December 7, 1937, 1, 12; "Labor Party

Plan Pressed in Jersey," *New York Times*, December 5, 1937, 36; "164 Jersey Unions from Labor Party," *New York Times*, December 6, 1937, 17; Troy, *Organized Labor in New Jersey*, 183, 117–18.

18. "U.S. Senator Defeats Minister Opponent," *Middletown (NY) Times Herald*, November 3, 1937, 1; "Moore Elected by Scant Vote in New Jersey," *Brooklyn Daily Eagle*, November 3, 1937, 4; "Jersey Recount to Be Demanded," *New York Times*, November 5, 1937, 8; "To Ask Legislative Action," *New York Times*, November 5, 1937, 8; "Move for Recount in Jersey Defied," *New York Times*, November 7, 1937, 71; "Clee to Ask for Jersey Recount Today," *New York Times*, November 13, 1937, 2; "Recount in Hudson Is Granted to Clee," *New York Times*, November 14, 1937, 5; N. Johnson, *Battleground New Jersey*, 99–101.

19. "Major CIO Aim Is to 'Lick' Hague," *New York Times*, December 18, 1937, 5; "CIO Leaders Talk of Machine Guns," *Jersey Journal*, December 18, 1937, exhibit D-1, TR 4, 61, *Hague* case file; "'No Machine Guns Will Be Used by Communistic Invaders Here'—Hague," *Jersey Observer*, December 18, 1937, 1.

20. RNB (Roger N. Baldwin), "Jersey City" and "Program on Jersey Situation for Week of December 20th," both undated internal memos, reel 153, vol. 1051, ACLU Papers; "Spaulding Frazer, a Newark Lawyer," *New York Times*, March 8, 1940, 26.

21. "CIO Plans Test on Ban by Hague," *New York Times*, December 19, 1937, 29; exhibit P-36, TR 4, 37–39, *Hague* case file; *Jersey City Board of Commissioners Minutes*, January 22, 1924, 473, and April 15, 1930, 579–80.

22. "Jersey City Gets Plea for CIO Rally," *New York Times*, December 24, 1937, 3; exhibit P-36.

23. Schedule F, CIO Bill of Complaint, January 7, 1938, TR 1, 27–35, *Hague* case file; "Jersey City Gets Plea for CIO Rally."

24. Abernathy, *The Right of Assembly and Association* , 12–53; State of New Jersey v. John C. Butterworth, et al., 104 N.J.L. 579 (1928); N. Johnson, *Battleground New Jersey*, 48–51.

25. "Hague Holds CIO Plots Labor Chaos," *New York Times*, December 28, 1937, 7; CIO Bill of Complaint, 39–44; "Meet Tonight at Armory to Fight Proposed Speech," *Jersey Observer*, December 28, 1937, 1, 10; "3,000 Veterans Back Hague Fight on CIO," *New York Times*, December 29, 1937, 14.

26. Exhibit P-33, postcard dated December 28, 1937, TR 4, 35, *Hague* case file; McKean, *The Boss*, 154, 236; Clarence Squires, letter to editor, *Jersey Observer*, January 21, 1938, 22; Ruotsila, "Leftward Ramparts," 174–93; Schrecker, *Many Are the Crimes*, 61–67, 72–75; Seaton, *Catholics and Radicals*, 68–69; "Hague Bares Full Record of Baldwin," *Jersey Observer*, December 27, 1937, 1, 4; "Final Installment of Expose by Mayor Hague of Baldwin's Activities," *Jersey Observer*, December 29, 1937, 11; CIO Bill of Complaint, 44.

27. CIO Bill of Complaint, 38–39, 45–46; "CIO Meeting Permit Denied," *Jersey Observer*, December 31, 1937, 1, 4; "Jersey City Bans Meeting of CIO," *New York Times*, December 31, 1937, 7; "'Mob Rule' of Hague Is Ridiculed by CIO," *New York Times*, January 4, 1938, 6; exhibit P-13, TR 4, 10–11, *Hague* case file; testimony of James Sweeney, TR 1, 295–97, 301–8, *Hague* case file.

28. Davis. v. Massachusetts, 167 U.S. 43 (1897); Gitlow v. New York, 268 U.S. 652 (1925); Whitney v. California, 274 v. 357 (1927); Stromberg v. California, 283 U.S. 359 (1931); Near v. Minnesota 283 U.S. 697 (1931); DeJonge v. Oregon, 299 U.S. 353 (1937); Senn v. Tile Layers Protective Union, 302 U.S. 468 (1937); Cantwell v. Connecticut, 310 U.S. 296 (1940); Chaplinsky v. New Hampshire, 315 U.S. 568 (1942); Feiner v. New York, 340 U.S. 315 (1951); Terminiello v. Chicago, 337 U.S. 1 (1949); Hague v. CIO, 307 U.S. 496 (1939); Edwards v. South Carolina, 372 U.S. 229 (1963); and Adderly v. Florida, 385 U.S. 39 (1966). On the civil libertarian transition, see also Weinrib, "Civil Liberties Outside the Courts," 322–28.

29. McKean, *The Boss*, 150–61; Connors, *Cycle of Power*, 87.

30. "Business and Labor Plan for Battle," *Jersey Observer*, December 29, 1937, 1, 15; "Civic Drive Backs Hague Ban on CIO," *New York Times*, December 30, 1937, 9; exhibit P-19, TR 4, 18–19, 21–23, *Hague* case file; editorial "'No Surrender to CIO' Is Jersey's Answer," *Jersey Observer*, January 3, 1938, 1; "Proclamation: Mayor Hague's Appeal to the People," *Jersey Observer*, January 4, 1938, 4; "Hague Bids All Attend Huge Rally," *Jersey Observer*, January 4, 1938, 1; "Polish League Inducts; Backs Hague on CIO," *Jersey Observer*, January 4, 1938, 2.

31. Franczak, "Fascist Game," 574–84; Gerstle, *Working-Class Americanism*, 11; L. Cohen, *Making a New Deal*, 333–49.

32. "Memorandum on the Jersey City Work," December 24, 1937, reel 153, vol. 1051, ACLU Papers; Roger Baldwin, "On Conference with Morris Ernst on Jersey Situation," memo January 3, 1938, reel 165, vol. 2040, ACLU Papers; "Orders by Baldwin on 'Invasion,'" and "Hague Gives Evidence to Show Baldwin Is 'Leading Communist,'" *Jersey Observer*, January 4, 1938, 1; "Hague Rally to Air His Stance Tonight," *New York Times*, January 6, 1938, 8; "Charge Hague Forces Tampered with Mail in Jersey City," press release, January 8, 1938, reel 165, vol. 2040, ACLU Papers; "Hague Leader Before Jersey Grand Jury on Mail Tampering," press release, May 6, 1938, reel 165, vol. 2040, ACLU Papers; "Hague Scoffs at Baldwin's Charge," *Jersey Observer*, January 6, 1938, 12; Dorsett, "Frank Hague," 28; "Hague and Thomas Almost Collide," *New York Times*, May 4, 1938, 12.

33. "Many Organizations to Be Represented at Big Mass Meeting Thursday," *Jersey Observer*, January 3, 1938, 1; "Moore Will Preside at Huge Rally," *Jersey Observer*, January 5, 1938, 1; "Predict 100,000 Will Storm Armory," *Jersey Observer*, January 5, 1938, 3; "Radio to Carry Plea to Country," *Jersey Observer*, January 6, 1938, 1; "Hague Rally to Air His Stand Tonight," *New York Times*, January 6, 1938, 8; "Hague and Carey Sit Side by Side," *Jersey Observer*, January 7, 1938, 1; "Nation Told of Peril at Huge Rally" and "Carey Pledges Help to Mayor," *Jersey Observer*, January 7, 1938, both on 1, 17; "Carey Rapped for Anti-CIO Address," *Jersey Observer*, January 11, 1938, 5; "Observations at Big Rally At Armory in Jersey City" and "Church, Civic and Veteran Leaders at Anti-CIO Rally," *Jersey Observer*, January 7, 1938, 13; "Vigilante Spirit Runs Hague Rally," *Daily Worker*, January 8, 1938, 3.

34. Hart, *Last Three Miles*, 172. List of officers and directors, and article, "Anti-Injunction Bill A Matter of Vital Concern," *Jersey City* 22, no. 3 (March 1937): 4, "Jersey City: An Ideal Industrial Center," *Jersey City* 22, no. 6 (June 1937): 1, and

"Amend, Supplement or Repeal the Wagner Act," *Jersey City* 22, no. 8 (September 1937): 4. "State Leader of AFL Sees Revolt in CIO," *Jersey Observer*, January 7, 1938, 17; McKean, *The Boss*, 193–194; Troy, *Organized Labor*, 117–18, 146–47.

35. "Legion Backs Hague's Drive," *Jersey Observer*, January 6, 1938, 7; Seaton, *Catholics and Radicals*, 68–69; Barrett, *The Irish Way*, 230.

36. Connors, *Cycle of Power*, 5–6; J. Owen Grundy to Richard J. Connors, February 17, 1965, pp. 2–3, and J. Owen Grundy, "Before 1949: Thirty Years War on Hagueism," unpublished manuscript, p. 12, both in Frank Hague Collection.

37. Editorial, "Jersey City's Unmistakable Answer to the CIO," *Jersey Observer*, January 8, 1938, 16; "Hoboken Knights Back Hague Fight," *Jersey Observer*, January 7, 1938, 8; "Support Is Given to Hague's Drive," *Jersey Observer*, January 14, 1938, 9; "Aid to Hague Denied by Jersey Veterans," *New York Times*, January 10, 1938, 4; "Wheeler Post Backs Hague's Fight on Reds," *Jersey Observer*, January 19, 1938, 4; "Jersey Churchmen Score Hague Stand," *New York Times*, January 11, 1938, 12; "Second Warders Get Hague Thanks," *Jersey Observer*, January 13, 1938, 4; "Democrats Re-elect Ertle; Urge Hague Continue Fight," *Jersey Observer*, January 14, 1938, 6; "Tenth Ward Club Thanked by Hague," *Jersey Observer*, January 12, 1938, 2; "Club Hears Hague Campaign Lauded," *Jersey Observer*, January 14, 1938, 2; "Law College Official Says Mayor's Duty Is to Protect Peaceful City from Invasion," *Jersey Observer*, January 12, 1938, 3; "Fomenting of Trouble by Radical Agitators Condemned by Engineers," *Jersey Observer*, January 17, 1938, 13; "Two Thousand at Dinner in Newark Back Mayor's Stand against Reds," *Jersey Observer*, January 10, 1938, 1; "Mayor Will Be Speaker Tonight at Dinner of Chamber of Commerce," *Jersey Observer*, January 12, 1938, 11; "No Dictator, Mayor Tells the Chamber," *Jersey Observer*, January 13, 1938, 1, 17; "Hague Begs Nation to Ban CIO Reds," *New York Times*, January 13, 1938, 13; Paul Gallico, "Hague Sells Self to Gallico in Interview," *Jersey Observer*, January 14, 1938, 1,8; "Hague Lays Strife to CIO Seamen," *New York Times*, January 17, 1938, 5; "Hague Keeps Hands Off CIO Walkout," *New York Times*, January 25, 1938, 7; "CIO Strikes in Jersey City," *CIO News*, February 5, 1938, 3.

38. "Clee Gain Goes Over 700 Mark," *Jersey Observer*, January 14, 1938, 1; "News of the Week in Review," *New York Times*," January 23, 1938, 59; "Jersey Voting Row Flares in Trenton," *New York Times*, January 25, 1938, 5; "Drastic Steps Due in Jersey Inquiry," *New York Times*, January 31, 1938, 10; N. Johnson, *Battleground New Jersey*, 99–104; Fleming, "The Political Machine II," 38; "Norris Sees Fight on Seating Milton," *New York Times*, January 20, 1938, 12; "Milton Appointment Fought," *New York Times*, January 21, 1938, 7; "Fight on Milton Pushed by Labor," *New York Times*, January 23, 1938, 21; "Milton Takes Seat as Labor Protests," *New York Times*, January 25, 1938, 5.

39. "Jersey Churchman Score Hague Stand"; "Labor Man Sought to Replace Hague," *New York Times*, January 12, 1938, 10; "Drastic Steps Due in Jersey Inquiry"; "Civil Liberties Union Upheld by Mgr. Ryan," *New York Times*, January 18, 1938, 2; Aron S. Gilmartin to Roger Baldwin, January 5, 1938, reel 176, vol. 2133, ACLU Papers; Minutes of the Executive Board Meeting, January 13, 1938, reel 165, vol. 2039, ACLU Papers; *WDL Upsets Jersey Gap Ordinances*, WDL bulletin, January 1938, reel 165, vol. 2040,

ACLU Papers; Neil Brant to Morris Ernst, January 7, 1938, and William J. Carney to Roger Baldwin, January 7, 1938, both reel 165, vol. 2040, ACLU Papers; "Is Hague Important?," *Labor Leader*, Vol. 1, no. 2, January 10, 1938, reel 165, vol. 2040, ACLU Papers; CIO press release, January 13, 1938, Information Department, RG20-003 AFL-CIO Press Releases, 1937–1995, AFL-CIO Records; "Hague in Hot Spot as Union Pushes on in Jersey Battle," January 22, 1938, Information Department, RG20-002, AFL-CIO Records; "Hague in Hot Spot as Union Drive Gains," *CIO News*, January 22, 1938, 3; "Hays Accepts Hague Challenge to Invade Jersey City," press release, December 31, 1937, reel 153, vol. 1051, ACLU Papers; "Hays Radio Speech Halted by Woman," *New York Times*, January 5, 1938, 22; "Ernst Denounces Hague as Radical," *New York Times*, January 7, 1938, 7; "Baldwin Assails Hague in Bayonne," *New York Times*, January 15, 1938, 16; Seaton, *Catholics and Radicals*, 68–69.

40. CIO press release, January 13, 1938; Henry C. Fleisher, "Mayor Tries to Hide Right to Organize," *CIO News*, January 14, 1938, 3; McAlister Coleman, "Hague's Record Shows Graft and Corruption," *CIO News*, January 14, 1938, 3; Art Shields, Hague's Hell in Harborside Bared," *Daily Worker*, January 19, 1938, 1; Art Shields, "In Hague's Slums, They Live on $1.72–1/2 a Week," *Daily Worker*, January 20, 1938, 5; editorial cartoon, "Trying to Stop the Flood!," *CIO News*, January 14, 1938, 3; "Hague in Hot Spot as Union Pushes"; "Hague in Hot Spot as Union Drive Gains."

41. "Hays Radio Speech"; "Ernst Denounces Hague"; "Baldwin Assails Hague"; Weinrib, *Taming*, 231–34.

42. "Hague's Stand against CIO Is Criticized by Bayonne Director of Public Safety," *New York Times*, January 14, 1938, 11; Gallico, "Hague Sells Self"; "Anti-Hague Labor Meeting Is Cancelled," *Jersey Observer*, January 18, 1938, 1; "Police Foil CIO Effort to Distribute Circulars," *Jersey Observer*, February 1, 1938, 1; Arthur T. Vanderbilt to Dayton McKean, February 21, 1940, folder A, box 96, Vanderbilt Papers; "Hague Foe Ousted by Bayonne Board," *New York Times*, January 16, 1938, 21; "Hague Lays Strife to CIO Seamen"; Grundy to Connors, February 17, 1965; Minutes of the [NJCLU] Executive Board Meeting, April 14, 1938, reel 165, vol. 2039, ACLU Papers.

43. CIO Bill of Complaint, 4–21.

44. "Injunction Asked against Hague in the U.S. Courts," *Jersey Observer*, January 8, 1938, 1, 5; "CIO to Confer This Week," *New York Times*, January 9, 1938, 9; "Hague Scoffs."

45. Advertisement, "Get Today's New York Post!", *Jersey Observer*, January 17, 1938, 4; Russell B. Porter, "Portrait of a 'Dictator,' Jersey City Style," *New York Times*, February 13, 1938, 5, 16; Denlinger, "Boss Hague"; "Jersey City's Mayor Hague: Last of the Bosses, Not First of Dictators," *Life*, February 7, 1938, 45; Robert Brupbacher, letter to the editor, *Life*, February 21, 1938, 3; Hart, *Last Three Miles*, 169–71; Katznelson, *Fear Itself*, 96–129; Vials, *Haunted*, 47–57; Vernon, *Life & Times*, 103–4.

46. "Jersey City's Mayor Hague," 45; Porter, "Portrait of a 'Dictator,'" 16; Denlinger, "Boss Hague," 134–37; Thomas, "No Democracy without Civil Liberty." On the capacity of popular movements to shape constitutional ideas, see Kramer, *The People Themselves*, 5–8, 207–8; Schmidt, *The Sit-Ins*, 67.

47. "Gains Power in Many States," *CIO News*, March 26, 1938, 3; W. J. Carney to John L. Lewis, February 5, 1938, Office of the President, CIO Files of John L. Lewis, Part 2: General Files of the CIO and AFL, 1929–1955, RG1–037, AFL-CIO Records; *CIO Theater Night: Bring Democracy to Jersey City* (pamphlet), February 20, 1938, reel 165, vol. 2040, ACLU papers.

48. ACLU press release, February 24, 1938, reel 165, vol. 2040, ACLU Papers; "Jersey Rule Scored," *New York Times*, February 27, 1938, 7; "Hague Target for Speakers from Capital," *Jersey Observer*, February 28, 1938, 1, 6; Weinrib, *Taming*, 236. "Charlie McCarthy" was a puppet used in Edgar Bergen's popular comedy routine during the 1930s.

49. Lovell v. City of Griffin, 303 U.S. 444 (1938); Weinrib, *Taming*, 236; "Jersey City Faces New Fight by CIO," *New York Times*, March 30, 1938, 16; testimony of Morris Milgram, TR 1, 421–22, *Hague* case file; "Ruling of Corporation Counsel James A. Hamill," April 1, 1938, reel 165, vol. 2041, ACLU Papers; Philip Aultman, "Constitutional Law—Freedom of the Press—Validity of Handbill Ordinances," 196; McAlister Coleman, "Jersey Joins the Union," *CIO News*, April 9, 1938, 2; "Instructions for Distribution of Pamphlets in Jersey City," NJCLU memo, August 8, 1938, reel 165, vol. 2041, ACLU Papers.

50. "Hague Foe Seized for Street Speech," *New York Times*, April 17, 1938, 8; list of meeting permit requests, TR 4, 29, *Hague* case file; Weinrib, *Taming*, 236. On Longo's fate, see Bryan, "Anti-Hague Revolt Led to Sentence."

51. "Labor Ranks Split for Rallies Today," *New York Times*, April 30, 1938, 16; petition, April 1938, TR 4, 20–21, *Hague* case file; list of meeting permit requests, 30; testimonies of Morris Milgram, Ashley Carrick, William Kernan, and William Callahan, TR 1, 406–10, 443–45, 447–49, 478, *Hague* case file; "Civil Rights in Jersey," *New York Times*, May 3, 1938, 22; "Protests on Hague Given to Cummings," *New York Times*, May 18, 1938, 10; "Thomas Sues for Permit," *New York Times*, September 8, 1938, 3; Weinrib, *Taming*, 236–37.

52. "Hague and Thomas Almost Collide"; "Hague to Testify in CIO Test Suit," *New York Times*, May 5, 1938, 5; "2,000 Hague Allies Protest at Rally," *New York Times*, May 6, 1938, 12; Weinrib, *Taming*, 237.

53. "Hague to Testify in CIO Test Suit," *New York Times*, May 5, 1938, 5; list of meeting permit requests, 31; "2,000 Hague Allies Protest at Rally"; testimonies of Timothy O'Brien, Joseph Zarella, and William Callahan, TR 1, 455–69, 474–77, 480–81, *Hague* case file; testimony of Charles C. Webber, TR 2, 884–88, *Hague* case file; "Statement by Vito Marcantonio," ILD press release, May 7, 1938, reel 165, vol. 2040, ACLU papers; "Sentence for Longo Put off for a Week," *New York Times*, May 13, 1938, 4; "Hague Foe's Charge Ignored by Center," *New York Times*, May 15, 1938, 2; "Jersey City Bars O'Connell Rally," *New York Times*, May 26, 1938, 12; "Broader Inquiry on Hague Urged," *New York Times*, May 22, 1938, 13; "Thomas Again Asks for Permit," *New York Times*, May 18, 1938, 10; "Jersey City Bars Thomas Talk Again," *New York Times*, May 21, 1938, 17; Bryan, "Anti-Hague Revolt."

54. "Jersey City Bars O'Connell Rally"; list of meeting permit requests, 30; "Civil Rights Truce with Hague Near," *New York Times*, May 27, 1938, 3; testimony of Nancy Cox, TR 1, 333–41, *Hague* case file; "Hague Plot Seen by CIO in Beating," *New York Times*, May 29, 1938, 9.

55. "Inquiries Begun into Thomas Riot," *New York Times*, June 7, 1938, 2; "Protest on Riot to Be Read in Pulpits," *New York Times*, June 11, 1938, 6; "Newark Grants Permit for Socialist Rally," *New York Times*, 17, 1938, 12; Minutes, NJCLU Board of Directors, July 29, 1938, reel 165, vol. 2039, ACLU Papers; Hart, *Last Three Miles*, 149–50; Grover, *Nazis in Newark*, 223.

56. "Attack on Reds Pressed by Hague," *New York Times*, June 3, 1938, 4; list of meeting permit requests, 31, and announcement, "Veterans Law and Order Committee," May 28, 1938, TR 4, 36, both in *Hague* case file; Foster Haley, "How Does Hague Do It?," *New York Times*, June 12, 1938, 69; "Hague Plot."

57. ACLU and NJCLU, *Candid Views of Mayor Hague* (pamphlet), ca. 1938, Frank Hague Collection; cartoon, "Der Big Boss Fuehrer," and article, "Tests on Free Speech Forced in Jersey City," *New York Times*, May 8, 1938, 71; Norman Thomas, *Last Night in Jersey City* (pamphlet), published by the WDL, 8–11, ca. May 1938, Frank Hague Collection; Thomas, *Hagueism Is Fascism*, 5–10; WDL, *Hagueism: What Is it?* (pamphlet), ca. June 1938, reel 165, vol. 2040, ACLU Papers; editorial, "Heil Hague," *CIO News*, June 11, 1938, 4.

58. Warren, *An Alternative Vision*, 36–37, 188–89; Thomas, *Hagueism Is Fascism*, 6; Thomas, *Last Night*, 10; Vials, *Haunted*, 33–35, 56; Berman, "A New Deal for Free Speech," 303–9.

59. Dorsett, *Franklin D. Roosevelt*, 84–93, 105–6; Stave, *The New Deal and the Last Hurrah*, 18–19.

60. Stave, *New Deal*, 5–16.

61. Murphy, *The Constitution in Crisis Times, 1918–1969*, 180–82.

## *Chapter 4. Into Federal District Court: Municipal Power and Civil Liberties in a New Forum*

1. McKean, *The Boss*, 199, 240–41; Steinberg, *The Bosses*, 57–58; Hart, *American Dictators*, 125; N. Johnson, *Battleground New Jersey*, 108; Weinrib, *The Taming of Free Speech*, 241–42.

2. The acronym "CIO-ACLU" indicates the partnership of CIO and ACLU litigants in the *Hague* case.

3. CIO Bill of Complaint, January 7, 1938, TR 1, 4–6, *Hague* case file.

4. Bernstein, *Turbulent Years*, 635–78; Walker, *In Defense of American Liberties*, 101, 106; Abernathy, *The Right of Assembly and Association*, 12–14, 110–12; Zick, *Speech Out of Doors*, 25–35.

5. ACLU, "Broad Injunction Suit to Test Jersey City CIO Ban," press release, January 15, 1938, reel 165, vol. 2024, ACLU Papers; CIO Bill of Complaint, January 7, 1938, 7–21; Weinrib, *Taming*, 230–31, 240.

6. Walker, *In Defense*, 107–11; Palko v. Connecticut, 302 U.S. 319 (1937); U.S. v. Carolene Products Co., 304 U.S. 144, 152 (1938).

7. CIO Bill of Complaint, January 7, 1938, 16–17.

8. Answer of Frank Hague, et al., February 19,1938, TR 1, 56–61, *Hague* case file.

9. Lovell v. City of Griffin, 303 U.S. 444, 450–53 (1938); Peters, *Judging Jehovah's Witnesses*, 183–84; "Jersey City Faces a New Fight by CIO," *New York Times*, March 30,1938, 16; testimony of Morris Milgram, TR 1, 421–22, and testimony of Grace Milgram, TR 1, 419–20, both in *Hague* case file; "Ruling of Corporation Counsel James A. Hamill on the Jersey City Ordinance Relating to the Distribution of Literature on the Streets," April 1,1938, and "Instructions for Distribution of Pamphlets in Jersey City," August 8, 1938, both on reel 165, vol. 2041, ACLU Papers; Weinrib, *Taming*, 236.

10. Minutes of the [NJCLU] Executive Board Meeting, April 14, 1938, reel 165, vol. 2039, ACLU Papers; "Civil Rights in Jersey," *New York Times*, May 3, 1938, 22; "Hague to Testify in CIO Test Suit," *New York Times*, May 5, 1938, 5; ILD Press Release, "Statement by Vito Marcantonio," May 7,1938, reel 165, vol. 2040, ACLU Papers.

11. "Previous Clashes Cited," *New York Times*, November 26, 1953, 22; "William Clark, U.S. Judge Dies," *New York Times*, October 11, 1957, 27; Lender, *"This Honorable Court,"* 150, 153, 199.

12. In Equity, Committee for Industrial Organization et al. v. Frank Hague, et al., May 26, 1938, TR 4, 83–100, *Hague* case file; "Civil Rights Truce with Hague Near," *New York Times*, May 27, 1938, 3.

13. "Civil Rights Pact Rejected by Hague," *New York Times*, May 28, 1938, 3; "The Nation: Jersey City Visit," *New York Times*, May 29, 1938, 35.

14. Committee for Industrial Organization et al., v. Frank Hague, et al., TR 1, 160, 165–69, *Hague* case file; Russell B. Porter, "Hague at Hearing on His CIO Ban," *New York Times*, June 2, 1938, 25.

15. Testimony of Daniel J. Foley, TR 1, 177–200, *Hague* case file.

16. Foley testimony, TR 1, 210–11, *Hague* case file.

17. Testimony of David L. Clendennin, TR 1, 215–231, testimony of David Silverstein, TR 1, 246–67, testimony of James Sweeney, TR 1, 284–95, testimony of Nancy Cox, TR 1, 310–20, testimony of Jules Nydes, TR 1, 346–48, testimony of Aaron Gilmartin, TR 1, 357–65, testimony of Harry Ahren, TR 1, 374–76, testimony of Bella Kussy, TR 1, 381–85, testimony of Sol Chernofsky, TR 1, 388–96, all in *Hague* case file; Morris Milgram testimony, TR 1, 402–5, Grace Milgram testimony, TR 1, 415–18.

18. Clendennin Testimony, TR 1, 214–15, 241–42; Morris Milgram testimony, TR 1, 411–12; Kussy testimony, TR 1, 385–88; Gilmartin testimony, TR 1, 367–71.

19. Discussion, TR 1, 280–84, *Hague* case file.

20. Cox testimony, TR 1, 310–13, 325–40; testimony of Frances McKee, TR 1, 429–38, *Hague* case file; Grace Milgram testimony, TR 1, 415–20;, Kussy testimony, TR 1, 381–83; Zieger, *The CIO, 1935–1955*, 86–88; testimonies of Mary Padla, Jean Palmieri, Lila Rocco, and Grace Pecore, TR 2, 858–70, *Hague* case file. On the black population, see table C-35, "Age by Race and Sex for Jersey City," *Sixteenth Census (1940)*, vol. 2, *Characteristics of Population*, 917.

21. Testimony of Ashley Carrick, TR 1, 443–45, testimony of William C. Kernan, TR 1, 447–50, and testimony of William Callahan, TR 1, 478–81, all in *Hague* case file; Morris Milgram testimony, TR 1, 406–10; Cox testimony, TR 1, 333–39.

22. Testimony of Samuel Macri, TR 2, 890–964, *Hague* case file; Russell B. Porter, "Hague Subpoenas all CIO Records," *New York Times*, June 10, 1938, 2.

23. Macri testimony, TR 2, 964–1019.

24. Testimony of Daniel Casey, TR 2, 767–81, *Hague* case file; Russell B. Porter, "Hague Police Head Backs 'Ejection,'" *New York Times*, June 9, 1938, 8.

25. Casey testimony, TR 2, 729–56, 782–83; Porter, "Hague Police."

26. Casey testimony, TR 2, 756–62; Porter, "Hague Police."

27. "An Ordinance to Preserve Public Peace and Good Order," Petitioner's Brief, appendix A, 129–30, *Hague* case file; Casey testimony, TR 1, 544–71, TR 2, 609–36, *Hague* case file; "Hague Aid Says He Banned Thomas," *New York Times*, June 8, 2918, 18.

28. Casey testimony, TR 2, 665—96, *Hague* case file.

29. Amendment by Way of Supplement, TR 1, 61, and testimony of Dorothy Opitz, TR 2, 871–76, 880–83, both in *Hague* case file; Macri testimony, TR 2, 950; Porter, "Hague Subpoenas ."

30. Discussion during Macri testimony, TR 2, 946–47, discussion, TR 3, 1496–538, *Hague* case file; Porter, "Hague Subpoenas"; Russell B. Porter, "Hague Loses Point in Attack on Reds," *New York Times*, June 21, 1938, 22.

31. Testimony of Frank Hague, TR 3, 1272, *Hague* case file; "Put Away the Pencils, Boys," *CIO News*, June 11, 1938, 8. For typical characterizations of Hague's testimony, see Weinrib, *Taming*, 241–42; Hart, *American Dictators*, 125.

32. Hague testimony, TR 2, 1049–51, TR 3, 1068–70.

33. Hague testimony, TR 3, 1395–1459.

34. Hague testimony, TR 2, 1039–41, 1068–69, 1082.

35. Hague testimony, TR 2, 1047–48, 1099–107.

36. Hague testimony, TR 2, 1082, TR 3, 1155–61; "CIO Strikes in Jersey City," *CIO News*, February 5, 1938, 3.

37. Hague testimony, TR 3, 1157–72.

38. Hague testimony, TR 3, 1179–84.

39. Hague testimony, TR 2, 1058–67, 1076–77.

40. Hague testimony, TR 2, 1078–80, 1109–14.

41. Hague testimony, TR 2, 1089, 1146–51, TR 3, 1185–90; "Hague Gets Thousands of Fan Letters," *New York Times*, June 16, 1938, 17. On the McCarthy-era outlook, see Schrecker, *Many Are the Crimes*, 199–200.

42. Hague testimony, TR 3, 1252–375.

43. Hague testimony, TR 3, 1395–483; affidavit of Morris L. Ernst, TR 1, 62–68, *Hague* case file.

44. Russell B. Porter, "Hague as Witness Is Star Performer," *New York Times*, June 19, 1938, 58.

45. Editorial, "Heil Hague," *CIO News*, June 11, 1938, 4.

46. "Hague-CIO Row Nears a Decision," *New York Times*, August 9, 1938, 5; "Clark Defers Ruling," *New York Times*, September 7, 1938, 7; News of the Week in Review,"

*New York Times*, June 26, 1938, 51; editorial, "The President's Address," *New York Times*, June 26, 1938, 58; Arthur Krock, "In the Nation: Some Practical New Idealism in Jersey," *New York Times*, August, 19, 1938, 18; "Hague Is Cleared in Federal Inquiry," *New York Times*, September 8, 1938, 3; "Thomas's Charges Go to Grand Jury," *New York Times*, September 29, 1938, 3; Weinrib, *Taming*, 237–39, 242; N. Johnson, *Battleground New Jersey*, 110–11.

47. Lender, *"This Honorable Court,"* 198–99; Katznelson, *Fear Itself*, 114–17.

48. Opinion, TR 1, 75–76, 131, *Hague* case file; Weinrib, *Taming*, 243.

49. Opinion, TR 1, 75–95; Weinrib, *Taming*, 243.

50. Opinion, TR 1, 95–104.

51. Ibid., 104–12; "The Hague Injunction Proceedings," 261–64, 270–71.

52. Opinion, TR 1, 114–26; "Hague Injunction Proceedings," 165–70.

53. Opinion, TR 1, 126–29.

54. Ibid., 129–31; editorial, "Hague Row Opens New Phase," *New York Times*, November 6, 1938, 81.

55. "Hague Restrained," *New York Times*, October 30, 1938, E2; Weinrib, *Taming*, 243.

56. Discussion, 132–39, Objection to the Form of Proposed Decree, 139–41, Comments and Objections to Findings, 141–45, Objections and Comments to the Proposed Conclusions of Law, 145–46, all in TR 1, *Hague* case file.

57. Findings of Fact and Conclusions of Law, 147–54, TR 1, *Hague* case file; Weinrib, *Taming*, 243–44.

58. Final Judgement and Decree, 155–59, TR 1, *Hague* case file; Weinrib, *Taming*, 244.

59. "Hague Restrained by Sweeping Writ," *New York Times*, November 8, 1938, 48; ACLU, "Injunction against Hague a 'Clear Cut Victory,'" press release, November 12, 1938, reel 165, vol. 2041, ACLU Papers.

60. Notice of Appeal, TR 1, 159, *Hague* case file; "Hague Plea on Ban Today," *New York Times*, November 9, 1938, 17; "'Free Speech' Writ Appealed by Hague," *New York Times*, November 10, 1938, 20; Weinrib, "The Liberal Compromise," 408.

61. William Clark, Judge to Spaulding Frazer, Morris Ernst, Edward O'Mara, and John Matthews, memo November 7, 1938, reel 165, vol. 2041, ACLU Papers.

## *Chapter 5. The U.S. Supreme Court Decisions: "Time Out of Mind"?*

1. Hague v. Committee for Industrial Organization, 101 F.2d 774 (3d Cir. 1939); Hague v. CIO, 307 U.S. 496, 516–17 (1939).

2. "Hague Plea on Ban Today," *New York Times*, November 9, 1938, 17; "'Free Speech' Writ Appealed by Hague," *New York Times*, November 10, 1938, 20.

3. "'Free Speech' Writ Appealed"; "Hague Foes Charge 'Packing' of Court, *New York Times*, November 20, 1938, 23; "CIO Challenges Hague Court Case," *New York Times*, November 24, 1938, 32; "Two Extra Judges Quit Hague Case," *New York Times*, December 2, 1938, 14; Kaplan, "The Great Civil Rights Case of *Hague v. CIO*," 921–23; Casey v. ACLU, 100 F.2d 354, 354–55 (1938). The acronym "CIO-ACLU" refers to the partnership of CIO and ACLU attorneys in the *Hague* case.

4. "Hague Is Assailed as 'Heresy Hunter,'" *New York Times*, December 24, 1938, 3.

5. Editorial, "A Brief for Free Speech," *New York Times*, December 23, 1938, 18; Weinrib, *The Taming of Free Speech*, 244–55; Murphy, *The Constitution in Crisis Times, 1918–1969*, 175–76.

6. N. Johnson, *Battleground New Jersey*, 99–107, 110.

7. "Lawyers Seek Ban on Mail Divorces," *New York Times*, January 11, 1939, 3; "Attacks Bar Group for Fight on Hague," *New York Times*, July 14, 1939, 3.

8. "Brief 'Engineered,' Mayor Hague Says," *New York Times*, December 24, 1938, 3; "Hague Lays Attack by Bar to 3 'Reds,'" *New York Times*, December 27, 1938, 10.

9. See biographies for judges John Biggs Jr., Joseph Buffington, John Warren Davis, Albert Branson Maris, and Joseph Whitaker Thompson at Federal Judicial Center, "U.S. Court of Appeals for the Third Circuit."

10. Frank Hague, et al. v. Committee for Industrial Organization, et al., U.S. 3d Cir., October Term, 1938, no. 6939, in TR 4, 101–28, *Hague* case file; Weinrib, *Taming*, 255–56; Casebeer, "Public . . . Since Time Immemorial," 172–74; Abernathy, *The Right of Assembly and Association*, 120.

11. *Hague*, U.S. 3d Cir. in *Hague* case file, 141–63; Casebeer, "Public," 174.

12. Weinrib, *Taming*, 256; Johnson, *Battleground New Jersey*, 108; Judgment, Hague v. CIO, U.S. 3d Cir., January 26, 1939, in TR 4, 164, *Hague* case file.

13. *Hague*, U.S. 3d Cir. in *Hague* case file, 116–17; Weinrib, *Taming*, 256.

14. "Labor Bodies Seek New Hague Ruling," *New York Times*, December 15, 1938, 12; "Jersey City Injunction Appeal Argued this Week," press release, reel 165, vol. 2041, ACLU Papers; CIO press release, January 26, 1939, RG20-003, Information Department, AFL-CIO Press Releases, 1937–1995, AFL-CIO Records.

15. Petition for Writ of Certiorari and Brief in Support Thereof, February 6, 1939, *Hague* case file.

16. Respondents' Statement Joining in Petitioners' Prayer for a Writ of Certiorari, February 6, 1939, *Hague* case file; U.S. Supreme Court Order Granting Certiorari, TR 4, 165, *Hague* case file.

17. P. Hoffer, W. Hoffer, and Hull, *The Federal Courts*, 167–243; Leuchtenburg, *The Supreme Court Reborn*, 238–43.

18. Rabban, *Free Speech in Its Forgotten Years*, 15–20, 23–176, 248–98, 342–71; Leuchtenburg, *Supreme Court Reborn*, 240–45; P. Hoffer, W. Hoffer, and Hull, *Federal Courts*, 266–68; U.S. v. Cruikshank, 92 U.S. 542 (1876); Davis v. Massachusetts, 167 U.S. 43 (1897); Patterson v. Colorado, 205 U.S. 454 (1907); Schenck v. U.S., 249 U.S.47 (1919); Abrams. v. U.S., 250 U.S. 616 (1919); Gitlow v. New York, 268 U.S. 652 (1925).

19. Leuchtenburg, *Supreme Court Reborn*, 245–50; Rabban, *Free Speech*, 374; P. Hoffer, W. Hoffer, and Hull, *Federal Courts*, 272–73, 291–98; Donelski, "The Hughes Court and Era," 144–45; Stras, "Pierce Butler," 719–20, 725; W. Ross, *The Chief Justiceship of Charles Evans Hughes, 1938–1941*, 172, 176, 182–83; Cortner, *The Supreme Court and the Second Bill of Rights*, 83–96; Parrish, *The Hughes Court*, 9–45.

20. Berman, "A New Deal for Speech," 291–317; Bernstein, *Turbulent Years*, 657–60, 675–78; Weinrib, *Taming*, 224–25; Senn v. Tile Layers Union, 301 U.S. 468 (1937); DeJonge v. Oregon, 299 U.S. 353 (1937); Herndon v. Lowry, 301 U.S. 242 (1937).

21. Brief on Behalf of Petitioners, February 27, 1939, 28–37, in *Hague* case file; Weinrib, *Taming*, 261.

22. Petitioners' Brief, 38–50, quoted at 41; Weinrib, *Taming*, 261.

23. Petitioners' Brief, 9–22.

24. Petitioners' Brief, 70–83; Judicial Code and Judiciary, 28 U.S.C. sections 41(1) and 41(14) (1934), with 1937 supplement; Aliens and Citizenship, 8 U.S.C. section 1 (1934); Forty-Second Congress, ch. 22, April 20, 1871; Barrineau, *Civil Liability in Criminal Justice*, 7–9; Schwartz and Kathryn R. Urbonya, *Section 1983 Litigation*, 1–3. Sections 24(1) and 24(14) in the Federal Judicial Code were numbered sections 41(1) and 41(14) in the general federal code.

25. Slaughterhouse Cases 83 U.S. 36, 73–77, 80–81 (1873); Labbe and Lurie, *The Slaughterhouse Cases*, 215–18.

26. Cruikshank, 551–53; Goldman, *Reconstruction and Black Suffrage*, 100–106.

27. Slaughterhouse, 77–78; Labbe and Lurie, *Slaughterhouse Cases*, 218; U.S. v. Wheeler, 254 U.S. 281 (1920).

28. Petitioners' Brief, 85–101, 128.

29. Respondents' Brief, February 27, 1939, 51–66, *Hague* case file.

30. Respondents' Brief, 17–52, 69–94; Weinrib, *Taming*, 261–62.

31. Respondents' Brief, 5–13, 74–89; Weinrib, *Taming*, 261–62.

32. Respondents' Brief, 42–43, 101–3, 128–41; Gitlow, 666 (1925); Near v. Minnesota, 283 U.S. 697, 707 (1931).

33. Respondents' Brief, 121–25, 148–85.

34. Respondents' Brief, 63; Weinrib, *Taming*, 261–62.

35. Brief of the Committee of the Bill of Rights, of the American Bar Association, as Friends of the Court, February 27, 1939, i, 1–2, 7–8, *Hague* case file; Weinrib, *Taming*, 251.

36. ABA Amicus Brief, 3–6, 14–24, 27–28; Weinrib, *Taming*, 254–55.

37. ABA Amicus Brief, 29–40; Weinrib, *Taming*, 253; Abernathy, *Right of Assembly*, 121–22.

38. Weinrib, *Taming*, 252–53, 256.

39. "Hague Tells Court He Protects Public," *New York Times*, February 28, 1939, 13; "Right of Assembly—Where?," *New York Times*, February 28, 1939, 15; "United States Supreme Court," *New York Times*, February 28, 1939, 20; "United States Supreme Court," *New York Times*, March 1, 1939, 21.

40. "Hague Tells Court"; "Court Ruling Waited on Red Deportation," *New York Times*, March 27, 1939, 2.

41. Donelski, "Hughes Court," 144–45; White, *The American Judicial Tradition*, 208–15; Parrish, *Hughes Court*, 41.

42. Cortner, *Supreme Court*, 63–96; Stras, "Pierce Butler," 719–20, 726–27; Leuchtenburg, *Supreme Court Reborn*, 245–58; W. Ross, *Charles Evans Hughes*, 182–83; Stromberg v. California, 283 U.S. 359, 368 (1931); Near, 697, 707, Butler dissenting, 723–24, 732.

43. Leuchtenburg, *Supreme Court Reborn*, 250–51; U.S. v. Carolene Products, 304 U.S. 144, 152–53 (1938).

44. R. G. Wolfe to Mr. Hugo Black, February 9, 1939; John R. Longo to Hugo L. Black, April 14, 1939, folder 651, box 256, October Term 1938, Hugo Lafayette Black Papers.

45. Felix Frankfurter to (Harlan Fiske) Stone, memo spring 1939, folder 651, box 64, Harlan Fiske Stone Records; Solomon, *FDR v. the Constitution*, 211–12.

46. White, *American Judicial Tradition*, 211–12; Cushman, *Rethinking the New Deal Court*, 92–105; Solomon, *FDR v. the Constitution*, 212, 215; Pfohl, "*Hague v. CIO* and the Roots of the Public Forum Doctrine," 560.

47. *Hague*, 307 U.S. 500–506.

48. *Hague*, 307 U.S. 507–14; Weinrib, *Taming*, 262; Abernathy, *Right of Assembly*, 122–23.

49. Herndon v. Lowry, 301 U.S. 242, 259–60 (1937); Schneider v. New Jersey, 308 U.S. 147, 160–62 (1939); Casebeer, "Public," 175–76; Harlan Fiske Stone to Owen Roberts, memo May 18, 1936, folder 651, box 64, Harlan Fiske Stone Records; Weinrib, *Taming*, 262–63; Abernathy, *Right of Assembly*, 123; Pfohl, "*Hague*," 561.

50. *Hague*, 307 U.S. 514–17; Zick, *Speech Out of Doors*, 183–86; Abernathy, *Right of Assembly*, 123–24; Pfohl, "*Hague*," 561–64.

51. *Hague*, 307 U.S. 517–18.

52. *Hague*, 307 U.S. 518–32; White, *American Judicial Tradition*, 215–21; Weinrib, *Taming*, 263; Abernathy, *Right of Assembly*, 123; Pfohl, "*Hague*," 564–65; Casebeer, "Public," 176–77.

53. *Hague*, 307 U.S. 532.

54. *Hague*, 307 U.S. 532–33; Zick, *Speech Out of Doors*, 183–186; Abernathy, *Right of Assembly*, 124; Stras, "Pierce Butler," 720.

55. McIntire and Rhyne, "Civil Liberties and Municipal Powers—The Hague Case," 35–36.

56. Abernathy, *Right of Assembly*, 128; Zick, *Speech Out of Doors*, 184; Murphy, *Constitution in Crisis Times*, 180–82; Weinrib, *Taming*, 263–64; Tanenhaus, "Picketing as Free Speech"; Berman, "New Deal," 319.

## *Epilogue: Aftermath and Legacy*

1. Editorial cartoon, "Old Tanglefoot," *CIO News*, June 12, 1939, 4.

2. "The Nation: Free Speech," *New York Times*, June 11, 1939, E2; Dean Dinwoodey, "A Fundamental Liberty Upheld in Hague Case," *New York Times*, June 11, 1939, E7. On Roberts's oversight in regard to the cities' long-standing violation of outdoor speech rights before the late 1930s, see Rabban, *Free Speech in Its Forgotten Years*, 372.

3. "Hague Promises to Obey Verdict," *New York Times*, June 6, 1939, 19; "Bar Urged to Set Up Hyde Parks," *New York Times*, July 12, 1939, 17. The acronym "CIO-ACLU" indicates the partnership of CIO and ACLU litigants in the *Hague* case.

4. Morris Ernst to William Carney, April 11, 1939, RG1–037, Office of the President, in the CIO Files of John L. Lewis, Part 2: General Files of the CIO and AFL, 1929–1955, AFL-CIO Records.

5. ACLU press releases June 7, 1939, and June 9, 1939, both on reel 177, vol. 2134, ACLU Papers.

6. Flyer, "Monster Public Meeting, June 12, 1939," typewritten speech transcripts marked "NJ Meeting," and press release, "Union Holds Unmolested Mass Meeting in Jersey City," bulletin 873, June 17, 1939, all on reel 177, vol. 2134, ACLU Papers; Weinrib, *The Taming of Free Speech*, 265–67.

7. Thomas v. Casey, 123 N.J.L. 447, 447–49 (1939).

8. Press release, June 5, 1939, RG20-003, Information Department, AFL-CIO press releases, 1937–1995, AFL-CIO Records; editorial, "The United States v. Hague," *CIO News*, June 12 1939, 4; Lee Pressman, "Labor and the Law: Significance of the Hague Case," *CIO News*, June 12, 1939, 7; CIO Legal Bulletin, "The Hague Case," August 15, 1939, RG1-037, Office of the President, CIO files of John L. Lewis, Part 2: General Files of the CIO and AFL, 1929–1955, AFL-CIO Records; Auerbach, *Labor and Liberty*, 53–60; Gall, *Pursuing Justice*, 109–10; Carlson v. California, 310 U.S. 106 (1940).

9. CIO press release, June 5, 1939; editorial, "The United States v. Hague"; "Girls Jailed by New Orleans Cops," *CIO News*, July 2, 1938, 1; "Attack on New Orleans Union Violated Civil Rights, CIO Charges," *CIO News*, July 2, 1938, 3, 6; "New Orleans CIO Strike Still On," *CIO News*, July 9, 1938, 3; "Victim Describes Brutality of Police in New Orleans," *CIO News*, July 9, 1938, 5; editorial cartoon, "Wings over New Orleans," *CIO News*, July 9, 1938, 4; "Police Terror Unabated in New Orleans Strike," *CIO News*, July 16, 1938, 3; "New Orleans Trucking Firms Agree to Poll by Labor Board," *CIO News*, February 13, 1939, 2.

10. "Hague Promise to Obey Verdict"; "CIO Hails Victory," *CIO News*, June 12, 1939, 1; Henry C. Fleisher, "High Court's Ruling Gives CIO Green Light for Jersey City Drive," *CIO News*, June 12, 1939, 3; Weinrib, *Taming*, 266.

11. "Jersey City Lets CIO Hail 'Victory,'" *New York Times*, June 29, 1939, 6; photograph and caption, "Build CIO in Jersey," *CIO News*, July 3, 1939, 1; "8,000 Cheer CIO at Rally in Jersey," *CIO News*, July 3, 1939, 3; Isserman, "CIO v. Hague," 32.

12. Clark, "A Federal Prosecutor Looks at the Civil Rights Statutes," 177–83; Barrineau, *Civil Liability in Criminal Justice*, 6–13; Low and Jeffries, *Civil Rights Actions*, 11–13; Schwartz and Urbonya, *Section 1983 Litigation*, 1–3; Weinrib, *Taming*, 260–61; U.S. v. Classic, 313 U.S. 299 (1941); Screws v. U.S. 321 U.S. 91 (1945); Monroe v. Pape, 365 U.S. 167 (1961).

13. Berman, "A New Deal for Free Speech," 311–21; Tanenhaus, "Picketing as Free Speech," 402–17; Tanenhaus, "Picketing-Free Speech," 4–20, 47–49; Gall, *Pursuing Justice*, 109–110; Zick, *Speech Out of Doors*, 152–53; Garden, "Citizens, United and *Citizens United*," 18–30; Truax v. Corrigan, 257 U.S. 312 (1921); Thornhill v. Alabama, 310 U.S. 88 (1940); Amalgamated Food Employees v. Logan Valley Plaza, 391 U.S. 308 (1968); Lechmere v. NLRB, 502 U.S. 527 (1992).

14. Garden, "Citizens, United," 21; Cantwell v. Connecticut, 301 U.S. 296, 303–4 (1940); Cox v. New Hampshire, 312 U.S. 569, 577–78 (1941); Niemotko v. Maryland, 340 U.S. 268, 272–73 (1951); Zick, *Speech Out of Doors*, 45–50; Peters, *Judging Jehovah's Witnesses*, 183–85, 208–9; Abernathy, *The Right of Assembly and Association*, 135–36, 140.

15. Cox v. New Hampshire, 574–75.

16. Edwards v. South Carolina, 372 U.S. 229, 334–39 (1963); Cox v. Louisiana, 379 U.S. 536, 546–58 (1965); Adderly v. Florida, 385 U.S. 39, 41–48 (1966); Zick, *Speech Out of Doors*, 47–49.

17. Hall, *American Patriotism, American Protest*; Zick, *Speech Out of Doors*, 45–64, 74–101, 105–30, 144–81, 183–206; Joe Heim, "Recounting a Day of Rage, Hate, Violence and Death," *Washington Post*, August 14, 2017, https://www.washingtonpost.com/graphics/2017/local/charlottesville-timeline/?utm_term-.b553e557d49a (accessed August 10, 2018); Kessler v. Charlottesville (August 11, 2017), in Justia Dockets and Filings, https://docs.justia.com/cases/federal/district-courts/virginia/vawdce/3:2017cv00056/108351/21 (accessed August 10, 2018).

18. L. Cohen, *Making a New Deal*, 303; "Hague Aids the CIO in Jersey Labor Row," *New York Times*, August 2, 1939, 7; Kermit Jaediker, "Jersey City Turns 'Open Door' to CIO," *New York Times*, August 6, 1939, E7; Weinrib, *Taming*, 266.

19. "Jaediker, "Jersey City Turns 'Open Door.'"

20. Weinrib, *Taming*, 266; Isserman, "CIO v. Hague," 32; Connors, *A Cycle of Power*, 5–6; Steinberg, *The Bosses*, 58.

21. "Another Pact in Hague's Jersey City," *CIO News*, December 9, 1940, 1; "Win Contract," *CIO News*, August 14, 1939, 2; "Special Drive at Gypsum Factories," *CIO News*, October 28, 1940, 2; Allan S. Haywood, "Organizing," *CIO News*, April 5, 1943, 7; "Jersey Shoe Workers Win Contract," *CIO News*, October 29, 1939, 1; "Shoe Union Wins Strike," *CIO News*, October 28, 1940, 7; "Shipyard Meeting Sept. 8," *CIO News*, August 28, 1939, 2; "Jersey Council to Hold Meeting in Hague-Town," *CIO News*, November 13, 1939, 8; "Hague Stronghold Site of Meeting," *CIO News*, November 27, 1939, 6; "CIO Back the Attack with Bonds," *CIO News*, October 11, 1943, 1.

22. Dorsett, *Franklin D. Roosevelt and the City Bosses*, 106–11; Hart, *The Last Three Miles*, 176–78; Connors, *Cycle of Power*, 158–97; Fleming, "The Political Machine II," 44–48.

# Bibliography


## *Archives*

ACLU Papers. American Civil Liberties Union Records. Public Policy Papers. Department of Rare Books and Collections, Princeton University Library, Princeton, NJ.

AFL-CIO Records. George Meany Memorial AFL-CIO Archives, Special Collections and University Archives, University of Maryland Libraries, College Park, MD.

Black, Hugo Lafayette, Papers. Manuscript Reading Room, Library of Congress, Washington, DC.

Hague, Frank, Collection. New Jersey Room, Jersey City Free Public Library, Jersey City, NJ.

Stone, Harlan Fiske, Records. Manuscript Reading Room, Library of Congress, Washington, DC.

Vanderbilt, Arthur T., Political, Professional and Judicial Papers. Special Collections and Archives. Olin Library, Wesleyan University, Middletown, CT.

## *Court Cases*

Abrams v. U.S., 250 U.S. 616 (1919).

Adderly v. Florida, 385 U.S. 39 (1966).

Amalgamated Food Employees Local 590 v. Logan Alley Plaza, 391 U.S. 308 (1968).

American Steel Foundries v. Tri-City Trades Council, 257 U.S. 184 (1921).

Barron v. Baltimore, 7 Pet. 243 (1933).

Bedford Cut Stone Co. v. Journeymen Stone Cutters' Association, 274 U.S. 37 (1927).

Cantwell v. Connecticut, 310 U.S. 296 (1940).

Carlson v. California, 310 U.S. 106 (1940).

Casey v. ACLU, 100 F.2d 354 (1938).

Chaplinsky v. New Hampshire, 315 U.S. 568 (1942).

Collins v. Cody, 95 N.J.L. 65 (1920).

Cox v. New Hampshire, 312 U.S. 569 (1941).

Cox v. Louisiana, 379 U.S. 536 (1965).
Davis v. Massachusetts, 167 U.S. 43 (1897).
DeJonge v. Oregon, 299 U.S. 353 (1937).
Duplex Printing Press Company v. Deering, 254 U.S. 443 (1921).
Edwards v. South Carolina, 372 U.S. 229 (1963).
Feiner v. New York, 340 U.S. 315 (1951).
Frank Hague et al. v. Committee for Industrial Organization, et al. , Supreme Court of the United States, Case File, October Term 1938, No. 651. Abbreviated in the notes as *Hague* case file.
Gitlow v. New York, 268 U.S. 652 (1925).
Hague v. Committee for Industrial Organization, 101 F.2d 774 (3d Cir. 1939). The original Third Circuit slip opinion for this decision is cited from the Frank Hague v. Committee for Industrial Organization case file, or *Hague* case file.
Hague v. CIO, 307 U.S. 496 (1939).
Herndon v. Lowry, 301 U.S. 242 (1937).
Haywood v. Ryan, 85 N.J.L. 116 (1913).
Harwood v. Trembley, 97 N.J.L. 173 (1921).
Kessler v. Charlottesville (August 11, 2017), in Justia Dockets and Filings, https://docs.justia.com/cases/federal/district-courts/virginia/vawdce/3:2017cv00056/108351/21 (accessed August 10, 2018).
Lechmere, Inc. v. NLRB, 502 U.S. 527 (1992).
Lovell v. City of Griffin, 303 U.S. 444 (1938).
Monroe v. Pape, 365 U.S. 167 (1961).
Near v. Minnesota, 283 U.S. 697 (1931).
Niemotko v. Maryland, 340 U.S. 268 (1951).
Palko v. Connecticut, 302 U.S. 319 (1937).
Patterson v. Colorado, 205 U.S. 454 (1907).
Plessy v. Ferguson, 163 U.S. 537 (1896).
Schenck v. U.S. 249 U.S. 47 (1919).
Schneider v. New Jersey, 308 U.S. 147 (1939).
Screws v. U.S., 321 U.S. 91 (1945).
Senn v. Tile Layers Union, 302 U.S. 468 (1937).
Slaughterhouse Cases, 83 U.S. 36 (1873).
State v. Boyd, 86 N.J.L. 75 (1914).
State v. John C. Butterworth, et al., 104 N.J.L. 43 (1927).
State v. Butterworth, et al., 104 N.J.L. 579 (1928).
State v. Quinlan, 86 N.J.L., 120 (1914).
State v. Scott, 86 N.J.L. 133 (1914).
State v. Tony Tachin and Fred Fedodoff, 92 N.J.L. 269 (1919).
Stromberg v. California, 283 U.S. 359 (1931).
Terminiello v. Chicago, 337 U.S. 1 (1949).
Thomas v. Casey, 123 N.J.L. 447 (1939).
Thornhill v. Alabama, 310 U.S. 88 (1940).

Truax v. Corrigan, 257 U.S. 312 (1921).
U.S. v. Carolene Products Co., 304 U.S. 144 (1938).
U.S. v. Classic, 313 U.S. 299 (1941).
U.S. v. Cruikshank, 92 U.S. 542 (1876).
Whitney v. California, 274 v. 357 (1927).

## *Government Documents*

*Acts of the Legislature of the State of New Jersey.*
Aliens and Citizenship, 8 U.S.C. section 1 (1934).
Federal Judicial Center. "U.S. Court of Appeals for the Third Circuit: Judges." https://www.fjc.gov/history/courts/u.s.-court-appeals-third-circuit-judges. Accessed January 16, 2020.
Gibson, Campbell. "Population of the 100 Largest Urban Places: 1910." *Population of the 100 Largest Cities and Other Urban Places in the United States: 1790 to 1990.* Washington, DC: U.S. Bureau of the Census, June 1998. www.census.gov/population/www/documentation/twps0027/tab14.txt. Accessed July 30, 2015.
*Jersey City Board of Commissioners Minutes*, 1913–30.
Judicial Code and Judiciary. 28 U.S.C. sections 41(1) and 41(14) (1934), with 1937 supplement.
National (Wickersham) Commission on Law Enforcement and Observance. *Report No. 11, Report on Lawlessness in Law Enforcement*, and *Report No. 14, Report on Police.* Montclair, NJ: Patterson Smith Publishing Corporation, 1968, originally published by the U.S. Government Printing Office, 1931.
U.S. Department of Commerce. Bureau of the Census. *Census of Manufacturers, 1914.* Washington, DC: Government Printing Office, 1918.
———. *Fifteenth Census of the United States: 1930. Population.* Volume 6, *Occupations by States.* Washington, DC: Government Printing Office, 1933.
———. *Fourteenth Census of the United States, 1920.* Volume 9, *Manufacturers 1919 Reports for States with Statistics for Principal Cities.* Washington, DC: Government Printing Office, 1923.
———. *Sixteenth Census of the United States: 1940. Population, Nativity and Parentage of the White Population.* Washington, DC: Government Printing Office, 1943.
———. *Sixteenth Census of the United States: 1940. Population.* Vol. 2, *Characteristics of the Population*. Washington, DC: Government Printing Office, 1943.
———. *Thirteenth Census of the United States Taken in the Year 1910: Statistics for New Jersey.* Washington, DC: Government Printing Office, 1913.
———. *Thirteenth Census of the United States Taken in the Year 1910.* Vol. 3, *Population*. Washington, DC: Government Printing Office, 1913.

## *Newspapers and Newsletters*

*Brooklyn Daily Eagle*
*CIO News*
*Daily Messenger* (Canandaigua, NY)

*Daily Worker*
*Dunkirk Evening Observer*
*Jersey City.* Published by the Jersey City Chamber of Commerce. New Jersey Room, Jersey City Free Public Library, Jersey City, NJ.
*Jersey Journal*
*Jersey Observer*
*Middletown (NY) Times Herald*
*Newark Evening News*
*New York Times*
*Police Reporter* (Somerville, NJ). New Jersey Room, Jersey City Free Public Library, Jersey City, NJ.
*Trenton Evening News*
*Washington Post*

## Other Works

Abernathy, Glenn. *The Right of Assembly and Association.* 1st ed. Columbia: University of South Carolina Press, 1961.
Auerbach, Jerold S. *Labor and Liberty: The La Follette Committee and the New Deal.* Indianapolis: Bobbs-Merrill, 1966.
Aultman, Philip. "Constitutional Law—Freedom of the Press—Validity of Handbill Ordinances." *Ohio State Law Journal* 6, no. 2 (March 1940): 195–97.
Barrett, James R. *The Irish Way: Becoming American in the Multiethnic City.* New York: Penguin, 2012.
Barrineau, H. E. *Civil Liability in Criminal Justice.* Cincinnati: Pilgrimage, 1987.
Berman, Geoffrey D. "A New Deal for Speech: Free Speech and the Labor Movement in the 1930s." *Virginia Law Review* 80 (February 1944): 291–322.
Bernstein, Irving. *The Lean Years: A History of the American Worker, 1920–1933.* Boston: Houghton Mifflin, 1960.
———. *Turbulent Years: A History of the American Worker, 1933–1941.* Boston: Houghton Mifflin, 1970.
Boyer, Paul. *Urban Masses and Moral Order in America, 1820–1920.* Cambridge, MA: Harvard University Press, 1978.
Bryan, Allen. "Anti-Hague Revolt Led to Sentence." *Liberal Republican*, March 1939: 4.
Callow, Alexander B., Jr. *The City Boss in America: A Interpretative Reader.* New York: Oxford University Press, 1976.
Casebeer, Kenneth M. "'Public . . . Since Time Immemorial': The Labor History of *Hague v. CIO*." *Rutgers Law Review* 66 (2013–14): 147–78.
Chiles, Robert. *The Revolution of '28: Al Smith, American Progressivism, and the Coming of the New Deal.* Ithaca, NY: Cornell University Press, 2018.
Chudacoff, Howard P., and Judith E. Smith. *The Evolution of Urban Society.* 5th ed. Upper Saddle River, NJ: Prentice Hall, 2000.
Clark, Tom C. "A Federal Prosecutor Looks at Civil Rights Statutes." *Columbia Law Review* 147 (1947): 175–85.

Cohen, Andrew Wender. *The Racketeer's Progress: Chicago and the Struggle for the Modern American Economy, 1900–1940*. New York: Cambridge University Press, 2004.

Cohen, Lizabeth. *Making a New Deal: Industrial Workers in Chicago, 1914–1939*. New York: Cambridge University Press, 1990.

Colburn, David R., and George E. Pozzetta. "Bosses and Machines: Changing Interpretations in American History." *History Teacher* 9, no. 3 (May 1976): 445–63.

Connors, Richard J. *A Cycle of Power: the Career of Jersey City Mayor Frank Hague*. Metuchen, NJ: Scarecrow, 1971.

Cortner, Richard C. *The Supreme Court and the Second Bill of Rights: The Fourteenth Amendment and the Nationalization of Civil Liberties*. Madison: University of Wisconsin Press, 1981.

Cottrell, Robert C. *Roger Nash Baldwin and the American Civil Liberties Union*. New York: Columbia University Press, 2000.

Cushman, *Barry. Rethinking the New Deal Court: The Structure of a Constitutional Revolution*. New York: Oxford University Press, 1998.

Delgado, Richard, and Jean Stefancic. *Must We Defend Nazis? Why the First Amendment Should Not Protect Hate Speech and White Supremacy*. New York: New York University Press, 2018.

Denlinger, Sutherland. "Boss Hague." *Forum and Century* 99, no. 3 (March 1938): 131–37.

Denning, Michael. *The Cultural Front: The Laboring of American Culture in the Twentieth Century*. New York: Verso, 1997.

DiGaetano, Alan. "Urban Political Reform: Did It Kill the Machine?" *Journal of Urban History* 18 (November 1991): 37–67.

Donelski, David J. "The Hughes Court and Era." In *Encyclopedia of the American Judicial System*, edited by Robert J. Janosik, 136–45. New York: Scribner, 1987.

Dorsett, Lyle W. "Frank Hague, Franklin Roosevelt, and the Politics of the New Deal." *New Jersey History* 94, no. 1 (spring 1976): 23–36.

———. *Franklin D. Roosevelt and the City Bosses*. Port Washington, NY: Kennikat, 1977.

Dubofsky, Melvin. *The State and Labor in Modern America*. Chapel Hill: University of North Carolina Press, 1994.

———. *We Shall Be All: A History of the Industrial Workers of the World*. Urbana: University of Illinois Press, 1969.

Erie, Steven. *Rainbow's End: Irish-Americans and the Dilemmas of Urban Machine Politics, 1840–1985*. Berkeley: University of California Press, 1988.

Feldman, Stephen M. *Free Expression and Democracy in America: A History*. Chicago: University of Chicago Press, 2008.

Finan, Christopher M. *From the Palmer Raids to the Patriot Act: A History of the Fight for Free Speech in America*. Boston: Beacon, 2007.

Fischer, Nick. *Spider Web: The Birth of American Anticommunism*. Urbana: University of Illinois Press, 2016.

Fisher, James T. *On the Irish Waterfront: The Crusader, the Movie, and the Soul of the Port of New York*. Ithaca, NY: Cornell University Press, 2009.

Flanagan, Maureen A. *America Reformed: Progressives and Progressivisms, 1890s-1920s.* New York: Oxford University Press, 2007.

Flanagan, Richard M. "Roosevelt, Mayors, and the New Deal Regime: The Origins of Intergovernmental Lobbying and Administration." *Polity* 31, no. 3 (spring 1999): 415–50.

Fleming, Thomas J. "The Political Machine II: A Case History—I Am the Law." *American Heritage* 20, no. 4 (1969): 33–48.

Fogelson, Robert M. *Big-City Police.* Cambridge, MA: Harvard University Press, 1977.

Forbath, William E. *Law and the Shaping of the American Labor Movement.* Cambridge, MA: Harvard University Press, 1991.

Foster, Mark S. "The Early Career of Frank Hague." MA thesis, University of Southern California, 1969.

Franczak, Joseph. "The Fascist Game: Transnational Political Transmission and the Genesis of the Modern Right." *Journal of American History* 105 (2018): 563–88.

Gall, Gilbert J. *Pursuing Justice: Lee Pressman, the New Deal, and the CIO.* Albany: State University of New York Press, 1999.

Garden, Charlotte. "Citizens, United and *Citizens United*: the Future of Labor Speech Rights?" *William and Mary Law Review* 53 (2011): 1–53.

Gerstle, Gary. *Working-Class Americanism: The Politics of Labor in a Textile City, 1914–1960.* New York: Cambridge University Press, 1989.

Gibbons, John J. "*Hague v. CIO*: A Retrospective." *New York University Law Review* 52, no. 4 (October 1977): 731–44.

Goldman, Robert M. *Reconstruction and Black Suffrage: Losing the Vote in Reese and Cruikshank.* Lawrence: University Press of Kansas, 2001.

Goldstein, Robert Justin, ed. *Little "Red Scares": Anti-Communism and Political Repression in the United States, 1921–1946.* Dorcester, UK: Ashgate, 2014.

Goodall, Alex. "Red Herrings? The Fish Committee and Anti-Communism in the Early Depression Years." In Goldstein, *Little "Red Scares,"* 71–103.

Greene, Israel B. "Growth of New Jersey Equity—A Survey." *University of Newark Law Review* 4 (1938–39): 37–72.

Grover, Warren. *Nazis in Newark.* New Brunswick, NJ: Transaction, 2003.

Grundy, J. Owen. *The History of Jersey City, 1609–1976.* Jersey City: Progress, 1976.

"The Hague Injunction Proceedings." *Yale Law Journal* 48, no. 2 (December 1938): 257–72. doi:10.2307/791670.

Hall, Simon. *American Patriotism, American Protest: Social Movements Since the Sixties.* Philadelphia: University of Pennsylvania Press, 2011.

Hart, Steven. *American Dictators: Frank Hague, Nucky Johnson, and the Perfection of the Urban Political Machine.* New Brunswick, NJ: Rutgers University Press, 2013.

———. *The Last Three Miles: Politics, Murder, and the Construction of America's First Superhighway.* New York: Free Press, 2007.

Heale, M. J. "Citizens versus Outsiders: Anti-Communism at State and Local Levels, 1921–1946." In Goldstein, *Little "Red Scares,"* 45–69.

Hoffer, Peter Charles, WilliamJames Hoffer, and N. E. H. Hull, *The Federal Courts: An Essential History.* New York: Oxford University Press, 2016.

Holli, Melvin G. *The American Mayor: The Best & the Worst Big-City Leaders.* University Park: Pennsylvania State University Press, 1999.

"In the Field of Labor." *Iron Age*, August 26, 1920, 529.

Isserman, Abraham. "CIO v. Hague: The Battle of Jersey City." *Guild Practitioner* 36 (1979): 14–32.

"Jersey City's Mayor Hague." *Life*. February 7, 1938, 44–51.

Johnson, Marilyn S. *Street Justice: A History of Police Violence in New York City.* Boston: Beacon, 2003.

Johnson, Nelson. *Battleground New Jersey: Vanderbilt, Hague, and Their Fight for Justice.* New Brunswick, NJ: Rutgers University Press, 2014.

Kaplan, Benjamin. "The Great Civil Rights Case of *Hague v. CIO*: Notes of a Survivor." *Suffolk University Law Review* 25, no. 4 (winter 1991): 913–47.

Katznelson, Ira. *Fear Itself: The New Deal and the Origins of Our Time.* New York: Liveright, 2013.

Kessler-Harris, Alice. *Out to Work: A History of Wage-Earning Women in the United States.* New York: Oxford University Press, 1982.

Klehr, Harvey. *The Communist Experience in America: A Political and Social History.* New Brunswick, NJ: Transaction, 2010.

———. *The Heyday of American Communism: The Depression Decade.* New York: Basic Books, 1984.

Kramer, Larry. *The People Themselves: Popular Constitutionalism and Judicial Review.* New York: Oxford University Press, 2004.

Labbe, Ronald M., and Jonathan Lurie. *The Slaughterhouse Cases: Regulation, Reconstruction, and the Fourteenth Amendment.* Lawrence: University Press of Kansas, 2003.

Larson, Edward J. *Summer for the Gods: the Scopes Trial and America's Continuing Debate over Science and Religion.* New York: Cambridge University Press, 1997.

Lender, Mark Edward. *"This Honorable Court": The United States District Court for the District of New Jersey, 1789–2000.* New Brunswick, NJ: Rutgers University Press, 2006.

Leuchtenburg, William E. *The Supreme Court Reborn: The Constitutional Revolution in the Age of Roosevelt.* New York: Oxford University Press, 1995.

Low, Peter W., and John W. Jeffries. *Civil Rights Actions: Section 1983 and Related Statutes.* Westbury, NY: Foundation Press, 1994.

Luff, Jennifer. *Commonsense Anticommunism: Labor and Civil Liberties between the World Wars.* Chapel Hill: University of North Carolina Press, 2012.

Lumsden, Linda J. *Rampant Women: Suffragists and the Right of Assembly.* Knoxville: University of Tennessee Press, 1997.

McIntire, John A., and Charles S. Rhyne. "Civil Liberties and Municipal Powers—The Hague Case." *American City* 54, no. 7 (July 1939): 35–36.

McKean, Dayton David. *The Boss: The Hague Machine in Action.* Boston: Houghton Mifflin, 1940.

Meyer, Stephen. *Manhood on the Line: Working-Class Masculinities in the American Heartland.* Urbana: University of Illinois, 2016.

Miller, Zane L. *The Urbanization of Modern America: A Brief History.* New York: Harcourt, Brace, Jovanovich, 1973.

Mohl, Raymond A. *The New City: Urban America in the Industrial Age.* Arlington Heights, IL: Harland-Davidson, 1985.

Murphy, Paul L. *The Constitution in Crisis Times, 1918–1969.* New York: Harper Torchbooks, 1972.

Parrish, Michael E. *The Hughes Court: Justices, Rulings, and Legacy.* Santa Barbara, CA: ABC-CLIO, 2002.

Pearson, Chad. "Fighting the 'Red Danger': Employers and Anti-Communism." In Goldstein, *Little "Red Scares,"* 135–63.

Peters, Shawn Francis. *Judging Jehovah's Witnesses: Religious Persecution and the Dawn of the Rights Revolution.* Lawrence: University Press of Kansas, 2000.

Pfohl, Richard T. "*Hague v. CIO* and the Roots of the Public Forum Doctrine: Translating Limits of Power into Individual Rights." *Harvard Civil Rights-Civil Liberties Law Review* 28 (1993): 533–66.

Porter, David L. *Mary Norton of New Jersey: Congressional Trailblazer.* Lanham, MD: Rowman & Littlefield, 2013.

Rabban, David M. *Free Speech in Its Forgotten Years.* New York: Cambridge University Press, 1997.

Richardson, James F. *Urban Police in the United States.* Port Washington, NY: Kennikat, 1974.

Ruotsila, Markku. "Leftward Ramparts: Labor and Anti-Communism between the World Wars." In Goldstein, *Little "Red Scares,"* 165–93.

Ross, Jack. *The Socialist Party of America: A Complete History.* Lincoln, NE: Potomac Books, an imprint of University of Nebraska Press, 2015.

Ross, William G. *The Chief Justiceship of Charles Evans Hughes, 1930–1941.* Columbia: University of South Carolina Press, 2007.

Schmidt, Christopher W. *The Sit-Ins: Protest and Legal Change in the Civil Rights Era.* Chicago: University of Chicago Press, 2018.

Schrecker, Ellen. *Many Are the Crimes: McCarthyism in America.* Princeton, NJ: Princeton University Press, 1998.

Schwartz, Martin A., and Kathryn R. Urbonya. *Section 1983 Litigation.* 2d ed. Washington, DC: Federal Judicial Center, 2008.

Seaton, Douglas P. *Catholics and Radicals: The Association of Catholic Trade Unionists and the American Trade Union Movement, from Depression to Cold War.* Toronto: Associated University Presses, 1981.

Solomon, Burt. *FDR v. the Constitution: The Court-Packing Fight and the Triumph of Democracy.* New York: Walker, 2009.

Stave, Bruce M. *The New Deal and the Last Hurrah: Pittsburgh Machine Politics.* Pittsburgh: University of Pittsburgh Press, 1970.

———, John H. Allswang, Terrence J. McDonald, and Jon C. Teaford. "A Reassessment of the Urban Political Boss: An Exchange of Views." *History Teacher* 21, no. 3 (May 1988): 293–312.

Stras, David R. "Pierce Butler: A Supreme Technician." *Vanderbilt Law Review* 62, no. 2 (March 2009): 695–756.

Steinberg, Alfred. *The Bosses*. New York: Macmillan, 1972.

Strum, Philippa. *When Nazis Came to Skokie: Freedom for Speech We Hate*. Lawrence: University Press of Kansas, 1999.

Swanberg, W. A. *Norman Thomas: the Last Idealist.* New York: Charles Scribner's Sons, 1976.

Tanenhaus, Joseph. "Picketing as Free Speech: Early Stages in the Growth of the New Law of Picketing." *University of Pittsburgh Law Review* 14 (1953): 397–418.

———. "Picketing-Free Speech: The Growth of the New Law of Picketing from 1940 to 1952." *Cornell Law Review* 38 (1952): 1–50.

Teaford, Jon C. *The Twentieth-Century American City.* 2d ed. Baltimore, MD: Johns Hopkins University Press, 1993.

Thomas, Norman. "No Democracy without Civil Liberty." *Reference Shelf* 11, no. 10 (1938): 45–51.

Troy, Leo. *Organized Labor in New Jersey.* Princeton, NJ: D. Van Nostrand, 1965.

Varacalli, Joseph A. "Ethnic Politics in New Jersey: The Changing Nature of Irish-Italian Relations, 1917–1983," Paper read at 16th Annual Conference of the Italian Historical Association, State University of New York at Albany, November 11–12, 1983, held in the New Jersey Room, Jersey City Free Public Library, Jersey City, New Jersey.

Vernon, Leonard F. *The Life & Times of Jersey City Mayor Frank Hague: "I Am the Law."* Charleston, SC: History Press, 2011.

Vials, Christopher. *Haunted by Hitler: Liberals, the Left, and the Fight against Fascism in the United States.* Amherst: University of Massachusetts Press, 2014.

Walker, Samuel. *In Defense of American Liberties: A History of the ACLU.* New York: Oxford University Press, 1990.

———. *Popular Justice: A History of Criminal Justice.* New York: Oxford University Press, 1980.

Warren, Frank A. *An Alternative Vision: The Socialist Party in the 1930s.* Bloomington: Indiana University Press, 1974.

Weinrib, Laura M. "Against Intolerance: The Red Scare Roots of Legal Liberalism." *Journal of the Gilded Age and Progressive Era* 18 (2019): 7–31.

———. "Civil Liberties Outside the Courts." *Supreme Court Review* 2014 (2014): 297–362.

———. "The Liberal Compromise: Civil Liberties and the Limits of State Power, 1917–1940." PhD dissertation, Princeton University, 2011.

———. *The Taming of Free Speech: America's Civil Liberties Compromise.* Cambridge, MA: Harvard University Press, 2016.

Wertheimer, John William. "Free Speech Fights: The Roots of Modern Free Speech Litigation in the United States." PhD dissertation, Princeton University, 1992.

"What Constitutes Lawful Picketing in New Jersey." *University of Newark Law Review* 4 (1938–39): 331–35.

White, G. Edward. *The American Judicial Tradition: Profiles of Leading American Judges*. Expanded ed. New York: Oxford University Press, 1988.

Zieger, Robert H. *The CIO, 1935–1955*. Chapel Hill: University of North Carolina Press, 1995.

Zick, Timothy. *Speech Out of Doors: Preserving First Amendment Liberties in Public Places*. New York: Cambridge University Press, 2009.

# Index

DONALD W. ROGERS is a lecturer in the Department of History at Central Connecticut State University. He is the author of *Making Capitalism Safe: Work Safety and Health Regulation in America, 1880–1940* and editor of *Voting and the Spirit of American Democracy: Essays on the History of Voting and Voting Rights in America.*

## *The Working Class in American History*

Worker City, Company Town: Iron and Cotton-Worker Protest in Troy and Cohoes, New York, 1855–84 *Daniel J. Walkowitz*

Life, Work, and Rebellion in the Coal Fields: The Southern West Virginia Miners, 1880–1922 *David Alan Corbin*

Women and American Socialism, 1870–1920 *Mari Jo Buhle*

Lives of Their Own: Blacks, Italians, and Poles in Pittsburgh, 1900–1960 *John Bodnar, Roger Simon, and Michael P. Weber*

Working-Class America: Essays on Labor, Community, and American Society *Edited by Michael H. Frisch and Daniel J. Walkowitz*

Eugene V. Debs: Citizen and Socialist *Nick Salvatore*

American Labor and Immigration History, 1877–1920s: Recent European Research *Edited by Dirk Hoerder*

Workingmen's Democracy: The Knights of Labor and American Politics *Leon Fink*

The Electrical Workers: A History of Labor at General Electric and Westinghouse, 1923–60 *Ronald W. Schatz*

The Mechanics of Baltimore: Workers and Politics in the Age of Revolution, 1763–1812 *Charles G. Steffen*

The Practice of Solidarity: American Hat Finishers in the Nineteenth Century *David Bensman*

The Labor History Reader *Edited by Daniel J. Leab*

Solidarity and Fragmentation: Working People and Class Consciousness in Detroit, 1875–1900 *Richard Oestreicher*

Counter Cultures: Saleswomen, Managers, and Customers in American Department Stores, 1890–1940 *Susan Porter Benson*

The New England Working Class and the New Labor History *Edited by Herbert G. Gutman and Donald H. Bell*

Labor Leaders in America *Edited by Melvyn Dubofsky and Warren Van Tine*

Barons of Labor: The San Francisco Building Trades and Union Power in the Progressive Era *Michael Kazin*

Gender at Work: The Dynamics of Job Segregation by Sex during World War II *Ruth Milkman*

Once a Cigar Maker: Men, Women, and Work Culture in American Cigar Factories, 1900–1919 *Patricia A. Cooper*

A Generation of Boomers: The Pattern of Railroad Labor Conflict in Nineteenth-Century America *Shelton Stromquist*

Work and Community in the Jungle: Chicago's Packinghouse Workers, 1894–1922 *James R. Barrett*

Workers, Managers, and Welfare Capitalism: The Shoeworkers and Tanners of Endicott Johnson, 1890–1950 *Gerald Zahavi*

Men, Women, and Work: Class, Gender, and Protest in the New England Shoe Industry, 1780–1910 *Mary Blewett*

Workers on the Waterfront: Seamen, Longshoremen, and Unionism in the 1930s *Bruce Nelson*

German Workers in Chicago: A Documentary History of Working-Class Culture from 1850 to World War I *Edited by Hartmut Keil and John B. Jentz*

On the Line: Essays in the History of Auto Work *Edited by Nelson Lichtenstein and Stephen Meyer III*

Labor's Flaming Youth: Telephone Operators and Worker Militancy, 1878–1923 *Stephen H. Norwood*

Another Civil War: Labor, Capital, and the State in the Anthracite Regions of Pennsylvania, 1840–68 *Grace Palladino*

Coal, Class, and Color: Blacks in Southern West Virginia, 1915–32 *Joe William Trotter Jr.*

For Democracy, Workers, and God: Labor Song-Poems and Labor Protest, 1865–95 *Clark D. Halker*

Dishing It Out: Waitresses and Their Unions in the Twentieth Century *Dorothy Sue Cobble*

The Spirit of 1848: German Immigrants, Labor Conflict, and the Coming of the Civil War *Bruce Levine*

Working Women of Collar City: Gender, Class, and Community in Troy, New York, 1864–86 *Carole Turbin*

Southern Labor and Black Civil Rights: Organizing Memphis Workers *Michael K. Honey*

Radicals of the Worst Sort: Laboring Women in Lawrence, Massachusetts, 1860–1912 *Ardis Cameron*

Producers, Proletarians, and Politicians: Workers and Party Politics in Evansville and New Albany, Indiana, 1850–87 *Lawrence M. Lipin*

The New Left and Labor in the 1960s *Peter B. Levy*

The Making of Western Labor Radicalism: Denver's Organized Workers, 1878–1905 *David Brundage*

In Search of the Working Class: Essays in American Labor History and Political Culture *Leon Fink*

Lawyers against Labor: From Individual Rights to Corporate Liberalism *Daniel R. Ernst*

"We Are All Leaders": The Alternative Unionism of the Early 1930s *Edited by Staughton Lynd*

The Female Economy: The Millinery and Dressmaking Trades, 1860–1930 *Wendy Gamber*

"Negro and White, Unite and Fight!": A Social History of Industrial Unionism in Meatpacking, 1930–90 *Roger Horowitz*

Power at Odds: The 1922 National Railroad Shopmen's Strike *Colin J. Davis*

The Common Ground of Womanhood: Class, Gender, and Working Girls' Clubs, 1884–1928 *Priscilla Murolo*

Marching Together: Women of the Brotherhood of Sleeping Car Porters *Melinda Chateauvert*

Down on the Killing Floor: Black and White Workers in Chicago's Packinghouses, 1904–54 *Rick Halpern*

Labor and Urban Politics: Class Conflict and the Origins of Modern Liberalism in Chicago, 1864–97 *Richard Schneirov*

All That Glitters: Class, Conflict, and Community in Cripple Creek *Elizabeth Jameson*

Waterfront Workers: New Perspectives on Race and Class *Edited by Calvin Winslow*

Labor Histories: Class, Politics, and the Working-Class Experience *Edited by Eric Arnesen, Julie Greene, and Bruce Laurie*

The Pullman Strike and the Crisis of the 1890s: Essays on Labor and Politics *Edited by Richard Schneirov, Shelton Stromquist, and Nick Salvatore*

AlabamaNorth: African-American Migrants, Community, and Working-Class Activism in Cleveland, 1914–45 *Kimberley L. Phillips*

Imagining Internationalism in American and British Labor, 1939–49 *Victor Silverman*

William Z. Foster and the Tragedy of American Radicalism *James R. Barrett*

Colliers across the Sea: A Comparative Study of Class Formation in Scotland and the American Midwest, 1830–1924 *John H. M. Laslett*

"Rights, Not Roses": Unions and the Rise of Working-Class Feminism, 1945–80 *Dennis A. Deslippe*

Testing the New Deal: The General Textile Strike of 1934 in the American South *Janet Irons*

Hard Work: The Making of Labor History *Melvyn Dubofsky*

Southern Workers and the Search for Community: Spartanburg County, South Carolina *G. C. Waldrep III*

We Shall Be All: A History of the Industrial Workers of the World (abridged edition) *Melvyn Dubofsky, ed. Joseph A. McCartin*

Race, Class, and Power in the Alabama Coalfields, 1908–21 *Brian Kelly*

Duquesne and the Rise of Steel Unionism *James D. Rose*

Anaconda: Labor, Community, and Culture in Montana's Smelter City *Laurie Mercier*

Bridgeport's Socialist New Deal, 1915–36 *Cecelia Bucki*

Indispensable Outcasts: Hobo Workers and Community in the American Midwest, 1880–1930 *Frank Tobias Higbie*

After the Strike: A Century of Labor Struggle at Pullman *Susan Eleanor Hirsch*

Corruption and Reform in the Teamsters Union *David Witwer*

Waterfront Revolts: New York and London Dockworkers, 1946–61 *Colin J. Davis*

Black Workers' Struggle for Equality in Birmingham *Horace Huntley and David Montgomery*

The Tribe of Black Ulysses: African American Men in the Industrial South *William P. Jones*

City of Clerks: Office and Sales Workers in Philadelphia, 1870–1920 *Jerome P. Bjelopera*
Reinventing "The People": The Progressive Movement, the Class Problem, and the Origins of Modern Liberalism *Shelton Stromquist*
Radical Unionism in the Midwest, 1900–1950 *Rosemary Feurer*
Gendering Labor History *Alice Kessler-Harris*
James P. Cannon and the Origins of the American Revolutionary Left, 1890–1928 *Bryan D. Palmer*
Glass Towns: Industry, Labor, and Political Economy in Appalachia, 1890–1930s *Ken Fones-Wolf*
Workers and the Wild: Conservation, Consumerism, and Labor in Oregon, 1910–30 *Lawrence M. Lipin*
Wobblies on the Waterfront: Interracial Unionism in Progressive-Era Philadelphia *Peter Cole*
Red Chicago: American Communism at Its Grassroots, 1928–35 *Randi Storch*
Labor's Cold War: Local Politics in a Global Context *Edited by Shelton Stromquist*
Bessie Abramowitz Hillman and the Making of the Amalgamated Clothing Workers of America *Karen Pastorello*
The Great Strikes of 1877 *Edited by David O. Stowell*
Union-Free America: Workers and Antiunion Culture *Lawrence Richards*
Race against Liberalism: Black Workers and the UAW in Detroit *David M. Lewis-Colman*
Teachers and Reform: Chicago Public Education, 1929–70 *John F. Lyons*
Upheaval in the Quiet Zone: 1199/SEIU and the Politics of Healthcare Unionism *Leon Fink and Brian Greenberg*
Shadow of the Racketeer: Scandal in Organized Labor *David Witwer*
Sweet Tyranny: Migrant Labor, Industrial Agriculture, and Imperial Politics *Kathleen Mapes*
Staley: The Fight for a New American Labor Movement *Steven K. Ashby and C. J. Hawking*
On the Ground: Labor Struggles in the American Airline Industry *Liesl Miller Orenic*
NAFTA and Labor in North America *Norman Caulfield*
Making Capitalism Safe: Work Safety and Health Regulation in America, 1880–1940 *Donald W. Rogers*
Good, Reliable, White Men: Railroad Brotherhoods, 1877–1917 *Paul Michel Taillon*
Spirit of Rebellion: Labor and Religion in the New Cotton South *Jarod Roll*
The Labor Question in America: Economic Democracy in the Gilded Age *Rosanne Currarino*
Banded Together: Economic Democratization in the Brass Valley *Jeremy Brecher*

The Gospel of the Working Class: Labor's Southern Prophets in New Deal America *Erik Gellman and Jarod Roll*
Guest Workers and Resistance to U.S. Corporate Despotism *Immanuel Ness*
Gleanings of Freedom: Free and Slave Labor along the Mason-Dixon Line, 1790–1860 *Max Grivno*
Chicago in the Age of Capital: Class, Politics, and Democracy during the Civil War and Reconstruction *John B. Jentz and Richard Schneirov*
Child Care in Black and White: Working Parents and the History of Orphanages *Jessie B. Ramey*
The Haymarket Conspiracy: Transatlantic Anarchist Networks *Timothy Messer-Kruse*
Detroit's Cold War: The Origins of Postwar Conservatism *Colleen Doody*
A Renegade Union: Interracial Organizing and Labor Radicalism *Lisa Phillips*
Palomino: Clinton Jencks and Mexican-American Unionism in the American Southwest *James J. Lorence*
Latin American Migrations to the U.S. Heartland: Changing Cultural Landscapes in Middle America *Edited by Linda Allegro and Andrew Grant Wood*
Man of Fire: Selected Writings *Ernesto Galarza, ed. Armando Ibarra and Rodolfo D. Torres*
A Contest of Ideas: Capital, Politics, and Labor *Nelson Lichtenstein*
Making the World Safe for Workers: Labor, the Left, and Wilsonian Internationalism *Elizabeth McKillen*
The Rise of the Chicago Police Department: Class and Conflict, 1850–1894 *Sam Mitrani*
Workers in Hard Times: A Long View of Economic Crises *Edited by Leon Fink, Joseph A. McCartin, and Joan Sangster*
Redeeming Time: Protestantism and Chicago's Eight-Hour Movement, 1866–1912 *William A. Mirola*
Struggle for the Soul of the Postwar South: White Evangelical Protestants and Operation Dixie *Elizabeth Fones-Wolf and Ken Fones-Wolf*
Free Labor: The Civil War and the Making of an American Working Class *Mark A. Lause*
Death and Dying in the Working Class, 1865–1920 *Michael K. Rosenow*
Immigrants against the State: Yiddish and Italian Anarchism in America *Kenyon Zimmer*
Fighting for Total Person Unionism: Harold Gibbons, Ernest Calloway, and Working-Class Citizenship *Robert Bussel*
Smokestacks in the Hills: Rural-Industrial Workers in West Virginia *Louis Martin*
Disaster Citizenship: Survivors, Solidarity, and Power in the Progressive Era *Jacob A. C. Remes*
The Pew and the Picket Line: Christianity and the American Working Class *Edited by Christopher D. Cantwell, Heath W. Carter, and Janine Giordano Drake*

Conservative Counterrevolution: Challenging Liberalism in 1950s Milwaukee *Tula A. Connell*

Manhood on the Line: Working-Class Masculinities in the American Heartland *Steve Meyer*

On Gender, Labor, and Inequality *Ruth Milkman*

The Making of Working-Class Religion *Matthew Pehl*

Civic Labors: Scholar Activism and Working-Class Studies *Edited by Dennis Deslippe, Eric Fure-Slocum, and John W. McKerley*

Victor Arnautoff and the Politics of Art *Robert W. Cherny*

Against Labor: How U.S. Employers Organized to Defeat Union Activism *Edited by Rosemary Feurer and Chad Pearson*

Teacher Strike! Public Education and the Making of a New American Political Order *Jon Shelton*

Hillbilly Hellraisers: Federal Power and Populist Defiance in the Ozarks *J. Blake Perkins*

Sewing the Fabric of Statehood: Garment Unions, American Labor, and the Establishment of the State of Israel *Adam Howard*

Labor and Justice across the America *Edited by Leon Fink and Juan Manuel Palacio*

Frontiers of Labor: Comparative Histories of the United States and Australia *Edited by Greg Patmore and Shelton Stromquist*

Women Have Always Worked: A Concise History, Second Edition *Alice Kessler-Harris*

Remembering Lattimer: Labor, Migration, and Race in Pennsylvania Anthracite Country *Paul A. Shackel*

Disruption in Detroit: Autoworkers and the Elusive Postwar Boom *Daniel J. Clark*

To Live Here, You Have to Fight: How Women Led Appalachian Movements for Social Justice *Jessica Wilkerson*

Dockworker Power: Race and Activism in Durban and the San Francisco Bay Area *Peter Cole*

Labor's Mind: A History of Working-Class Intellectual Life *Tobias Higbie*

The World in a City: Multiethnic Radicalism in Early Twentieth-Century Los Angeles *David M. Struthers*

Death to Fascism: Louis Adamic's Fight for Democracy *John P. Enyeart*

Upon the Altar of Work: Child Labor and the Rise of a New American Sectionalism *Betsy Wood*

Workers against the City: The Fight for Free Speech in *Hague v. CIO* *Donald W. Rogers*

The University of Illinois Press
is a founding member of the
Association of University Presses.

---

Composed in 10.5/13 Minion Pro
by Lisa Connery
at the University of Illinois Press

University of Illinois Press
1325 South Oak Street
Champaign, IL 61820-6903
www.press.uillinois.edu